Living Together Separately

PRINCETON STUDIES ON THE NEAR EAST

Written under the auspices of the Jerusalem Institute for Israel Studies

A list of other publications by the Jerusalem Institute for Israel Studies appears at the back of the book.

Living Together Separately

ARABS AND JEWS IN CONTEMPORARY JERUSALEM

Michael Romann and Alex Weingrod

PRINCETON UNIVERSITY PRESS

PRINCETON, NEW JERSEY

Library of Congress Cataloging-in-Publication Data

Romann, Michael.
Living together separately : Arabs and Jews in contemporary Jerusalem /
Michael Romann and Alex Weingrod.
p.   cm. — (Princeton studies on the Near East)
Includes bibliographical references and index.
1. Jerusalem—Ethnic relations. 2. Palestinian Arabs—Jerusalem.
3. Jews—Jerusalem. 4. Jewish-Arab relations—1973– I. Title.
II. Series.
DS109.94.R66   1991   305.892′40569442—dc20   90-9073

ISBN 0-691-09455-1 (cloth)

Contents

Maps and Tables

Preface

JERUSALEM, and how it has developed as an Arab-Jewish city under Israeli sovereignty and control, is the major topic of this study. Throughout the analysis we show how members of these two opposed groups, Arabs and Jews, have responded to the new conditions of living together within this ancient Holy City. Emphasis is placed upon practical matters and everyday behavior—how persons belonging to both groups behave and interact with one another in a variety of concrete settings and circumstances. While our main goal is to provide a deeper understanding of the particular case of contemporary Jerusalem, the conceptualization of ethnic relations in this unique city also highlights broader issues regarding the role of ethnicity in everyday urban affairs, and, even more generally, how ethnic political conflicts and cultural differences are expressed in daily practice.

This study is the joint product of two field projects carried out separately by each of the authors during the early 1980s. Each project followed a somewhat different conceptual approach and used different methods of gathering data; what they had in common, however, was an interest in better understanding the real "on-the-ground" nature of Jewish-Arab relations in this city that is physically united but remains deeply divided socially and politically. Romann's research had as its main objectives an examination of how, following 1967, Jerusalem's two previously separate city systems became integrated in economic and spatial terms, and the practical expressions of the renewed relationships between the Jewish and Arab sectors. In the context of this broad macro-level approach a wide range of related issues were studied. These included the changing patterns of Jewish and Arab residential and business locations; how city space was perceived and organized by members of both groups; the differential economic development and distribution of public resources and services between the two sectors; and the scope and forms of intersectoral exchange between economic entities in the labor and consumer markets. Wherever possible quantitative and previously published material (ranging from official reports to newspaper accounts) were analyzed, and these were complemented by numerous field interviews and observations.

Weingrod's study was designed as an anthropological analysis of those particular Jerusalem contexts where, for a variety of reasons, Jews and Arabs were drawn into regular, ongoing contacts. More specifically, field research was carried out in two residential border neighborhoods where Arabs and Jews live in close proximity. Detailed investigations were also conducted in both a large factory and a major hospital where members of the two groups interact on a day-to-day basis; in addition, studies were made of those Arab and Jewish political actors who, at various levels and for different purposes, became engaged in continuing exchanges. Focusing upon these more micro-level places and social contexts, the data were collected by means of a series of interviews with both Jews and Arabs as well as lengthy periods of participant observation in each of the situations studied.

When we found that much of our empirical evidence and theoretical interpretations either coincided with or complemented each other, we decided to present our findings in this joint book. Three main features of Jewish-Arab contacts are given particular emphasis: (1) the spatial expressions of post-1967 relations between the two communities, especially with reference to their political and social dimensions; (2) the structure of economic ties in both sectoral terms and in regard to particular workplaces; and (3) the patterns of exchange between members of the two communities in the city's commercial markets, administrative frameworks, and political networks. The design of the book is such that each of these topics is initially presented in broad general terms focusing upon overall systemic features, followed by a more detailed analysis of particular contexts and illustrative cases. Chapters 2, 4, and 6 were written by Romann, while Weingrod wrote chapters 3, 5, 7, and 8. The first chapter, which provides a historical and conceptual background, as well as the final chapter, which evaluates and conceptualizes emerging contemporary patterns, were written jointly by both authors.

Two additional points need to be set out in this introductory section. The first refers to the highly partisan nature of the issues being presented and analyzed. If the Arab-Israeli dispute triggers waves of emotion and disagreement, these passions inevitably become even more inflamed when Jerusalem is the topic of debate. The basic terms of reference are themselves part of the dispute. To cite just two examples from among many, should post-1967 Jerusalem be defined as "occupied," "liberated," or "reunited"? Are Jewish-Arab relations properly categorized in terms of "coexistence" or "conquest"? What is more, whichever terms are selected appear to ally persons with one side or the other, and are thereby interpreted as "codes" signifying presumed allegiance and ideology.

The authors are well aware of the problems posed in studying this exceedingly sensitive urban arena. Both authors are Israelis, long-time residents of Jerusalem, and deeply involved and concerned with the city's current problems and future prospects. In this study we sought to understand Jerusalem's realities without ideological preconceptions, and to grasp the variety of everyday exchanges from the viewpoints of all the participants, both Jews and Arabs. We have, indeed, attempted to understand ethnic relations in this deeply divided city as they are rather than as we would wish them to be. We have not (at least not consciously) leaned in any direction so as to presumably present a "more balanced picture." In many instances our research experience revealed certain aspects of Arab-Jewish relations that contradicted our own preconceptions, and thus we were led to alter our understandings and conclusions. The reader will judge whether we have succeeded in presenting an accurate, fair analysis.

The second point has to do with the period or timing of the research. As noted previously, the data were mainly collected in the early 1980s, although more recent statistical and other material has also been incorporated. We completed a draft of the study in the latter half of 1987, or more or less at the same time that the Arab popular uprising, or *intifada*, broke out in the West Bank and Gaza Strip, and quickly spread to Jerusalem. There can be no doubt that the *intifada* represents a watershed: although many of the structural features governing Arab-Jewish relations in Jerusalem have not been altered, it has produced important changes along key dimensions. Throughout this book our analysis refers primarily to the two-decade period between 1967 and 1987, and in the final chapter we also point out how some of the rules and patterns have recently been changing as a direct result of the new circumstances. We therefore believe that our analysis presents an accurate view of "living together separately" both in the present as well as the recent past.

Finally, we wish to express our appreciation to the many Jerusalemites, both Arabs and Jews, who keenly and graciously helped us to understand their separate realities. We also wish to thank those who participated with us in the research projects. Israel Kimhi and Benjamin Ricardo took an active part in the study conducted by Romann, while Rina Ben Shaul, Nawaf Matar, Mazen Abu Ita, and Idan Yaron worked with Weingrod. We express our debt and gratitude to each of these colleagues. The Israel National Council for Research and the Israel Foundation Trustees of the Ford Foundation provided support for portions of the two studies, and we thank them for their assistance. Judith Friedgut provided invaluable help in typing many drafts of this manuscript. We express our gratitude to the staff and executive officers of the Jerusalem Institute for Israel Studies—in particular, Ora Achimeir, Amiran Gonen, and David Amiran—for their cooperation and support in bringing this book to its completion. Last but not least, Margaret Case of Princeton University Press provided warm encouragement and good suggestions, and we thank her for her assistance.

Living Together Separately

CHAPTER 1

Jerusalem between Past and Present

THIS IS A BOOK about Arabs and Jews in contemporary Jerusalem. It is an inquiry into the patterns of relationship—social, economic, and political—that emerged in Jerusalem between Jews and Arabs in the more than two decades since the entire city was brought under Israeli control in June 1967. As might be expected, it is a complex tale involving two different, antagonistic peoples who presently live within a single urban system. Mutual fear, violence, prejudice, and conflict are part of this intensive experience, just as working together, and, intermittently, a mutual groping for understanding, also characterize significant dimensions of their contacts. The chapters in this book document and analyze how persons on both sides, both Jews and Arabs, have entered into the complicated daily realities of living together separately.

Understanding the historical background of the present-day encounters between Arabs and Jews is obviously important. Since members of both groups have lived together in this Holy City for many decades, even centuries, today's patterns of contact may be influenced by the experiences, expectations, and above all, memories of the past. Before looking back into history, however, it is useful to observe several events that were recently celebrated in Jerusalem. These particular gatherings—festivities held on the same day by both Jews and Arabs—introduce some of the essential features, not to say ironies, of this special place. Examining them will help to clarify some dimensions of Jerusalem as a Jewish-Arab city.

Yom Yerushalayim, or "Jerusalem Day," was celebrated on the last Thursday in May 1983. (The full name of this observance is "Jerusalem Liberation Day," but in recent years the shorter title has been used.) This is a relatively recent Israeli occasion, initiated following Israel's lightning triumph in the Six-Day War of 1967. It is a secular holiday, and the participants are mainly youngsters and school-age children. For most adults this is a normal workday, although some may leave work early in order to watch or take part in the festivities. What is being celebrated, of course, is the post-1967 joining together of the previously divided city into a single city under Israeli rule.

Dancing through the streets of Jerusalem was the main motif of the holiday that year. Pre-event publicity reported that "5,000 dancers will dance down Jaffa Road," one of the central arteries located in West, or Jewish, Jerusalem. And, in fact, during the morning and early afternoon hours seemingly endless circles of Jewish dancers moved happily through the streets. Some were religious, others secular. They were dressed in festive costume—boys in white or colored shirts, girls mainly in white— and they transformed the normally noisy, traffic-filled streets into a merry scene as they danced to the rhythms of Israeli folk tunes. Along the route they were cheered by adults who clapped their hands and shouted their encouragement, as well as by occasional Israeli celebrities and political personalities. Later in the afternoon many walked the short distance to the Old City, where, in the large square facing what Jews call "the Kotel," or Western Wall of the ancient Jewish Temple Mount, the day's events continued. The Western Wall (or "Wailing Wall") is an awesome symbol for Jews: for centuries this was the focal point of their mourning the destruction of the holy temple and the exile and dispersion that followed. Since Jerusalem's unification under Israeli sovereignty in 1967, the Kotel represents their triumphant return and control over the entire city. In keeping with the festive atmosphere, the square was adorned with dozens of Israeli flags, and the crowds celebrated with a mixture of solemn prayers, song, and dance.

A second event also took place that day, but it was totally different. This second occasion was the yearly observance of the Muslim holiday of *al-Isra Wal-Mi'raj*, and it was conducted publically in and around the Dome of the Rock and the al-Aqsa mosque, Jerusalem's major Muslim holy places. At the exact same moment as the Jewish dancers were rejoicing over Jerusalem's unification, Muslim Arabs were observing their own version of Jerusalem's past and present.

Al-Isra Wal-Mi'raj commemorates the Prophet Mohammed's legendary night-voyage from Mecca to Jerusalem, where, as the Koran informs us, astride his mighty horse al-Burak, the Prophet leaped upward to heaven. The Dome of the Rock is the site where this journey began: this is, in fact, the place and event that made Jerusalem holy for Muslims throughout the world. On this particular day the holiday was publically celebrated with a mixture of prayer, speeches, and street theater. Several hundred Arab men, many of them young and most apparently residents of Jerusalem, gathered in and around the mosque. Following prayers, they listened to a number of speeches. The Cadi and other religious officials delivered sermons emphasizing the holy meaning of the holiday; several Jerusalem Arab dignitaries also addressed the crowd. The main motif of these speeches was the great religious importance of Jerusalem to Islam and to all Muslims, and the necessity to protect and defend the city and its holy places from enemies. This contemporary political message was at times shrouded by flowery, complex parables, while at other moments it was stated directly. Following these sermons two brief plays were presented. Local Arab youths depicted real situations of everyday life under Israeli occupation, and the audience alternated between laughter and hooting. The ceremony then ended. Some members of the crowd lingered to gossip and exchange pleasantries, while others made their way home in small groups.

These cameo descriptions illustrate many dimensions of our central theme. The conflicts are apparent—the Jews celebrated Israeli rule over all of Jerusalem at the same moment that the Arabs spoke of defending Jerusalem against her Israeli captors. Set within holy places claimed equally by both sides, these conflicts do not seem to be merely political and national, but ideological and religious as well. The messages were delivered practically simultaneously, but neither side heard or paid much attention to the other. The Israelis were unaware of the Muslim observance, just as the Arabs ignored the Israeli holiday. The Israeli press did not even mention the Muslim celebration, just as the Jerusalem Arab newspapers made no mention of *Yom Yerushalayim*. So close to one another in actual physical space, the two groups seemed to be on different planets.

And yet, during that day—just as on practically all other days of the year—most residents of Jerusalem, Jews and Arabs alike, went about their usual daily affairs. Thousands of Jerusalem Arabs went to work in Jewish-owned and -managed factories or businesses; Jews shopped in the Arab Old City markets; and the usual air of normalcy prevailed throughout the city's many neighborhoods. With all of its volatile mixture of celebration, gaiety, and hooded anger, when night fell this seemed like just another day in Jerusalem.

All of the subjects that have been mentioned thus far—political conflict, spatial division, economic exchange, social interaction—will become the central issues in the chapters that follow. However, a principal theme of this introductory chapter is Jerusalem in the past. In addition to roughly sketching out the overall contours of Jerusalem's history, three topics will be discussed: (1) Jerusalem's unique status as a holy city; (2) the relatively recent Arab-Jewish national conflict over Jerusalem; and (3) the systems of daily relationships between Jews and Arabs as they evolved during the past century.

THE THRICE HOLY CITY

Located between the Mediterranean Sea and the Judean Desert, perched high on a ridge of north-south hills, Jerusalem stands oddly by itself. This city is literally four thousand years old. Yet there are no obvious reasons or special advantages that can explain its location, or, for that matter, its fame. Jerusalem guards no rich trade routes, is not astride strategic resources or fertile lands, and more surprising, the city has always suffered from a lack of water. Why is it there at all?

Jerusalem's origins are "holy." For whatever mysterious reasons, the settlement that first began there was a religious or shrine center. Holiness, and intimately bound with it, power and myth, have always been the city's core features: it has, at one and the same time, been both a sacred, mythological city ("the heavenly Jerusalem") and a place where real people lived, ruled, and fought ("the earthly Jerusalem"). It has moved in and out of history—majestic (but, in fact, frequently barren), inspirational (but provincial), otherworldly (yet so much a part of this world).

Jerusalem is, of course, thrice holy. This ancient shrine center has been claimed by devout Jews, Christians, and Muslims alike. However, the city's significance differs in important ways for each of these three world religions, and, what is more, while the "heavenly Jerusalem" could remain a part of the prayers and dreams of believers in all times and places, throughout its long history the "earthly Jerusalem" was alternately controlled or fought over by one or another of the three religious groups.[1]

The Jews' attachment to Jerusalem dates back to biblical times. David conquered the city toward the end of the eleventh century B.C. and thereafter King Solomon built the first temple in Jerusalem. For many centuries, until its destruction by the Romans in A.D. 70, this was the political and spiritual center of the various Israelite kingdoms. Following Israel's loss of independence, and during the nearly two thousand years of exile, Jerusalem lived on in memory and myth: Jews everywhere in the world vowed (on the date of the temple's destruction) "Never to forget thee Jerusalem" and promised too (on Passover), "Next year in Jerusalem." Prayer in synagogues all over the world faced and was directed toward Jerusalem. Yet the Jews' aspirations for their lost capital were not confined to prayer and waiting for the Messiah. Although following the Roman conquest they were prohibited from entering the city, in later centuries small numbers of pious Jews repeatedly sought to return and settle there. In fact, under a lengthy series of regimes and rulers—Byzantines, Arabs, Crusaders, Mamlukes, and Ottomans—Jews from the diaspora succeeded in maintaining an almost continuous presence around their holy sites. Their living conditions were harsh and sometimes

---

[1] The number of studies devoted to Jerusalem's ancient and recent history and its holy status is practically endless. Regarding the particular issue of Jerusalem's religious significance for Jews, Christians, and Muslims, see, for example, Oesterreicher and Sinai 1974.

wretched, and yet a mystical link to the Holy City continued to attract them.

For Christians, Jerusalem's holiness derives from Jesus' ministry in and around its environs and his crucifixion there. These events sanctified the city for the growing number of Christians throughout the world; the mythic Jerusalem became enshrined in the dreams and prayers of Christian believers, while the city itself became the destination of pilgrimages made by both kings and commoners. When, in the fourth century, the emperor Constantine adopted Christianity, great cathedrals were built at the sacred places of Christ's life and death, and Jerusalem became a Christian city for three centuries of Byzantine rule. Christendom's presence in Jerusalem was once again forcefully expressed when, toward the end of the eleventh century, European Crusaders succeeded in seizing control of the city. For nearly a hundred years it became the center and major stronghold of the Latin kingdom of Jerusalem. The Christian world's interest in the "earthly Jerusalem" revived during the mid-nineteenth century. This was expressed by the reestablishment of official representatives of the major Christian denominations in the Holy City, and the construction of churches, monasteries, and hospices designed to serve the growing number of pilgrims and local Christian residents of all sects, beliefs, and nationalities. Indeed, there is no other place in the world where so many Christian churches are represented, ranging from the Eastern churches (Greek Orthodox, Coptic, Armenian, Assyrian, Ethiopian, Russian Orthodox) to the Catholic Church and its many orders, to various Protestant groups.

For Muslims, Jerusalem's primary religious significance springs from the Prophet's visionary experience. Mohammed's miraculous voyage from Mecca to Jerusalem, and from there to heaven, sanctified Jerusalem within Islamic religious belief. Following the seventh-century Arab conquest of the city, the Muslim rulers built the Dome of the Rock and the al-Aqsa mosque on the al-Haram al-Sharif, or Noble Sanctuary, on the very site of the Jews' ruined Temple Mount. Al-Quds, the holy, as the city is known in Arabic, thereby became third in importance following Mecca and Medina. What is more, the city's significance was strengthened following the successful holy wars against the Crusaders and Jerusalem's reconquest by Saladin's armies. For well over a millennium with a single interruption Jerusalem developed within the orbit of Muslim life and civilization. Throughout this long period—marked by epochs of growth and prosperity, often followed by steep decline—Jerusalem continued to be a ritual center and place of traditional learning. However, the "earthly Jerusalem" never attained more than a minor position within the various empires and changing regimes that ruled the region. The city remained a small, provincial administrative center.

Jerusalem's sacred character, its thrice holiness, has been a driving force throughout the city's history. Dreams of the "heavenly Jerusalem" have been translated into practice, and as a result members of all three groups have at times sought to establish *their* holy city within its walls. Under Islamic rule Christians and Jews were permitted to live there as *dhimmi*, the non-Muslim minority subjects of Muslim states. While this status granted them a large measure of internal communal autonomy, they were considered inferior to Muslims and subject to various restrictions as well as a special tax. Even though the structure of Muslim rule was uncontested, each religious group pressed its claim for control over its own holy places and, by implication or outright act, the denial or limitation of others. Thus during the many centuries of Muslim control the Jews were denied access to the Temple Mount, and the area of the Wailing Wall, their holiest shrine, became the property of the Muslim *Waqf*, or religious trust. Similarly, Jews and Christians faced restrictions regarding the repair or expansion of their synagogues and churches. Conflict between the different groups periodically flared in and around the holy places, those practically adjoining shrines where believers from all sides might, and sometimes did, offend and clash with one another.

During the nineteenth century, when the "Jerusalem problem" began to be an international issue, this primarily involved the status of the Christian shrines and the rights of the city's Christian residents. With the Ottoman Empire weak and floundering, the European powers were able to obtain special political concessions. These privileges were closely connected with competing church interests that focused primarily upon the Holy City. The major colonial powers, therefore, established consulates in Jerusalem, and their consuls were enabled to extend direct protection to their own citizens as well as others. As a result the political status of Christians and Jews, both foreign residents and Ottoman subjects, changed radically; in various respects they gained rights and privileges long denied them under Muslim rule.

Under these conditions religious disputes commonly involved rival Christian churches who were quarreling for control over their own holy places, and Muslims and Jews who fought for access to and prayer at the Wailing Wall. This compelled the Ottoman rulers, and later the British authorities, to repeatedly intervene and try to establish a status quo regarding the different religious claims. These smouldering disputes are the main reason why, since the First World War, various plans and resolutions have suggested that Jerusalem be granted a special *corpus separatum* status, or be internationalized, in order to guarantee free access to the city's holy places for all believers.

These bare historical strokes refer to the past; but they continue to have meaning in the present. Jerusalem's status as a holy city, and the clash between Muslim, Christian, and Jewish believers, is an essential dimension of present-day realities. Every day one sees, particularly in Jerusalem's Old City, mixed crowds of tourists and pilgrims on their way to visit or pray at their own holy shrines. Robed Franciscans or Greek Orthodox acolytes rub shoulders with black-garbed Jewish hasidim and bearded Muslim believers. The sights and sounds testify to a kind of ongoing competition. Pressed tightly within the same small space, Muslim minarets rise above Christian bell towers, Israeli flags and rebuilt synagogues announce the renewed Jewish presence in their own historic quarter, while the peal of church bells clashes with the muezzin's call to prayer. But there is more than the mere cacaphony of sounds or blending of colors. Zealots, true believers, fanatics of all kinds thrive in this holy atmosphere. Religious extremism flourishes in Jerusalem's clear air, and the merging of the "heavenly" with the "earthly" city continues to nourish conflicting sentiments and periodic outbursts of open conflict.

THE CONTESTED CAPITAL: THE NATIONAL CONFLICT

During the twentieth century, and in particular following the end of the First World War, the religious issues regarding Jerusalem gradually became overshadowed by the emerging struggle between two national groups, Jews and Palestinian Arabs. To be sure, religious belief and symbols have often been intertwined with the conflicting aspirations of Zionism and Arab nationalism. Yet the "Jerusalem problem" now involved the more fundamental issues of political control and ultimate sovereignty.

As the conflict over Palestine became more severe and violent, Jerusalem became a major focus of contention and struggle. For the Zionist national movement, restoration of independence to the Jews' biblical home naturally involved gaining control over its historic capital city; after all, Zionism derived its name from "Zion," as Jerusalem was called in biblical times. How could there be a Jewish state without Jerusalem as its capital? The same can be said for the Arabs. For Arabs, including both Muslims and Christians, the centrality of Jerusalem as "their city" was equally clear and obvious. Jerusalem had great religious significance for them, and more important, it had been an Arab city for more than a thousand years. Given these opposed, uncompromising claims, it is little wonder that Jerusalem became the focus of confrontation and conflict.

The national struggle over Jerusalem was a dominant feature throughout the three decades of British Mandatory rule.[2] This competition took a variety of forms and involved practically every public issue, ranging

[2] Among the numerous publications describing the events and political issues related to the Jewish-Arab conflict over Jerusalem since the beginning of the Mandatory period, a retrospective introductory analysis can be found in Kraemer 1980; Benvenisti 1976.

from demography (how many Jews, and how many Arabs lived in the city?) to land acquisition and land use, to the status of the Hebrew and Arabic languages, to erecting national symbols in public places, to the allocation of public resources, to the way that the city government should be elected and how it should conduct its affairs. All of these topics were passionately debated by Arabs and Jews, while both sides placed pressure upon the British authorities to act as arbitrators, or better still, resolve the issues in their favor.

The British colonial administration was frequently caught between the conflicting promises and political obligations made to both national groups. This was particularly the case when it came to the sensitive issues of ruling the Holy City. In order to work out compromises that might mollify both sides, the Mandatory authorities typically opted in favor of the status quo, seeking in this way to maintain the delicate balance between the opposed Jewish and Arab claims. This is well illustrated in what came to be called "the problem of the Jerusalem Municipality" which was a major sore point and unresolved issue throughout the Mandatory period. While elsewhere in mixed Arab-Jewish towns in Palestine a system of proportional representation was introduced, in Jerusalem the British basically retained the old Ottoman pattern. According to this system, eligible voters were limited to property owners who paid taxes, and City council members representing the three religious communities were elected or appointed by the reigning authorities. Despite the clear Jewish population majority in Jerusalem, under the British the Arabs were guaranteed a majority on the city council, and the mayor was to be a Muslim with both a Christian Arab and a Jewish vice-mayor. Designed to accommodate all interests, this system worked fitfully at best. The Jews refused to take part in council deliberations for a number of years, and later the Arabs also boycotted its meetings. Indeed, by the early 1940s the city council had ceased to exist, and decisions regarding Jerusalem were made by appointed British administrators. Not only did the mixed government system break down, but throughout this period the Jews repeatedly claimed that they were not allocated their due share of municipal and government-sponsored services, and that opportunities for employment in the Jerusalem Municipality as well as support for Jewish population growth and economic expansion were denied them. No wonder that during these decades they felt themselves to be a "frustrated majority." Of course, the Arabs also complained that the British favored the Jews, and that the growing Jewish population was endangering the traditional Muslim character of the city; if the Jews were frustrated, the Arabs were equally perturbed by their inability to control events as they had in the past.

This political debate periodically boiled over into open violence. As elsewhere throughout Palestine, communal riots or "hostilities" broke out in the capital in 1920, 1929, and repeatedly during the "Arab revolt" of 1936–1939. Lives were lost on both sides, and particularly in Jerusalem, where Arabs and Jews lived close to one another, the sense of communal danger and friction became increasingly intense. This process reached its peak when, toward the end of the Mandate in November 1947, the United Nations voted to partition Palestine into separate Jewish and Arab states, and to make Jerusalem an "international city" belonging to neither side. What began as intercommunal strife rapidly escalated into a full-scale war between the Israeli and Arab armies. The battle for Jerusalem lasted throughout 1948. For part of this time the besieged Jewish population was practically cut off from the newly created state by the surrounding Arab forces. Within Jerusalem itself fierce fighting took place over each house, neighborhood, and hilltop, resulting in heavy Arab and Jewish casualties. Moreover, warfare brought about the massive flight of Arabs from those areas of the city that were controlled by the Jewish forces, while, on the other side, Jews were evacuated from those sections of Jerusalem that had been occupied by the Jordanian Arab Legion.[3] When, in 1949, an armistice agreement was finally signed, Jerusalem had become entirely divided between Arabs and Jews.

During the nineteen-year period of Jerusalem's division, the political issues of control and sovereignty were seemingly resolved. There were two Jerusalems, each developing under its own state system. The area to the east of the dividing line, including all of the Old City, became Arab and was under Jordanian rule; not a single Jewish family remained there. The area to the west was Jewish and part of Israel, and there too the remaining Arabs and other non-Jews constituted no more than one percent of the total population.[4] In keeping with the Jews' national and ideological attachment to their historic capital—and despite widespread international opposition and nonrecognition—Jewish Jerusalem became Israel's capital and the seat of its government. For the Hashemite rulers of Jordan, controlling Arab Jerusalem with its sacred Muslim shrines also represented a triumph. However, the Palestinian Arabs who lived there felt no necessary allegiance to the new Jordanian regime that had incorporated them as citizens. Jordan's capital was located at Amman, on the

---

[3] The respective numbers of Arabs and Jews who fled or were evacuated during the war reflected their overall geographic distribution in the city on the eve of the war and its territorial outcomes. According to rough estimates, nearly two thousand Jews, mostly but not only from the Jewish Quarter in the Old City, and about twenty thousand Arabs and other non-Jews, were involved.

[4] This mainly refers to the Arab inhabitants of the village of Beit Safafa, which was divided between Jordan and Israel according to the 1949 Armistice Agreement. The Israeli section was later incorporated in the municipal area of West Jerusalem.

east side of the Jordan River, and relations between Amman and Arab Jerusalem continued to be tense and often turbulent.

Jerusalem's division was most emphatically expressed by the ugly, hostile border that ran directly through the city's center. The dividing line between Arabs and Jews was composed of damaged or destroyed buildings, stretches of rubble that had become a no-man's land, minefields, and long strings of barbed wire. At various points high concrete walls were put up in order to protect residents from the occasional outbursts of sniper fire. The only passage between the two cities was the Mandelbaum Gate, through which a convoy of Israeli armored buses was allowed to pass each fortnight on their way to the Israeli-held enclave on Mount Scopus. An occasional diplomat, churchman, or pilgrim was also permitted to cross over, but for Jerusalemites, both Jews and Arabs, the border was sealed and impenetrable.

As time passed, Jerusalem residents on both sides turned away from the border zone and generally ignored what was taking place on "the other side." Even though it was near at hand, for both Arabs and Jews "the other side" represented an unknown, hostile territory. Arab tourist maps printed in East Jerusalem showed Israeli Jerusalem as a blank white space, as if it did not exist. Jews occasionally climbed rooftops to peer at their inaccessible holy places, often commenting that their failure to conquer the Old City in 1948 was a "grievous lost opportunity" (Heb. *behia l'dorot*). In effect, both Jews and Arabs had grown reconciled to the fact that their Holy City was split in two.

Just as Jerusalem was divided by war, so too it was reunited as a result of war. The war began on June 5, 1967, the first day of what became known as the Six-Day War. It happened suddenly, unexpectedly, in a great rush of events. The Jordanian army positions began firing into Israeli Jerusalem; the fire was returned, and the fighting immediately spread to various points along the dividing line. Four days later the warfare ended with a total Israeli victory: the whole of Arab Jerusalem as well as the entire West Bank was occupied by the Israeli army.

The response of Arabs and Jews to these unanticipated events was, as might be expected, diametrically opposed. The Jewish population was exhilarated by the near-miraculous changes. Jerusalem, the Holy City, was suddenly united under their control, and, among other things, for the first time in two decades Jews could walk through the Old City and pray at the Western Wall. The Arab population was, in turn, shocked. The sight of the Israeli flag hoisted on top of the Dome of the Rock symbolized the trauma of defeat, and worse still, the Arabs found themselves living under Israeli occupation.

Looking back, it is possible to see how the terms and outcomes of the national conflict over Jerusalem have been profoundly changed. At the turn of this century and for hundreds of years prior to that, the Arab hegemony in Jerusalem was uncontested. Later, during the period of British colonial Mandate, Jews and Arabs maintained an equal, competitive, yet subordinate political status since neither side had ultimate sovereignty. Following the 1948 war, the issue of sovereignty was solved by Jerusalem's division into two different cities, the one Israeli and the other Jordanian. This situation was, of course, reversed in 1967, when Jews gained absolute control over the entire city—including its large Arab population. Nevertheless, even under these circumstances the sovereignty issue was not settled. Under Israeli rule the collective political rights of the Arab Jerusalem community are not recognized; on the other hand, the Arabs contest and reject the right of Israel to govern them and their part of the city, and they consider themselves to be living under an illegal Israeli military occupation. The political terms have, in short, been enormously changed yet hardly resolved.

JEWISH-ARAB DAILY RELATIONS IN THE PAST

In spite of the fact that religious tensions and political conflict have been the overriding issues, throughout this century as in previous time periods Jerusalem's Arabs and Jews have established and maintained a variety of ongoing relationships. Sharing the same city space, they have been linked by a complex web of social, economic, and political exchanges. Taken as a whole, their contacts derived from two sets of factors. First, Arab-Jewish interactions have been largely determined by the kinds of political conditions and developments that have prevailed in the course of the various regimes that ruled the city—under the Ottomans, later during the British Mandate, and in the more recent time period when Jerusalem was divided. Second, these everyday ties also reflect a number of basic underlying features and long-term processes. These include in particular the different social characteristics and structures that typify each group, as well as selective trends in Jewish and Arab population growth and economic development. The interplay between these features is underscored in the following brief review of recent history.

Jerusalem in Late Ottoman Times

At the beginning of the nineteenth century Jerusalem was at one of the lowest ebb-points in its long history. Enclosed within its sixteenth-century walls, its inhabitants numbering no more than a few thousands, Jerusalem was a neglected provincial town in an unimportant corner of the Ottoman Empire. No wonder that when, in 1799, Napoleon and his armies arrived in Palestine they laid siege to Acre, then the country's most important center, while Napoleon never even journeyed the short distance to Jerusalem.

Yet, as we have seen, it was precisely because of the European colonial "opening of the Orient" and Jerusalem's unique religious status that new interest began to focus upon the Holy City. This is the major reason why, toward the mid-nineteenth century, Jerusalem again began to grow and develop. Competition between the rival colonial powers and Christian churches, together with special economic concessions granted to foreign associations, led to extensive investments in construction, more public services, and the creation of new economic opportunities. Similarly, the increased personal safety of pilgrims and foreign residents directly contributed to the growing number of Christian institutions and residents in the Holy City.

These changing circumstances also led to a revival of the Jewish presence in Jerusalem. In addition to the old established community of Sephardic Jews who were Ottoman subjects and had lived there for many generations, an increasing number of religious European (Ashkenazi) Jews made their way to the Holy City. Like the European Christian newcomers, they did not become Ottoman subjects but lived as foreign nationals under the protection of their consuls. These clusters of religious Jews also benefited from financial support sent by their brethren living in the diaspora. In fact, the renewed presence of these religious Jews preceded—and, in certain respects, even heralded—the modern Zionist immigration which began during the late nineteenth century.

This influx of new residents was reflected in the slow but continuous growth in Jerusalem's population, as well as in its widening religious and ethnic diversity. Estimated at about 15,000 in the mid-nineteenth century, the Jerusalem population numbered 55,000 by the beginning of this century, and 75,000 on the eve of the First World War. Significantly, from the 1870s on the Jews became the largest group, and from the 1880s they composed a majority of the entire population.[5] By the end of the nineteenth century the Christians, including both local and foreign residents, constituted the second largest group. The Muslim population also grew in size, as a result of both natural increase and migration from nearby villages and towns, but its pace of growth was slower and it gradually lost its demographic majority.

Even though growing in size and diversity, during the late Ottoman period Jerusalem continued to be organized according to patterns com-

[5] In the absence of official reliable statistics for this period, population figures represent the generally accepted estimates based on the critical evaluation of various contemporary sources, such as travelers' and consuls' reports or partial, periodical enumerations of the Jewish inhabitants of the city. See Ben-Arieh 1970; Schmelz 1960, 1987.

mon to traditional Middle Eastern cities.[6] Religious affiliation was the crucial marker in regard to personal status, access to community services, and, to a large extent, economic specialization and sources of income. Schools, while limited, were mainly organized separately by the various religious institutions and endowments; this was also the case in regard to medical care and related services. There was, in addition, a long-standing division of labor among the three main religious groups. The Muslim population was primarily engaged in construction and providing the city with agricultural and other regional produce, while the Jews and Christians specialized in artisanry and related trades, as well as a range of commercial activities that included importing products, money changing, and providing services for the growing number of foreign institutions and visiting pilgrims.

In keeping with the classic Middle Eastern pattern, residence was segregated along religious and ethnic lines. Jerusalem's ancient Old City had for centuries been divided into four separate quarters (Muslim, Jewish, Christian, and Armenian). This traditional pattern was also followed when, during the latter half of the nineteenth century, Jerusalem expanded beyond the Old City walls. In the New City separate, homogeneous residential neighborhoods developed according to fine-grained religious or ethnic affiliation. Thus at the close of the Ottoman period Jerusalem was composed of several dozen different neighborhoods, many of whose names immediately identified their inhabitants. To cite several examples, there was a Muslim Mughrabi Quarter, the Christian Greek or German Colony, and the Jewish Bucharan or ultraorthodox Hungarian quarters.

Although segregated residentially and in many other ways, persons from all groups—Jews and Arabs, Muslims and Christians—nonetheless had frequent contacts with one another. The very facts of economic specialization and geographic proximity implied a wide scope of daily exchange. Within the congested Old City the boundaries between the Arab and Jewish quarters became blurred; in particular, as the Jewish population grew in size it expanded into the Muslim Quarter. Similarly, along the major commercial arteries in both the Old and New Cities, Arab and Jewish shops were often located side by side, competing for the business of local residents and visitors. Jewish and Christian clinics and hospitals served all of the city's inhabitants, including many Arabs. Local politics was also a forum for periodic interaction. Throughout the late nineteenth and early twentieth centuries a majority of the Jerusalem city council

[6] Regarding the particular characteristics of Jerusalem's urban structure and development, see, for example, Amiran, Shachar, and Kimhi 1973. A more comprehensive description of the daily realities of the city during the late Ottoman period can be found in Ben-Arieh 1977, 1979.

members were Muslims, and the mayor too was a Muslim, but Jewish and Christian councilors also were appointed or elected. Factional struggles in the council's deliberations occasionally brought about temporary coalitions that crossed ethnic lines. Finally, there was a broad base of cultural understandings common to all of Jerusalem's residents: many Arabs and Jews conversed with each other in Arabic, practiced some of the same customs, and intuitively understood the rules and codes that informally ordered their life together.

Jerusalem under the British Mandate

Britain's Mandatory rule over Palestine set off a series of important changes. Jerusalem again became, for the first time in many centuries, a capital city: the British made it the official seat of their colonial government and administration. In their custodial role they were anxious to preserve the city's traditional historical-religious character. At the same time, however, Jerusalem under the British rapidly grew in size and population, developed economically, and took on a more modern Western urban appearance.[7] The population ratios of the three major religious groups were generally retained, although the relative number of Jews gradually but steadily increased, mainly due to the continuous influx of new immigrants from European countries. By the end of the Mandatory regime the city's population had more than doubled to include about 165,000 inhabitants, of whom nearly 100,000 were Jews, 34,000 Muslims, and 31,000 Christians, the latter almost equally divided between ethnic Arabs and various other nationals including Armenians, Greeks, British, and others. In this sense Jerusalem retained its multireligious, heterogeneous cultural flavor, with the additional new features of a colonial capital city.

Under British rule and the terms of the Mandate over Palestine, the Arab and Jewish communities officially benefited from a largely autonomous status and separate institutional structures. Inasmuch as they had become subject to a non-Muslim regime, the Arabs formed a Supreme Muslim Council; based in Jerusalem, the council was designed to manage Islamic religious assets and affairs as well as provide some communal services in addition to those guaranteed by the central government. On the other side, as part of its attempt to develop a framework for the future Jewish national home, the Jewish community set about establishing a

---

[7] Relevant material concerning the demographic, economic, and urban characteristics and developments of Jerusalem in general, and Jews and Arabs in particular, was compiled during the Mandatory period in a host of official statistics and reports, and can be found in many contemporary and later studies. See Amiran, Shachar, and Kimhi 1973; Oesterreicher and Sinai 1974.

highly independent state-wide communal structure. To this end, the Zionist "national institutions" were located in the capital, and they organized separate Jewish public services, ranging from education and health systems to labor exchanges, public transportation, and housing programs. In addition, as elsewhere in Palestine, purely demographic and economic trends also brought about the differential development of the two ethnic sectors. Occupationally, while the Arabs tended to provide pools of cheap unskilled and semiskilled labor, the more Westernized Jews were to a greater extent concentrated in higher-skilled professional roles. The increasing gap in levels of education, personal income, and public resources both reflected and explained this overall tendency. As a result, throughout the Mandatory period not only did the practical segregation between Arabs and Jews become more institutionalized and apparent, so too the socioeconomic differentiation between the two communites grew more pronounced.

As Jerusalem grew in size and its economy became more complex, Jews and Arabs entered into a wider series of cooperative exchange relations. Jewish employers hired Arab labor, particularly in construction, while Jewish lawyers and physicians served a wider Arab clientele. Economic exchanges continued to take place in the Old City markets, and in the New City's main business center Arabs and Jews intermingled as buyers and sellers. In addition, the Mandatory regime introduced several new points of contact. Members of both groups worked together in the Jerusalem Municipality and Mandatory government offices, just as in several foreign establishments, such as the British-owned electric company and some of the large commercial banks. Although Jerusalem continued to be a city composed of many different ethnically defined homogeneous neighborhoods, several new mixed residential areas developed. In these areas Jews and Arabs lived on the same streets, and in some instances in the same apartment buildings. This was particularly the case in several middle-class neighborhoods where the Muslim or Christian property owners rented apartments to Jews as well as to British civil servants. In these as in other settings, social encounters sometimes took place among members of all three groups—Jews, Arabs, and the British administrators and officials. Indeed, because of their longer experience in living together it is fair to conclude that ethnic daily contacts in Jerusalem were more widespread than in Mandatory Palestine as a whole.

However, with the passage of time the intensification of the national conflict inevitably led to greater divisions between Jews and Arabs. The repeated periodic violence forced Jews to move away from exposed residential zones that were within larger Arab population concentrations (such as in the Old City) and seek housing within exclusively Jewish neighborhoods. Moreover, during the "Arab revolt" of the late 1930s, the

Palestinian Arab population declared a general economic boycott on co-operation with Jews, and this in particular had a dampening effect upon daily interactions between them. The Jewish community also sought to disengage itself from its dependence upon the Arab sector, and the creation of a kind of dual economy was thereby further encouraged. For all of these reasons, toward the end of the Mandate the separation of Jerusalem into Arab and Jewish sectors—including the city's residential zones and main commercial centers—had become increasingly apparent. Jerusalem was, in fact, about to become two cities.

The Divided City

Following the 1948 war and its total physical and political division, Jerusalem grew and developed as two completely separate and unrelated urban entities.[8] This partition meant that the city's infrastructure systems—water, electricity, telephone, roads, and the like—were split in two and disconnected. Indeed, the only systems that remained connected and functioning following 1948 were the underground sewers! Since most of the central facilities were located in the New City, almost entirely occupied by Israel, they had to be replaced by the Arabs living across the border. Similarly, with Jerusalem's main business district also in Israeli hands, an entirely new Arab commercial center was built just outside the Old City walls at a safe distance from the border. Menacing and dangerous, the border continued to repel development. Urban growth in both Arab and Jewish Jerusalem tended to expand away from the border, and consequently, in opposite directions.

For the next two decades these two cities grew within their own separate state systems. What is more, their differential growth on each side of the dividing line broadly reflected the varied rates and levels of development of Israel and Jordan, as well as the different positions and priorities assigned to Jewish and Arab Jerusalem within these two neighboring states. Israeli Jerusalem underwent a process of rapid expansion and change. Following a temporary decline in the city's Jewish population during the 1948 siege, it grew rapidly and had reached nearly 200,000 inhabitants on the eve of the 1967 war. As an outlying city precariously attached to the rest of Israel by a narrow corridor, Jerusalem and its economic development received high priority by Israeli policy makers. Many of the new immigrants then pouring into the country were directed to the city; at first they were settled in homes that had been abandoned by Arabs. Later large public housing estates were hastily erected to ac-

[8] For the main features and practical issues related to the divided city, see Benvenisti 1976.

commodate this continuous influx of new residents. Public resources were funneled to Jerusalem in order to strengthen its economic base; a number of factories were built, new campuses for the Hebrew University and Hadassah Hospital (which remained inaccessible on the Arab side) were developed, and new government offices and public institutions were also put up. Above all it was Israel's decision to designate Jerusalem as its national capital that secured it a relatively broad economic base as an urban center providing a wide range of public services to the rest of the country.

On the Arab side of the dividing line, Jordanian Jerusalem's urban and economic development was relatively slower and far more limited. As a direct consequence of the 1948 war, the dislocation of thousands of Arab refugees meant that many among them, and particularly the foreign nationals and Arab Christians, left the city altogether. Under the Jordanian regime Arab Jerusalem did not receive a high development priority: the local Palestinian residents were opposed to Jordanian rule and, what is more, the city was exposed to a potential Israeli military threat. State-controlled resources were mainly allocated to the development of the East Bank of the Jordan and its capital city, Amman. Lacking modern industries and national public functions, Jerusalem was relegated to the position of a secondary regional center. Since most of the Holy City's religious and historical sites were situated on its side of the dividing line, it was mainly the local tourist industry that became the mainspring of Arab Jerusalem's economic life. However, in common with the West Bank region, it suffered from insufficient employment opportunities, and as a result many Arabs migrated to the East Bank of the Jordan or to the oil-rich Arab countries. As a result of these long-term demographic trends, as well as the second massive flight immediately after the Six-Day War, the number of Arabs remaining in East Jerusalem after June 1967, did not exceed 44,000, and if we add to that the entire area annexed by Israel following the city's reunification the total was approximately 65,000. This latter figure is about the same as the total number of non-Jews who lived within the city twenty years earlier at the end of the Mandatory period.

Jerusalem Reunited: The Dilemma of Political Unification

Immediately following the military occupation of Arab Jerusalem, the Israeli authorities took a series of steps designed to consolidate the city's physical and political reunification under Jewish control.[9] To begin with,

[9] Detailed descriptions of the process of reunification and the establishment of Israeli rule over East Jerusalem following 1967 are found in Benvenisti 1976; Kraemer 1980.

as soon as the fighting stopped, a concentrated effort was made to do away with the marks of nineteen years of Jerusalem's division. The concrete walls along the border were torn down, debris left from two wars was cleared away, and the divided roads, watermains, and telephone and electricity networks were once again reconnected. Moreover, in spite of the obvious security risks, three weeks after the cease fire civilians were allowed to pass freely from one side to the other. At first tentatively, but then in the thousands, both Arabs and Jews swarmed across the old dividing line. There were, briefly, some excited meetings between old friends, nostalgic strolls down familiar streets, and a genuine curiosity to see what "the other side" looked like. More than anything else, this appeared to symbolize the extraordinary fact of Jerusalem's reunification. Then too, despite the protests of the Muslim religious authorities, for the first time since the destruction of their temple Jews were permitted to freely enter the historic site of the Temple Mount. Shortly thereafter an area of Arab homes built next to the Western Wall was torn down in order to create an open square where thousands of Jews could gather in celebration of Jerusalem's reunification. These too were deeply symbolic acts, in effect expressing Israel's hegemony over the Holy City.

Determined to secure its control throughout the city, Israel moved quickly to establish permanent legal-political control over all Jerusalem. On June 28, 1967, the Israeli Knesseth passed a law formally extending Israeli laws, jurisdiction, and civil administration over Arab East Jerusalem. In addition, the Israeli Ministry of the Interior issued a special decree dissolving the Jordanian Municipal Council and extending the jurisdiction of the Jewish municipality over the entire annexed area. The territory thereby incorporated ranged from Ramallah in the north to Bethlehem in the south, and comprised seventy square kilometers; the new boundaries of the annexed area extended beyond the municipal limits of the Jordanian city, and actually tripled the previous area of Israeli Jerusalem. It is important to emphasize that with respect to East Jerusalem, Israel acted differently than it had with the other Arab territories occupied in 1967. In the rest of the West Bank, including many villages and suburbs adjoining East Jerusalem, the previous Jordanian law and municipal structure were retained, while both the territory itself and the Arab population that lived there were placed under military rule. By quickly and unilaterally annexing East Jerusalem the Israeli government was proclaiming its determination that henceforth Jerusalem would remain united under its sovereignty.

In addition to these formal political-legal acts, Israel also set in motion a series of policies designed to "create facts on the ground." A twofold strategy was adopted and implemented with great speed and energy. First, as a means of establishing a strong Jewish physical presence over all of East Jerusalem, a massive program of Jewish settlement was carried out beyond the pre-1967 dividing line. Second, the Israeli authorities sought to maintain—and if possible even enlarge—the Jewish demographic majority by encouraging Jews to settle in Jerusalem, while at the same time limiting the migration of Arabs from the West Bank into the newly annexed areas of East Jerusalem. The fact that at the time of reunification the Jews, who represented almost three-quarters of the population living within the expanded city limits, had access to far greater economic means and public resources than the Arabs, was in itself a crucial factor in implementing these policies. But it was primarily Israel's total political, legal, and administrative control that allowed her to pursue these goals in a forceful, uncompromising fashion.

However, even under these circumstances, Israeli policies faced a number of political constraints and perplexing dilemmas. These derived primarily from the problems of governing a large, opposed, and in many respects hostile Arab population, while at the same time demonstrating to the international community that she could be entrusted with the control of a place as sensitive as the Holy City. The issues that arose were, to say the least, complicated, and so too were the ways in which they were addressed. A prime example was the question of the legal position of East Jerusalem Arabs: if the annexed territory of East Jerusalem was henceforth Israel, then what would be the legal status of the Arabs living there?

Rather than directly imposing Israeli citizenship upon them, this option was, in principle, made available to all those who formally requested Israeli nationality. In practice, however, a tiny number of Arabs opted for this choice, while the overwhelming majority continued to be citizens of Jordan, a country still officially at war with Israel. At the same time, all of the Arabs living in East Jerusalem were granted the status of Israeli "residents" (toshav). They were issued Israeli identity cards and became subject to Israeli laws and regulations. This dual, ambiguous legal position had various practical applications. As Israeli "residents" Jerusalem Arabs were required to pay Israeli taxes, and they also became eligible to receive social security benefits and other related services. They were entitled to vote in local Jerusalem elections, but since they were not Israeli citizens they could not vote in Israeli national elections. By retaining their Jordanian passports Arabs were allowed to cross the bridges into Jordan, and from there they were free to travel to Amman or any place in the Arab world. Finally, the status of "residents" needs to be clearly distinguished from two other legal categories of Arabs living in and around Jerusalem. These include "Israeli Arabs,"—persons who were either born in West Jerusalem or had migrated there from elsewhere in Israel, and consequently were Israeli citizens with full citizenship rights;

and "West Bank Arabs,"—persons who lived beyond the municipal limits under military rule, but who were nonetheless free to travel and work in Jerusalem. This situation was, as noted before, anything but simple.

In more general terms, while Israel wished to exercise its exclusive sovereignty over the entire city, in practice the government and Jerusalem Municipality frequently abstained from fully applying state laws and power to the Arab population. The Israeli authorities were constantly compelled to agree to various compromises that, in effect, acknowledged the particular requirements and different status of Arab institutions and individuals. This was thought to be necessary in order to make Israeli rule more tolerable, if not acceptable. Moreover, these policies were perceived by many Israelis as an indication of the city's "liberal administration" in its relationships with the Arab population. Negotiations mainly focused upon the problems Arabs faced as a religious-cultural minority with special needs, separate autonomous organizations, and ethnic ties with the West Bank population or with Arabs in other countries. From the Israeli point of view, these compromises were legitimate so long as they did not imply that East Jerusalem Arabs had collective rights as a recognized, separate political entity.

For their part, the Arabs held diametrically opposed political positions. They refused to accept the moral and legal basis of Israeli rule over their part of the city, and rejected the distinction between East Jerusalem and the rest of the West Bank territories. As they saw it, they were all Palestinians living under the temporary rule of a foreign power. While the Israeli military presence in Jerusalem was never as massive or obvious as in the nearby occupied territories that were under direct military rule, East Jerusalem Arabs never made these distinctions. For them the repeated experience of Israeli soldiers carrying arms and patrolling their neighborhoods, or the constant check by the police of Arab identity papers, was an endless reminder of their comparatively powerless situation. And, indeed, in a basic sense it was Israel's military power that not only brought about reunification but also kept the Arab population under control. In spite of this, however, Arab resistance to Israeli rule was expressed from the very beginning. This took various forms, ranging from strikes called by merchants to student demonstrations to acts of terror aimed primarily at Jewish civilians. More generally, Arab political resistance was primarily expressed by policies of noncooperation with the Israeli authorities.

Yet despite their total rejection of Israeli rule, the Arabs also faced a series of difficult dilemmas. So long as they lived in Jerusalem, an Israeli-administered city, and were under Israeli political and economic hegemony, they were in effect compelled to make or accept various compromises. On the one hand, Arab political leaders refused to present their candidacy to an all-Jerusalem municipal council, Arab lawyers refused to argue cases in Israeli courts, and various Arab professional organizations categorically opposed merging with parallel Jewish organizations—all because of the fact that this would be interpreted as an implicit recognition of Israeli sovereignty over East Jerusalem. On the other hand, however, most Arab employees of the reunited Jerusalem Municipality kept their positions; others were willing to work for a variety of Israeli administrative and law enforcement bodies, or receive Israeli government social welfare payments. It is fair to say that, over time, working for or otherwise interacting with Jewish individuals, employers, or institutions became widely practiced and acceptable within the Arab community. These attitudes were justified in political terms by the necessity to survive and "hold out" economically under the new conditions of Israeli occupation.

To be sure, the precise line to be drawn between basic political principles and more pragmatic daily considerations was not always easy to define, and it was also subject to changing attitudes and all sorts of seemingly contradictory practices. Together with their formal policy of mutual, total political nonrecognition, Jews and Arabs alike had to constantly renegotiate their respective positions, all the while taking account of one another's political attitudes and constraints. What emerged is a process that Meron Benvenisti, an acute observer of the contemporary Jerusalem scene, has termed a "dialogue through actions."[10]

ARAB-JEWISH RELATIONS IN PRESENT DAY JERUSALEM: ISSUES, PROBLEMS, CONTEXT

Our goal in this study is to understand how Jews and Arabs have gone about their daily lives within an overall context of deep political conflict. We argue that focusing attention upon everyday practical exchanges provides a key to understanding the realities of contemporary Jerusalem, that is, how persons on both sides negotiate their daily activities between confrontation and cooperation, or ways in which they navigate their encounters between conflict and accommodation. This is not to say that their beliefs and ideologies, or the prevailing organization of political and economic power, are not crucial features; nor do we maintain that Arabs and Jews are always able to negotiate their relationships so that conflicts are averted. Rather, by focusing upon everyday relations we are better able to understand how ideologies and power relations frame the encounters between members of these groups, or why conflicts may in fact erupt under certain circumstances.

In the process of elucidating the nature of daily contacts between

10 See Benvenisti 1983.

Arabs and Jews, our analysis directs attention to two general topics. The first of these focuses upon a unique feature of post-1967 Jerusalem. It poses the intriguing question of what takes place when a previously divided city is once again brought together to form a single interactive system. At one level this inquiry focuses upon particular local features: we examine the processes that were set off when two formerly separate urban entities, which differed in social structure, economic size, and level of development, were forcefully reunited. At another level it is important to understand how reunification and the process of reintegration and structural adjustment in themselves had an effect upon the emerging patterns of Arab-Jewish relations. Namely, to what extent and in what types of activity did the pre-1967 patterns of ethnic separation prevail or continue to be significant? Did both Jews and Arabs equally benefit from Jerusalem's reunification, and what were the implications for their differential opportunity structures and patterns of growth? Most important, how were these processes affected by Israeli policies?

The second topic relates to interethnic relations conceived more broadly. Living within a single urban, economic, and political system has brought members of the two ethnic groups into a variety of social contacts: some Arabs and Jews again reside close to one another, many more interact in various work settings, and others have exchanges in a number of commercial, administrative, and political frameworks. The major questions posed in this regard seek to better understand the nature, implications, and interpretation of these relationships. To what extent have everyday contacts between Arabs and Jews grown over time as a result of mutual interests, or, on the contrary, have cultural and political divisions produced deepening avoidance and segregation? Have members of both groups adopted modes of cooperation that are mutually acceptable, or are their everyday contacts characterized by hostility, prejudice, and various forms of asymmetric relations? Finally, how did ethnic identity influence Jewish-Arab interactions, and what informal rules were adopted in order to sustain relationships in the light of the ongoing political and other conflicts?

To some extent our analysis has been informed by previous research and publications on the topic of Arab-Jewish relations in Jerusalem. It is useful at this point to briefly indicate the directions taken by these earlier studies, and also to suggest how their findings are relevant to our research.

The general topic of Jews and Arabs in post-1967 Jerusalem has been the subject of a large number of scholarly books and articles, as well as many more journalistic reports. This literature focuses mainly upon political problems, examining their historic background and future prospects, and to a large extent it also reflects the political outlooks of Jewish,

Arab, and foreign analysts.[11] While much of the literature was written by Israeli and Jewish authors, it is interesting to note that their perceptions and evaluations of Arab-Jewish coexistence in the united city have gradually shifted over time. This changing mood is well illustrated by the different titles given to books written about Jerusalem since 1967.

In the initial heady years following the city's reunification, one of the first studies was entitled *Jerusalem: A City without a Wall* (Benziman 1973); in another book title, problems were related to prospects for their solutions (Kraemer 1980); and these were outlined in yet another study in terms of bridging the four walls (Cohen 1977). In the Israeli press, too, special newspaper sections published on Jerusalem Day typically described Jerusalem as "a city brought together" and proclaimed any new revelation of Jewish-Arab cooperation. Over the years, however, a greater pessimism, or perhaps realism, may have set in. This is again reflected in titles, such as *Jerusalem: A Torn City, A City with a Wall in Its Midst,* and *Jerusalem: A Polarized Community* (Benvenisti 1976, 1981, 1983). This change in perspective indicates not only that basic political antagonisms have continued, but also that the schism between the two communities persists in many aspects of everyday life.

Turning directly to this body of research, several studies provide documentation of the events that took place during and immediately after Jerusalem's reunification. Books by Benziman (1973) and Benvenisti (1973) render detailed descriptions of the decision-making process that accompanied the imposition of Israeli administrative and political control. Studies by Romann (1967), Amir (1969), Weigert (1973), and Farchi (1980) demonstrate how Jerusalem's reunification, as well as the specific policies imposed by the Israeli authorities, had, in the short run, direct social and economic consequences for the Arab population. Cohen (1977) takes up some of these same topics, and also puts forward proposals that are meant to draw Jews and Arabs more closely together.

Various other dimensions of post-1967 Jerusalem have also been examined. These include demographic (Schmelz 1987) and socioeconomic (Kimhi and Hyman 1978; Hyman, Kimhi, and Savitzki 1985) characteristics of the city, as well as composite views of Jerusalem's overall urban structure (Amiran, Shachar, and Kimhi 1973) and problems of city planning and design (Kroyanker 1982, 1985). Several collective volumes have

---

[11] Most of the major works on contemporary Jerusalem in general, and the various issues arising since the city's reunification in particular, have been written by Jewish authors. Arab writers have not agreed with some of the basic terms commonly employed in these works. See, for example, Bin Talal 1979; Abdul-Hadi 1985. Similarly, most Jews and Arabs alike would reject (at least in part) descriptions and interpretations presented by foreign observers—from Lapierre and Collins (1971) to Shipler (1987)—who attempt to present a "balanced" picture of this highly contested contemporary history.

also reviewed key aspects of Jerusalem's socially and culturally hetero-geneous population (Prawer and Ahimeir 1988).

All of these studies, as well as other published material, provide important basic information showing how the new circumstances of a unified and rapidly growing Jerusalem led to changes for members of both ethnic groups. However, in most instances they tend to examine each group separately, without analyzing the patterns of everyday or longer-term interactions between them. Nor have they provided a widescale overall analysis of the structure of contemporary Jewish-Arab relations in Jerusalem. There is, on the other hand, a literature in which these topics have been considered. With regard to the issue of Arab-Jewish daily interactions, much of the relevant source material is composed of newspaper reports and feature articles that have appeared in the Hebrew and Arabic press, as well as several books based mainly upon lengthy personal experience and reporting (Heilman 1986; Shipler 1987). Among the studies that provide a more systematic, comprehensive analysis and interpretation, two in particular should be noted. Kaplan (1977) studied Jewish-Arab encounters in various Jerusalem settings, such as in Israeli administrative bureaus, the Old City market, and similar frameworks where members of the two groups were engaged in daily exchanges. Based upon his experience as a mental health practitioner and mediator of intercommunity conflicts, Kaplan concludes that many of the misunderstandings and conflicts in everyday Jewish-Arab contacts can be explained in terms of the concept of "cultural dissonance." Particular mention should also be made of the work of Benvenisti, who has made continuing important contributions to understanding the nature and development of Jewish-Arab relations in Jerusalem. Based in part upon his own personal experience as the first Israeli municipal official responsible for Arab East Jerusalem, his publications have emphasized the conflicts and contradictions that arise from "living together" and attempting to administer a Jewish-Arab city. In contrast with Kaplan, Benvenisti argues that the many divisions and misunderstandings between Jews and Arabs are essentially the result of overwhelming political antagonism and mutual, collective nonrecognition (Benvenisti 1982, 1983, 1985, 1986). What this suggests is that, whatever the point of departure, the scope and nature of Jewish-Arab day-to-day exchanges are expressions of deeper cultural and political factors, and that they will need to be conceptualized in these terms.

In addition to these studies of Jerusalem, there is a second pertinent body of literature, namely, research dealing with Arab-Jewish relations in Israel. The empirical evidence on this topic, and more importantly, its theoretical interpretation, may provide us with a relevant precedent and general model for analysis.[12] Briefly summarized, the position of Arabs who remained in Israel differs in several respects from East Jerusalem Arabs. In contrast with the latter, after 1948 Israeli Arabs comprised a small minority of roughly 10 percent of the total population, and they mainly constituted a rural population dispersed in several peripheral regions and a small number of mixed cities. Moreover, those Arabs that remained after the 1948 mass exodus lacked both effective leadership and autonomous central institutions; in addition, for the next two decades they were completely cut off from the rest of the Palestinian population and Arab world. On the other hand, they were all granted Israeli citizenship, and over the years they have grown in number (by the 1980s they made up about 15 percent of the total population) and have become more integrated into the social, economic, and political systems of the Jewish state.

These differences notwithstanding, Arab-Jewish relations in Israel provide a relevant comparative case. Following Smooha's model of structural pluralism, we briefly outline some of the salient features of Israeli Arab-Jewish interactions as these have evolved over the past four decades.

According to this approach the underlying factors and their revealed patterns are multidimensional and reflect the major divisions and power relations between the two social groups. Conceived of in these terms, Jews and Arabs can initially be distinguished from one another along four major dividing lines: language, religion, national affiliation, and ethnic-group membership. Their different identities are unequivocal, and find expression in contrasting cultural values and social norms that both groups are anxious to preserve. What is more, Israeli Arabs consider themselves to be a part of the Palestinian people and the Arab world at large, and consequently their status as both "Arabs" and "Israelis" has been problematic. By the same token, in light of the ongoing Arab-Israeli conflict the Jewish majority often mistrusted the Arabs' basic loyalty and considered them to be an undependable minority.

These underlying features are expressed in a deep, thoroughgoing segregation that can be found at many levels. Since their coexistence as Israelis was basically nonvoluntary and neither group aspires to assimilation, the desire for segregation has been shared by both groups and is often institutionalized. Jews and Arabs reside in separate homogeneous

[12] Since Jewish-Arab relations have for many decades been a major focus of interest and concern, a large number of studies and publications have been devoted to analyzing this complex topic. These range over political, cultural, social, economic, and territorial aspects as examined by Middle East specialists, political scientists, anthropologists, sociologists, geographers, and many others. For a comprehensive, detailed discussion and evaluation of the different overall conceptual approaches and interpretations of Jewish-Arab relations in Israel, see Smooha 1978.

villages and towns; and even in those cities that do have mixed populations Arabs and Jews tend to concentrate in separate neighborhoods.
Close-knit social relations between them, and intermarriage in particular,
have been rare. Issues of marriage and divorce are considered in separate
Jewish, Muslim, and Christian religious courts, and Jews and Arabs commonly attend their own schools with distinct curriculum and language
instruction. In many government agencies special departments are assigned to handling "Arab affairs." At the same time, however, a range of
interpersonal contacts between Jews and Arabs takes place. These are
mainly concentrated in the workplace and marketplace, or within the
framework of public institutions such as hospitals and universities. Despite the fact that these encounters tend to be instrumental in character
and limited in scope, they provide regular avenues of interaction.

An additional defining feature of Arab-Jewish relations in Israel is their
basic inequality. Although Arabs and Jews are formally accorded equal
personal rights, in practice Arabs, who are exempted from serving in the
Israeli army, do not receive the same state-allocated benefits or opportunities that are made available to Jews. What is more, at a society-wide
level Jews typically monopolize higher-prestige positions, while Arabs
are in lower-status ranks. There is, therefore, a basic structural inequality
between the two groups, and it finds expression in such important domains as education, occupation, income, consumption level, and related
features. These inequalities are particularly acute with regard to access
to strategic economic and political resources. Arabs have hardly been
represented in the higher-rank command positions within Israeli political, administrative, and economic organizations; lacking their own resources, they remain dependent upon the Jewish sector and consequently they have often been coopted by the reigning Jewish
establishment. The non-Jewish minority has been allowed a relatively
broad religious, cultural, and municipal-level autonomy—but in this regard too final authority rests with the Israeli-Jewish state officials. Arabs
have been discouraged from forming their own national political or other
organizational frameworks, and the Jewish majority has not granted them
a separate minority status.

Over the years, however, there has been an increased Arab upward
mobility, especially in regard to educational attainments. This has also
been associated with a heightened Arab political consciousness. Israeli
Arabs have actively protested against discriminatory practices, demanding full exercise of their political rights within the Israeli system. Given
these circumstances, Israeli Arab sociopolitical responses have ranged
from antagonism and alienation to the demand that inequalities be recti-
fied and they receive equal rights and allocations of resources.

This model may prove illuminating for understanding Jewish-Arab relations in Jerusalem. Comparing the two systems should indicate, for example, whether both are characterized by plural structures, a high level of ethnic segregation, and systematic inequalities, and, moreover, the extent to which processes of ethnic accommodation and conflict are similar in both Jerusalem and Israel as a whole.

Taking an even broader perspective, we can also view Jerusalem as an instance of a plural society in which different ethnic groups share the same political-territorial environment or live together in mixed cities. Overall, ethnic groups differ with regard to place of origin, race, nationality, religion, language, and other attributes that signify their distinct collective identity. The vast literature dealing with ethnic relations indicates that group contacts are influenced by numerous historic, social, and political variables, as well as by the specific setting in which they take place.[13] Fundamental underlying conditions arise from the definition of group membership, whether initial contacts were voluntary or imposed, and the extent to which different collective goals are conflicting or can be accommodated. Additional relevant aspects include population proportions, geographic distribution, and economic status of majority versus minority groups, as well as the overall structure of the society and its political regime. Depending on these and other factors, intergroup relations range from relative cohesion with mild cultural divisions and competition over scarce resources, to deeper social cleavages and generalized political conflict. Such major divisions and conflicts are more likely where these have persisted over a long time period and where contradictory aspirations cannot be met or agreed upon. This occurs when a large collectivity cannot realize its political objectives or feels economically and socially discriminated against and deprived; this often is the case when a subordinate status coincides with ethnic affiliation. In extreme instances all social issues are considered in zero-sum political terms, and lacking any consensus, the very legitimacy of the political regime is contested by the subordinate group.

Structural pluralism also finds expression in the nature of daily intergroup relationships. In ethnically divided societies close social relationships, like friendship or marriage, are limited. Segregation can take the form of separate residential areas, schools and other public facilities, or voluntary associations; these may also be associated with a distinct legal status. Indeed, it is the extent of segregation in everyday life and the degree of segregation in each particular area which largely measure the

---

[13] The abundant empirical and theoretical literature regarding plural societies in general and ethnic relations in particular draws upon several disciplines: from political science, anthropology, and sociology to social psychology and social geography. For a review of this literature, the different concepts of pluralism, and related aspects of intergroup relationships, see Clarke, Ley and Peach 1984; Jackson and Smith 1981.

extent of the structural division within a given society. By the same token, dimensions of segregation should be measured and compared with
aspects of integration; both represent two ends along a continuum of possible intergroup interactions. The scope as well as trends over time of
these dimensions of practical relationships are key indicators of the factors underlying ethnic group divisions.

The second major aspect of ethnic interactions concerns the nature and
terms of society-wide power relationships. Positions of dominance as
against subordination are generally expressed in the differential access to
personal material status and symbolic rewards as well as to collective economic resources and political control. In order to protect and maintain
its privileges, the dominant group tends to unequally allocate national
public resources, and sometimes also exercises measures of social closure
and discrimination toward the less powerful group. In certain cases, exclusive discriminatory policies involve legal or coercive measures, and,
in extreme instances, the removal of the minority from the political process altogether.

In all these respects ethnic relations in mixed cities mirror the national-level structure, and are even more sharply expressed due to the
closer proximity in spatial terms and daily interactions.[14] One of the major expressions of cultural differentiation is the tendency of ethnic groups
to concentrate in separate urban neighborhoods. The scope and patterns
of residential segregation may vary in time and between cities, depending on the relative size, differential growth rates, and related processes
of infiltration of certain groups into the urban sections of others. Generally speaking, the degree of residential segregation is one of the best
comparative indicators of the social distance between ethnic groups who
reside in the same city. The underlying reasons for this are largely voluntary. Separation enables different groups to maintain their distinct life-
styles, create their own community organizations, and, in conflicting situations, preserve a sense of security. At the same time, residential
clustering, particularly in the case of minority groups, is often imposed,
whether as a result of purely economic constraints or because of individual or institutional practices of closure by the dominant group. These
divisions are reinforced by other aspects of separation in everyday life,
such as education or religion. In addition, while ethnic groups normally
compete for a greater share in the housing market and other urban public
commodities, the options and opportunities open to them are rarely
equal. This too depends on various choices and constraints that are not

---

[14] Among the many studies introducing and discussing ethnic relations in cities, see Cohen 1974; Ley 1983; Peach, Robinson, and Smith 1981.

only economic, but also vary according to the kind of organization of city space and the distribution of public resources.

Ethnic interactions in cities normally take place in the economic field, in urban workplaces, or within the framework of the local business community and similar settings. Exchanges of this kind are usually conducted in the city's main commercial centers and have a rather impersonal, utilitarian character. However, ethnicity also plays a role in these contexts. This may be the case regarding separate economic specializations and business or consumer norms, or be expressed in the different familiarity, sense of estrangement, and patterns of movement throughout the various sections of the city. Consequently, intragroup models of exchange often differ from intergroup patterns in analogical contexts. Indeed, group identities and social boundaries are constantly negotiated; ethnic daily relations should be viewed from an interactionist perspective and conceptualized in negotiable, transactional terms. These oft-times subtle aspects are commonly related to the identity of ethnic-group members and the forms and terms of exchange between different ethnic groups. They are often conducted from positions of dominance or subordination, expressing in turn society-wide power relations.

In deeply polarized urban environments, aspects of division and power relations take extreme forms. Spatial segregation is not confined to residence, but includes many urban, economic, and public functions. Territorial ethnic boundaries are clearly marked, and the use of urban space assumes primordial significance. The exclusionary practices of the hegemonic group are responded to, in turn, by similar practices by subordinate group members, designed to strengthen their own separate institutions and intragroup cohesion. Socioeconomic gaps and competition for public resources are largely interpreted in terms of ethnicity rather than social class. To be sure, daily movement and interactions across ethnic boundaries take place as dictated by mutual needs and interests. Yet, as a general rule, deeply divided cities are characterized by dichotomous urban, social, economic, and perceptual spheres, where ethnic identity invariably plays a crucial role in everyday encounters.

It is against this general background that the empirical evidence regarding Jewish-Arab daily relations in contemporary Jerusalem can also be examined. The issues and variables that have been identified are relevant throughout our analysis, and in the last chapter we also compare Jerusalem with other deeply divided cities. Jerusalem's unique features—the city's thrice holiness and the special unfolding of the national Jewish-Arab conflict within it—can thereby be interpreted and understood from these wider comparative perspectives.

CHAPTER 2

A Tale of Two City Sides:
Spatial Division within a United City

THE FIRST STEP in this analysis of contemporary Jerusalem is a consideration of how urban space is organized and used. This is a cardinal issue: the spatial pattern arranges Jews and Arabs into particular configurations, and it is therefore important to examine the ways in which this system of "living together separately" is organized and how it works. The questions are intriguing: how has the urban spatial pattern changed during the two decades since Jerusalem has been under Israeli hegemony? In particular, to what extent is the pre-1967 division into an Arab eastern and a Jewish western city still viable? What new spatial patterns have emerged during the postunification period?

To the foreign visitor, Jerusalem appears to be a city of striking physical diversity; the major contrasts seem to be between the Old and the New City, or between traditional oriental architectural styles and modern residential or commercial developments. While strolling through the city, visitors and tourists rarely become aware of the border zone where Jerusalem was formerly divided, or distinguish between Jewish and Arab neighborhoods. For local Jerusalemites, however, the most important differentiation of urban space is the one made between Jewish and Arab zones. This demarcation is expressed not only in the persistent patterns of residential segregation, but also in various other ways in which ethnic boundaries continue to have significance in everyday life. Moreover, territory in Jerusalem is never "neutral" but always assumes symbolic, national value in the ongoing struggle between Arabs and Jews for control of space. It is for this reason that the changing spatial patterns reflect not only the social distance between these groups, but also the continuing political conflict between them.

ARAB ZONES VERSUS JEWISH ZONES

During the two-decade period following Jerusalem's unification, the basic separation between Jewish and Arab zones has been maintained, and to a large extent continues to express the pre-1967 patterns characteristic of the divided city. All of West Jerusalem—that is, the section of the city that was Israeli since 1948—remains an almost exclusively Jewish zone.

Similarly, the Arab residential and commercial areas continue to be confined to the former eastern section of the city and to adjacent sections outside of Jerusalem's municipal boundaries located on the West Bank. However, taking the urban area as a whole, major changes have occurred as a result of massive new Jewish construction and settlement across the former dividing lines in East Jerusalem. These large-sized building projects have practically transformed the city's shape, and more particularly, they have altered the overall distribution of Jewish and Arab zones throughout the city.

The new Israeli building projects in East Jerusalem were begun almost immediately following the 1967 war. This program had as its major objective establishing a Jewish physical presence within the former Arab sections of the city; the Israeli authorities wished to "create facts" so that newly united Jerusalem could not again be divided into two cities. In order to carry out this program effectively, they first took steps to expropriate large sections of unoccupied Arab land that could be developed for residential or industrial use. These areas were located at a distance from the then existing urban core areas. Ultimately, nearly one-third of the total area of East Jerusalem was expropriated by the Israeli government.[1]

Once the land itself had become available, Israeli government companies were made responsible for planning and then implementing the new construction. The building projects advanced in several stages. In the first stage, initiated only several months following the end of the fighting, construction was started in two places. The Jewish Quarter in the Old City began to be rebuilt, and construction also started in several residential neighborhoods (Ramat Eshkol, French Hill, and others) that stretched between West Jerusalem and the former Israeli enclave on Mount Scopus. In the second stage, beginning in 1970, four large suburban satellite developments were created (Neve Ya'akov, Ramot Allon, Gilo, and East Talpiyyot) in strategic locations dominating the major approaches to the city. In the third and most recent stage, still another major housing project (Pisgat Ze'ev) was built on the northeast edge of the city; the purpose of this program was to create a continuous Jewish residential area ranging from Neve Ya'akov to Mount Scopus. Each of these new housing developments was large in scope, involving several thousand dwelling units; they were, in fact, on the scale of a medium-

[1] According to Israeli land ordinances, expropriation for public purposes, including public housing projects, is allowed and often practiced. Land expropriation in East Jerusalem by the Israeli authorities was carried out in three stages between 1968 and 1980, and altogether included about 21,000 dunams out of the total of 70,000 dunams annexed after 1967. While most of the expropriated land consisted of state- and Arab-owned uninhabited areas, it also included Jewish-owned land such as in the Jewish Quarter of the Old City, Mount Scopus, and other lands owned by Jews prior to 1948.

sized new Israeli town, complete with their own infrastructure and service centers—and clearly separate from the neighboring Arab areas. These satellite communities were exclusively occupied by Jewish residents, and thus they became an integral part of Jerusalem's overall Jewish residential space.

In addition to housing developments, the Israeli authorities also planned and built a number of large public centers and industrial zones on the other side of the former dividing line. A good example of this are the new Hebrew University campus and Hadassah Hospital on Mount Scopus; rebuilt and vastly enlarged, they now dominate the Old City and the northern sections of East Jerusalem. A new government center was built close by, and a major industrial zone (Atarot) was also established on the city's northern edge. In these ways the Israeli presence in East Jerusalem was widened to include functionally different zones that covered large portions of what previously had been exclusively Arab space (see map 1).

Two major outcomes emerged from Israeli settlement policies in East Jerusalem. First, the distinction between East and West Jerusalem no longer coincides with the Arab-Jewish divide. By 1983, over 21,000 new dwelling units were completed and inhabited by Jews across the former dividing line; according to the census conducted that year, more than 76,000 Jewish residents were then living in the eastern sections of the city (see tab. 2.1). This figure represents roughly one-quarter of the total Jewish population of Jerusalem, and is almost two-thirds the size of the entire Arab population.[2] Indeed, in a certain sense the East-West population distribution has been reversed: in the northern portions of the city the Jewish areas are now located to the east of the Arab zones. Second, the previously clear-cut continuous dividing lines separating Jewish from Arab zones can no longer be said to exist. In their place a kind of mosaic or checkerboard pattern has evolved in which Jewish and Arab neighborhoods are juxtaposed and spread throughout East Jerusalem. In some instances, the new Jewish zones are enclaves within Arab areas, while in others the Jewish areas practically engulf what have become Arab residential islands. In several of these locations the Arab or Jewish neighborhoods are only—or most effectively—accessible by crossing through "the other side."

While this new checkerboard pattern has been imposed upon Jerusalem as a whole, at the local level spatial segregation can be said to prevail: Jews and Arabs continue to reside in separate, homogeneous, and well-

[2] Evidently, as the building projects continued to progress the absolute and relative number of Jews living beyond the former partition line also increased. According to official estimates, by the end of 1987 this figure approached the 110,000 mark, or nearly one-third of the total Jewish population of Jerusalem. See Bigelman 1987.

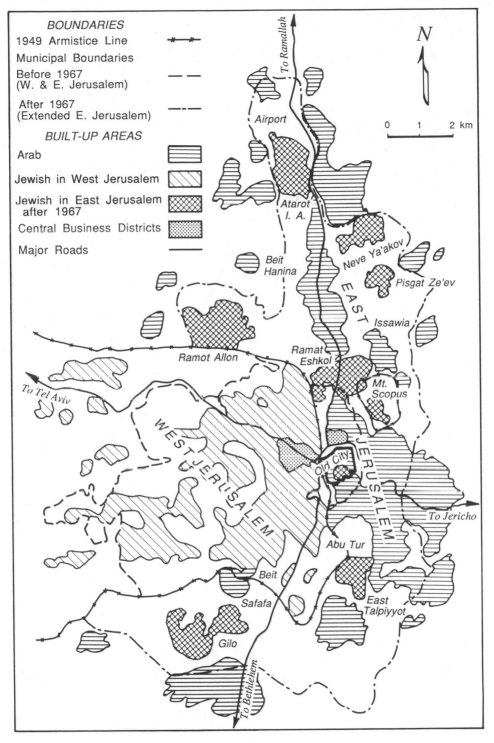

1. Boundaries and Ethnic Areas in Jerusalem

TABLE 2.1

Jewish Residents in New East Jerusalem Neighborhoods, 1983

	No. of Dwelling Units Planned	No. of Units Completed	Population
Jewish quarter	670	600	1,700
Ramat Eshkol and vicinity	5,500	5,500	22,900
Neve Ya'akov	4,200	3,790	13,000
Ramot Allon	9,200	3,130	11,500
East Talpiyyot	4,600	2,760	9,700
Gilo	9,000	5,340	17,200
Pisgat Ze'ev and northern Jerusalem	12,000	—	—
TOTAL	45,170	21,120	76,000

Sources: Data on dwelling units—Israel Ministry of Housing, unpublished internal reports; data on population—Israel, CBS, Census of Population and Housing, 1983.

defined neighborhoods. This fundamental urban feature can best be illustrated by examining the overall distribution of Jewish and non-Jewish (Muslim and Christian) residents by urban statistical subquarters as recorded in the 1983 census (see tab. 2.2). In twenty of the thirty-five subquarters the residents are exclusively Jewish or non-Jewish, with members of the other group amounting to no more than one percent. Even in those cases where the proportion of non-Jews residing in Jewish areas, or vice versa, was higher, the statistics may be misleading. Since community affiliation is classified by religion rather than nationality, many of the non-Jews residing in Jewish areas actually are Christian non-Arabs, such as Christian clergy or Christians married to Jews. In addition, the crude division of urban space into statistical areas necessarily produces cases of overlap where these boundaries do not coincide with Jewish and Arab neighborhoods, most notably in the Jewish and Armenian quarters of the Old City. Indeed, in the two decades that have elapsed since Jerusalem's reunification, no mixed Jewish-Arab residential areas have been created. At most, in certain places Arabs and Jews now live in closer proximity to each other along border zones, or are scattered in small numbers on the "other side" of the ethnic boundary.

While the overall pattern of segregation is clear, it is enlightening to examine the few exceptions to this rule. Shortly after the Six-Day War, a small number of Jewish families sought to establish residence in Arab areas and succeeded in renting homes or apartments in several middle-class neighborhoods in East Jerusalem. The reasons for these individual,

TABLE 2.2
Jewish and Non-Jewish Residents of Jerusalem
by Subquarter, 1983

Subquarter	Total	Jews	Non-Jews	Jews	Non-Jews
		(thousands)[a]		%	
11. Ramat Eshkol	14.8	14.5	0.3		1.7
12. Beit Yisrael, Me'a She'arim	23.2	23.2	0.1		0.2
13. Morasha	2.4	2.2	0.3		10.5
14. Town Center	5.7	5.5	0.1		2.5
15. Rehavia	8.3	8.3	0.1		1.0
16. Nahla'ot	9.5	9.5	. .		. .
17. Geu'la	21.4	21.4	. .		. .
21. Romema	12.4	12.4	. .		. .
22. Giv'at Sha'ul	6.9	6.9	. .		. .
23. Beit ha-Kerem	17.5	17.5	0.1		0.3
24. Giv'at Ram	2.6	2.5	0.1		5.4
25. Bayit Vagan	17.2	17.2	0.1		0.3
31. Kiryat ha-Yovel (South)	10.0	9.9	0.1		0.1
32. Kiryat ha-Yovel (North)	12.2	12.0	0.2		1.8
33. Ir Ganim	10.0	9.9	0.1		0.6
41. Gonen	24.0	23.6	0.1		0.4
42. Rassco, Giv'at Mordekhay	13.5	13.4	0.1		0.4
51. Emeq, Refaim, German Colony	11.6	11.4	0.2		1.7
52. Talbieh	4.2	4.1	0.1		3.1
53. Ge'ulim	9.5	9.3	0.2		2.4
54. Talpiyyot	10.6	9.6	1.0		9.4
61. Christian Quarter[b]	4.3	-	4.3	-	
62. Armenian Quarter[b]	2.0	0.5	1.5	23.0	
63. Jewish Quarter[b]	2.0	1.7	0.3		16.5
64. Muslim Quarter[b]	17.1	. .	17.1		
71. Atarot, Beit Hanina, Shu'afat	30.3	0.1	30.2	0.4	
72. Ramot Allon	11.7	11.5	0.1		1.3
73. Neve Ya'akov, Pisgat Ze'ev	13.3	13.0	0.3		2.3
74. Gi'vat Shappira, Mount Scopus	9.1	8.3	0.8		8.9
75. Al-Tur, Isawiyya	19.8	. .	19.8	. .	
76. Sheikh Jarrah, American Colony	7.6	-	7.6	-	
81. Abu Tur, Silwan	22.3	. .	22.3	. .	
82. Sur Baher, Beit Safafa (South)	14.4	-	14.4	-	
83. East Talpiyyot	9.7	9.7	. .		. .
84. Gilo	17.5	17.2	0.3		1.6
TOTAL	428.7	306.3	122.3	71.5	28.5

Sources: Jerusalem Municipality and the Jerusalem Institute for Israel Studies, *Statistical Yearbook of Jerusalem, 1984*; based on Israel, CBS, *Census of Population and Housing, 1983.*

Note: - = no cases; . . = insignificant.

[a] Figures are rounded off and hence do not always add up to the total.

[b] The division of the Old City into statistical subquarters does not correspond to the present ethnic distribution of residents.

spontaneous initiatives were varied. Some of the Jews were motivated ideologically, caught up in the high drama of Jerusalem's unification and believing that Jews and Arabs could and should live together again; others were mainly motivated by the opportunity to obtain better housing at a low price. The number of Jewish families who actually moved into Arab neighborhoods was small and never exceeded an estimated sixty families, or two hundred persons in all. Most of these Jewish residents eventually moved out, however, so that by the early 1980s only a handful remained. Daily difficulties, such as the necessity to transport their children to distant Jewish schools, or minor friction with their Arab neighbors, were among the principal reasons why they left. In addition, as time passed the Arab landlords were also reluctant to continue renting their property to Jewish tenants.

In recent years another movement of Jews into Arab neighborhoods has been taking place: small numbers of mainly orthodox Jewish families and religious groups have gradually penetrated the congested Muslim Quarter of the Old City. In contrast with the cases described previously, the motive for this movement is ideological, or more precisely, a religious-nationalist ideology. Those who have moved there were determined to reoccupy all of the structures previously inhabited by Jews in the Muslim Quarter that were abandoned in the 1920s and 1930s, in spite of their decaying condition and the availability of modern housing in the renovated Jewish Quarter located nearby. Indeed, these individuals claim that Jews have the right to settle anywhere in the Arab sections of Jerusalem, even if this provokes violence and ongoing friction.

In contrast, there are no known cases of East Jerusalem Arabs having moved to West Jerusalem, or, for that matter, who settled in the new Jewish neighborhoods in the eastern part of the city. It should be emphasized that by virtue of their legal status as "residents" they are not formally barred from purchasing real estate or from renting apartments in any section of the city. On the other hand, in several reported instances East Jerusalem Arabs who wished to reside in Jewish neighborhoods were prevented from doing so by strong Jewish opposition. This was expressed most clearly in the Old City's reconstructed Jewish Quarter. A number of Arab families who had been living there in abandoned Jewish properties between 1948 and 1967, and who wished to remain, were forced to leave their homes in order to permit the reestablishment of a totally homogeneous Jewish residential zone.[3] There are, of course,

---

[3] In this particular case the eviction of Arab families was upheld by a ruling of the Israeli High Court of Justice. The court rejected an appeal by an Arab family against the Jewish Quarter's Development Corporation on the grounds that its refusal to allow an Arab Jordanian citizen to remain in his home could not be considered an act of discrimination in light of Jordan's expulsion of Jews and the demolition of the Jewish Quarter in 1948. It

Arabs who live in West Jerusalem, but they are Israeli Arabs who have been citizens of Israel since 1948. For the most part they live in the Arab village of Beit Safafa—a village that was incorporated into the Israeli section of the city following the 1948 war—as well as several hundred others who have taken up residence in West Jerusalem.

Even though the rule of residential separation holds for most Jerusalemites, Arabs and Jews alike, it is interesting to note that there are two particular groups for whom the entire city consists of a single potential residential zone. One group is composed of the Israeli Arabs who study or work in Jerusalem; since they are both "Israelis" and "Arabs" they can and normally do consider the alternative choice of living in either Jewish West Jerusalem or Arab East Jerusalem. Interestingly, many prefer to take up residence in the Jewish sections of the city. This is particularly true of Arab students and single persons who live in the Hebrew University "integrated" dormitories, or rent apartments in various parts of West Jerusalem. This has been the case despite the difficulties involved; Jewish landlords have often refused to rent their premises to Arabs. One reason for their preference is the even greater reluctance of Arab landlords to rent to single persons; rental units in East Jerusalem are typically an integral part of family homes, and Arab landlords do not wish to expose their own family members—particularly females—to unmarried outsiders. In addition, many Arab students prefer living in the Jewish sector where they have greater social and personal freedom as well as the advantage of being closer to better developed public services and places of entertainment. In contrast, Israeli Arab families more often choose to settle in Arab East Jerusalem, where their children can attend Arab schools and women are in a more protected social environment. Indeed, some of the Arab families who remained in West Jerusalem after 1948 subsequently moved to the eastern section following reunification.

The second group that may elect to live anywhere in the city is Jerusalem's sizable "foreign community": Christian clergymen, members of the diplomatic or United Nations (UN) staff, foreign journalists, and other "temporary residents." During the initial years following the city's reunification, many such persons chose to live in the Arab section because rents were lower there. Since then, rental quarters in East Jerusalem have become less available, and consequently living in the Jewish section has become more common for many of them. Thus, for example, in the early 1980s, most of the foreign UN staff members took up residence in Jewish West Jerusalem, close to the UN Observers Headquarters located

---

further justified the restoration of a purely Jewish Quarter besides the Muslim and Christian Quarters in the Old City in terms of broader historical, political, and security considerations. See Benvenisti 1983.

on the former dividing line. Paradoxically, Jerusalem seems to be more of a "united city" for outsiders and foreigners than for its own permanent residents.

Turning next to the question of where economic activities are located, here too the basic rule of ethnic spatial segregation tends to be followed. Reunited Jerusalem retains its two separate central business districts, the major one wholly Jewish and located in West Jerusalem, and the other entirely Arab, situated in and adjacent to the Old City. In addition, there continue to be parallel Jewish and Arab hotel areas, industrial zones, garages, vegetable markets, and the like, all reflecting Jerusalem's persistent sectoral division.

However, in contrast with the residential patterns, in the case of economic functions a number of Jewish public institutions and commercial enterprises did become established within the Arab business districts. Soon after the imposition of Israeli authority over East Jerusalem, the Israeli government and the municipality took over a number of Jordanian public premises located throughout this section of the city. These included Jordanian government and municipal offices, army facilities, the small airport, police stations, as well as a number of other institutions previously maintained by Arab countries. In several cases the change from Jordanian to Israeli control was nominal. For example, post offices and public schools continued to employ and serve an exclusively Arab population. In other cases, however, the Israeli authorities transferred government or municipal central functions to East Jerusalem, which then began to serve the entire population, both Arabs and Jews. These included, for example, the Israeli Ministry of Justice (relocated in the former Jordanian Jerusalem district offices), the Jerusalem district court, and the city's central abattoir.

A small number of Israeli or Jewish-owned institutions also moved to the Arab area. Several government agencies and Jewish public institutions, such as offices and clinics sponsored by the Histadruth (the General Federation of Jewish Workers) located themselves in East Jerusalem in order to extend their services to the local Arab population. In addition, a handful of Jewish businesses—most notably branches of Israeli banks— also opened their offices in this section of the city. However, in common with the renting of residential housing, these rental contracts were all established immediately after the city's reunification and were few in number. Jewish public offices or private firms that later wished to extend their physical presence to East Jerusalem found it practically impossible to rent space from Arab owners, and there is no case in which a Jewish enterprise was openly able to purchase Arab-owned property for this purpose. This is well illustrated by the fact that in spite of the great demand by Jewish hotel companies for favored locations close to the Old City, no

Jewish-owned hotel was built within the Arab section of Jerusalem after 1967.

This basic pattern of segregation accompanied by asymmetrical opportunities of "penetration into the other side" can also be seen by reversing the angle of observation. When looked at from the Arab side, there are practically no cases in which an East Jerusalem Arab enterprise has been opened in West Jerusalem or in any other Jewish area. This is even more striking than the absence of East Jerusalem Arab residences across the ethnic line; after all, many Arab stores and workshops in East Jerusalem serve mainly Jewish customers, and many small enterprises in West Jerusalem (for example, garages) are operated by Arab workers. Here again, even when the possibility arose, Arab willingness to subcontract or open business locations in West Jerusalem has stopped short in the face of Jewish opposition.

This ongoing spatial segregation is further underscored by the fact that despite the emerging checkerboard pattern of Jewish and Arab residential areas and the widespread economic links between the two communities, hardly any major reorientation of business locations has taken place on either side of the ethnic dividing line. To be sure, a few sites along the old boundary between East and West Jerusalem have become attractive places for Jewish residents and selected businesses, especially the tourist trade; but this should be attributed to their central location and proximity to the Old City rather than their accessibility to the Arab sector. On the Arab side, the removal of the hostile border and the desire to cater to Jewish customers have encouraged minor relocations of businesses in the direction of the Jewish sector. This can be seen in front of the Old City's Damascus Gate, where Arab taxis, haulage vehicles, watermelon sheds, and unorganized workers waiting for an occasional Jewish employer have become concentrated in an open area facing West Jerusalem. However, the basic orientation of business locations has continued to develop in opposite directions in the two parts of the city, and in an "inward" fashion at the local neighborhood level. Significantly, the modern commercial centers built in the new Jewish neighborhoods in East Jerusalem were all located well within the Jewish zones, rather than along the contact areas close to the Arab neighborhoods.

Following the city's reunification, early urban planning proposals considered the reorientation and eventual linkage of the two major business centers of West and East Jerusalem. But these were later rejected in the new master plan for reunited Jerusalem that was finally adopted. This "integrative" planning concept has reemerged in proposals regarding the future development of two particular areas that are close to both Jewish and Arab zones. One plan is concerned with the so-called seam area that stretches north of the Damascus Gate along the former no-man's land;

here a mixture of Jewish and Arab public and commercial facilities are planned to serve as a meeting point or "bridge" between the two sections of the city. The second plan refers to future urban growth in the northeastern section of the city. According to this proposal, extensive Jewish and Arab residential and commerical development is to take place separately, with a major thoroughfare dividing them. Along this axis higher-level services for both Arabs and Jews are planned.[4] Neither of these proposals has thus far been put into practice. Indeed, over the years integrative planning has generally received low priority, while much of the construction that has taken place (building new roads, for example) mainly serves as a physical barrier rather than as a bridge between Jewish and Arab zones.

Another closely related issue concerns the spatial organization of public services. The question to be asked is whether service distribution is organized according to functional-geographical principles regardless of the Jewish-Arab spatial divisions, or instead on a sectoral-ethnic basis. Putting it differently, do public service centers of various kinds and levels serve all of Jerusalem's residents, both Arabs and Jews, or are separate service areas provided for members of each group? This topic is particularly meaningful since, as we have seen, Jewish and Arab zones are presently juxtaposed and in close proximity, and public services are mainly delivered by the Israeli authorities.

The emerging picture indicates that the "functional" pattern was adopted in most matters having to do with the city's physical infrastructure. Thus, since 1967, Jerusalem has one water and sewer system and a single telephone network. Subareas of telephone exchanges are also organized functionally; the newly installed telephone exchanges in the Jewish residential areas in East Jerusalem include the Arab subscribers in the surrounding areas. Similarly, the subdivision of the urban area into postal distribution or garbage collection zones is organized irrespective of whether the residential areas are Arab or Jewish; the central post office in East Jerusalem, for example, is responsible for sorting and delivering mail to nearby Jewish neighborhoods by Arab postmen. Hospitalization zones are also determined according to geographic criteria; however, this includes only the Jewish hospitals since the Arab hospitals do not take part in this system. Most notably, the new Hadassah Hospital on Mount Scopus is responsible for serving the entire northern section of the city comprising both Arab and Jewish residents. It is important to add, however, that in most cases in which the entire city is covered by a single

[4] Regarding the overall planning concepts and problems following Jerusalem's reunification and some of the particular plans related to Jewish-Arab contact zones, see Kutcher 1973; Kroyanker 1982, 1985.

service center, it is usually located in Jewish West Jerusalem. This is the case for nearly all the central government and municipal offices; to cite a few examples, the international telephone exchange, emergency ambulance station, and vehicle licensing authority are all situated in West Jerusalem. In these instances, Arabs have to travel to the Jewish zone in order to receive these and other essential services. The opposite is far less common and applies only to those few instances in which government or municipal central functions have been relocated within the Arab sections of East Jerusalem.

In contrast, the sectoral-ethnic pattern, based upon ethnic-group membership, was also applied in a number of significant instances. As a general rule, wherever the official subdivisions of urban space were determined by residential areas, the zoning has strictly followed the Jewish-Arab neighborhood boundaries; this applies, for example, to taxation areas or building licensing zones. Another example is the spatial allocation of municipal well-baby clinics; with few exceptions, the zoning of these local-level services also followed ethnic lines. This was also the case with a whole range of national-level public services in which special needs or administrative requirements called for the creation of a separate Arab East Jerusalem office. Thus, Arabs and Jews go to different income tax offices or labor exchange agencies.

In most cases, however, an interesting and sometimes unique combination of these two basic patterns has emerged. This reflects the complicated reality of applying a single administration to two previously separate city systems and two distinct, rival ethnic communities. The spatial organization of police work in united Jerusalem is one case in point. Since 1967, the Israeli police force has been the only body responsible for keeping law and order; consequently, Arab policemen serve under Jewish command. As a general rule, these Arab policemen are stationed in the former Jordanian central police station in the Old City, and are responsible for maintaining order within East Jerusalem. Interestingly, during the first years following 1967 this police post was also responsible for the Old City's Jewish Quarter which is situated nearby. In the course of time responsibility for the Jewish Quarter was shifted to the central police station located in West Jerusalem, so that Jewish policemen would be called in cases involving Jews. Of course, in practice it is not always possible to differentiate; police cases are often ambiguous and frequently involve disputes between Arabs and Jews. In addition, Arab policemen may be assigned to West Jerusalem on specific tasks that involve the Jewish population, and Jewish policemen also deal with major cases or incidents involving Arabs.

A similar system has evolved with regard to Jerusalem's fire-fighting apparatus. Following 1967, the parallel services of the two city sectors were formally integrated under the Jewish municipality's control; the East Jerusalem station (which continued to be operated by Arab firemen) became a secondary post responsible to the major station in West Jerusalem. However, in everyday practice the first engine sent to put out a fire is not selected on the basis of geographic proximity, but rather according to whether the fire is located in an Arab or a Jewish area. Only in cases of emergency are reinforcements sent from either or both stations. Problems related to security, as well as group sensitivities, are apparently responsible for these practices.

Sectoral divisions are even more clearly maintained in the operation of parallel Arab and Jewish urban services. The best example is the way in which the city's bus system has been organized. Following reunification, both the Jewish West Jerusalem and the Arab East Jerusalem bus companies continued to operate as separate entities serving their pre-1967 parts of the city. However, the service area of the Arab buses was confined to the Arab sections of the city, and only in one instance were they authorized to run through West Jerusalem en route to nearby Bethlehem. On the other hand, the Jewish bus company was awarded the concession for the routes between West Jerusalem and the new Jewish neighborhoods in East Jerusalem, and also, in several cases, within the Arab areas of the city proper (see map 2). This has resulted in some highly unique features. First, the basic sectoral pattern has generally been maintained: two parallel systems continue to operate side by side, each designed to serve the transportation needs of members of its own community. Hardly any effort was made to link the two networks, and in several instances two different bus companies—the one Jewish, the other Arab—travel along the same route. The numbering system was not even changed: Jewish and Arab buses displaying the same number may travel to different destinations, sometimes running parallel to one another for a certain distance! Second, the spatial organization of public transportation once again indicates the basic asymmetry with regard to Jewish and Arab access to urban space. Whereas Jews may travel on a Jewish bus to any "Jewish destination" located in West or East Jerusalem, this is not the case for Arab passengers. Arabs from East Jerusalem and its environs have no direct connections to employment and service centers in Jewish West Jerusalem, and they are always obliged to avail themselves of a Jewish bus whenever they cross over. On the other hand, within the Arab zones of East Jerusalem Arab passengers are often able to choose between Arab and Jewish bus services.

Another problem concerns electricity. Prior to 1967 there were two parallel electrical companies: West Jerusalem was linked to the Israeli-wide electrical system, while East Jerusalem was supplied by a local Arab-owned and -operated electrical corporation. After 1967, the two

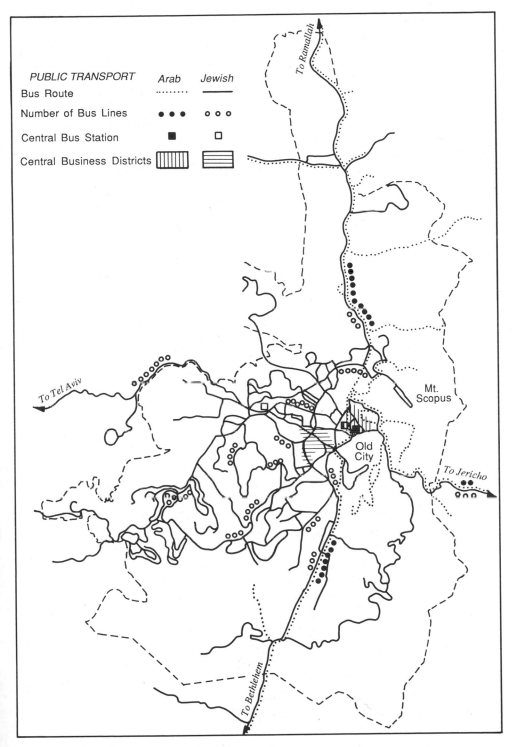

PUBLIC TRANSPORT | Arab | Jewish
Bus Route
Number of Bus Lines
Central Bus Station
Central Business Districts

To Ramallah

To Tel Aviv

Mt. Scopus

Old City

To Jericho

To Bethlehem

2. Jewish and Arab Bus Routes in Jerusalem

systems were connected, yet each of the two companies retained its pre-1967 concession areas. Unlike the limited concessions preserved by the Arab bus companies, in the case of the East Jerusalem Electric Corporation the Israeli authorities fully respected the Arab pre-1967 monopoly rights, including supplying electricity to the new Jewish residential areas and service centers in East Jerusalem. The spatial pattern of electrical supply was thus exceptional compared to the other cases cited: in this instance "Arab electricity" was supplied to Jewish consumers. This represents one of the rare cases in which the old East-West dividing line was retained, rather than the now predominant Jewish-Arab ethnic boundary. More significantly, this was the only important instance in which Jewish customers and zones were dependent on an essential public service originating in the Arab sector.

THE SIGNIFICANCE OF ETHNIC BORDERS

We turn next to a closer examination of how space is distinguished within any particular urban zone, either Jewish or Arab. What are the features that mark off and identify the ethnic boundaries, and how are they maintained and made meaningful?

Jerusalemites are intuitively sensitive to the different signs and markers that are represented in each portion of their city. As we noted earlier, in a fundamental sense all of the city space is either "Jewish" or "Arab," and consequently its residents are always aware whether they are within "their own" zone or that of "the others." There are no longer walls that separate Jews and Arabs, but numerous boundary signs are ever-present and significant.

These spatial markers have both visible and invisible expressions. Beginning with the former, Jewish and Arab residential zones and business centers can be distinguished by their contrasting levels of physical development, land-use patterns, and architectural styles. Whereas the built-up areas in Jewish zones are typified by the intensive development of high-rise construction and extensive public housing apartment blocks, the Arab areas are characterized by low-density occupation of space, traditional-style family homes, and a comparatively lower level of infrastructure. These contrasts are particularly striking where new Jewish developments were built close to the Arab residential areas in East Jerusalem; for example, they stand out visually when comparing the newly reconstructed Jewish Quarter and the decaying Muslim Quarter in the Old City, or the modern high-rise Jewish development around Mount Scopus and the nearby Arab residential areas of village-like family homes. The interface that divides these areas is further dramatized by the massive supporting terraces surrounding the Jewish neighborhoods—they present a kind of "solid front" facing the adjacent Arab areas.

Ethnic spatial divisions are also expressed in other ways: Hebrew versus Arab shop signs, different contents and styles in displaying merchandise, cafes occupied by the two sexes (in the Jewish sector) or by men only (in the Arab sections of the city), differently colored local buses, other contrasting colors and sounds. The time dimension is also highly indicative, particularly with respect to the weekly Sabbath and annual round of holidays observed by Jews and Arabs. Friday noon dramatically illustrates the coexistence of Jerusalem's two distinct worlds. Whereas in the commercial center of Jewish West Jerusalem streets, shops and cafes are at that moment packed with customers concluding their weekly activities on the verge of the Jewish Sabbath, less than a mile away the Old City alleys overflow with streams of traditional Muslims pouring out from the great mosque on the Temple Mount following the Friday noon prayer. On Saturdays and Jewish holidays when stores in West Jerusalem are closed and its commercial center is practically abandoned, bazaars and business districts in Arab East Jerusalem experience their peak activity and are crowded with Arabs, Jews, and tourists.

There are, in addition, a variety of less apparent ways in which the city space is divided and the ethnic boundaries are given practical meaning. City-planning norms and regulations, as well as land-use requirements and practices, are important in this regard. In Jerusalem's Jewish areas, urban development is regulated by statutory town plans and laws which conform to standards required of all Israeli cities. These norms were applied as well in the new Jewish zones of East Jerusalem where the extensive development projects were carried out in accordance with up-to-date and comprehensive planning concepts. In contrast, Israeli planning codes have rarely been applied to the Arab zones of East Jerusalem, and two decades after reunification no overall town-planning scheme has been approved for this section of the city. Several reasons for this may be cited. Unclear land ownership and registration in vast sections of East Jerusalem was one reason. In addition, different norms are followed regarding land use. For example, according to Israeli planning codes sizable sections of land are required to be set aside for public purposes. While this is an accepted practice in the Jewish sector, the Arab land owners have generally opposed this provision. Political sensitivities also explain the reluctance of the Israeli authorities to apply their more demanding building regulations to the Arab sector of the city. As a result, orderly urban development has been held back there; building permits have been issued—or refused—on an ad hoc basis, thereby adding further legal and practical dimensions to the ethnic boundary.

The differential use of city space is also apparent in the persistence of two different housing and real estate markets. Residential development in the Jewish sector generally takes the form of multi family apartment buildings built by construction companies for private-owner purchase. In contrast, in the Arab sector most dwellings are single-family homes, although rental housing is common in East Jerusalem, even among the affluent. In the Jewish sector real estate brokers play a major role; this activity is practically unknown in East Jerusalem, where various informal networks fill this function. In fact, the absence of any institutionalized diffusion of information (through real estate agencies or newspaper advertisements) on housing opportunities on "the other side" best illustrates Jerusalem's divided housing market.

No less significant, two scales of land value also exist. As a general rule, land values in the Jewish zones of Jerusalem are higher than those in the Arab zones. This is mainly due to the absence of clear title deeds on large portions of land, the lower level of infrastructure development, and the lack of approved zoning regulations. Different scales of land values also exist depending upon whether Arab land is being sold to Arabs or Jews. Although infrequent, Arab land offered for sale to Jews is typically so problematic (with regard to location or proof of ownership) that it would rarely be purchased by other Arabs. Transactions which do occur are always complicated, secretive, and costly. Needless to say, under the circumstances of "united Jerusalem" Jewish land is never sold or in other ways transferred to Arab ownership.

In addition to the features already described, there also are perceptual and behavioral dimensions to the ethnic spatial division. These can be seen in the different perceptions of city space made by Arabs and Jews— a kind of "division in the mind"—and also in the different patterns of conduct that take place whenever members of one community cross over to "the other side."

To begin with, when referring to the urban area of Jerusalem, Jews and Arabs perceive the scope and outlines of the city and its boundaries quite differently. The Israeli authorities and the Jewish population regard "united Jerusalem" as it was defined by the city's post-1967 municipal boundaries, greatly enlarged when East Jerusalem and significant sections of its peripheral Arab suburbs and villages were incorporated under Israeli rule. The Arab population not only refuses to recognize this act of annexation, but continues to consider just the former, far more limited, East Jerusalem city area when referring to "their Jerusalem." In a related fashion, while Jews think of the new residential neighborhoods built on the periphery of East Jerusalem as an integral part of both Jerusalem and Israel, thereby separating their status from that of the Jewish settlements created beyond the city limits in the West Bank territory, the Arabs rarely make such a distinction. For the Arabs these are all equally instances of illegal Israeli settlements built on their territory.

Jews and Arabs also make use of different names when referring to various sections and landmarks within Jerusalem. The city itself is called "Yerushalayim" in Hebrew and "al-Quds" (the Holy) in Arabic. The ancient gates to the Old City are called by different names; thus, for example, what is the Jaffa Gate or "Sha'ar Yafo" for the Jews is "Bab al-Khalil" or Hebron Gate for the Arabs. Names have symbolic as well as practical meaning. Following reunification, the Israeli authorities changed several street names in East Jerusalem that referred to Arab national heroes or victories (such as Port Said or Suleiman Street), replacing them with more "neutral" names or even names that referred to their recent victory in the Six-Day War ("al-Zahra" or Flower Street, and "Hatsanhanim" or Paratroopers Street). The Arab population nevertheless continues to employ their own traditional designations; for example, to the dismay of the Jewish residents the East Jerusalem Electric Company for many years billed its customers in new Jewish residential neighborhoods in East Jerusalem according to the previous Arab names of these areas ("Jabal al-Mukabber" rather than "East Talpiyyot").

Crossing the ethnic boundary is, for both Arabs and Jews, a highly conscious act that is normally done under specific circumstances and for well-defined purposes. Indeed, because of the deep spatial segregation of residential and business areas, interaction between members of the two communities necessarily involves crossing over to the other side. However, the practice of "open bridges" between the two city sections is complemented by the principle of "closed gates": the substantial intermingling of the Arab-Jewish daytime population is followed by the general retreat and segregation of the same population at night.

East Jerusalem Arabs—and, for that matter, Arabs from the surrounding West Bank territory—are commonly present in West Jerusalem in great numbers and spread throughout the Jewish sections of the city. Thousands of Arabs cross over daily for employment purposes or to make use of Jewish service and commercial facilities. On weekends, Arab families also make use of several recreation areas located in West Jerusalem; popular among these are a few centrally located parks that are situated close to the Arab zones. For their part, the Jewish population crosses over to Arab East Jerusalem in order to visit the many religious and historical sites that are located there, or to shop in the Arab market and workshops in order to purchase particular consumer items or obtain related services. Many Jews are attracted by the quaint charm of the Old City, and the sights and smells of the Arab *souk*. As mentioned previously, on Saturdays and Jewish holidays East Jerusalem's commercial streets and the Old City's tourist itineraries are crowded with Jewish visitors and customers from Jerusalem and elsewhere.

At the same time, however, significant numbers of both Jews and Arabs rarely or never cross over to the other side of the city. This is typically the case for those who can or prefer to provide for their needs on their own side, as is often true of many Arab housewives and some religious orthodox Jews. In addition, many others are reluctant to venture across the ethnic boundary and tend to avoid "the other side" because of their fear that violence may break out in unpredictable ways. Jews fear acts of Arab terrorism or the hostile demonstrations that have periodically occurred in East Jerusalem, just as Arabs are apprehensive about the constant Israeli police checks and other preventive measures, as well as the possibility that Jewish reprisals may take place should a bomb explode somewhere in West Jerusalem. When, as periodically happens, a violent incident takes place somewhere in Jerusalem, the number of Arab and Jewish visits to the other side greatly decreases for several days and sometimes weeks. Indeed, Jewish visits or excursions to the Arab sections have over the years tended to be less frequent in comparison with the years immediately after the city's reunification. This undoubtedly reflects the cumulative effect of the attacks and other violence that Jews have been exposed to in East Jerusalem. It is also one of the reasons why, with nightfall, Jews and Arabs alike retreat back to their own areas and avoid staying on in what seems to be menacing, dangerous territory.

There are, in addition, two general rules that are followed regarding crossing to the other side and preserving the ethnic boundaries. First, while both communities are strongly opposed to persons from the other side establishing a permanent presence within their own territory, they are much more permissive with regard to its temporary use. This is true not only with respect to residence, but also regarding the daily economic activities of members of one ethnic group on the territory of the other. Many Arab petit entrepreneurs cross over and follow their trade in West Jerusalem on the implicit understanding that they do not remain there permanently. These include, for example, village women selling their products, occasional gardeners and repairmen, or Arab children distributing Israeli evening newspapers in West Jerusalem's commercial center. On a larger scale, this is represented by various "mobile" functions such as East Jerusalem-based tourist buses and haulage vehicles that have become active in the Jewish sections of the city. Similarly, East Jerusalem taxis regularly cross over in search of Jewish passengers, and according to estimates, about one-half of their activity takes place in West Jerusalem. While taxis from both sectors are authorized to circulate freely throughout the city, they nevertheless have their permanent stations in their own respective zones.

Second, the conditions and constraints related to crossing over are not symmetrical. Whereas Arabs are obliged on various occasions to travel to and remain within the Jewish area, Jews are generally free to choose whether and when they wish to be in the Arab sections of the city. The Arabs' dependence on Jewish employment or public service centers results in this kind of "spatial dependence." Indeed, thousands of Arabs from East Jerusalem—particularly those employed in Jewish-owned workplaces—are obliged to travel daily to West Jerusalem and remain there whatever the circumstances. In many instances Arabs find themselves alone throughout the day in a purely Jewish zone, as isolated maintenance personnel in a remote residential area, workers in a small workshop, or as patients in a Jewish hospital. Jews, on the other hand, can be more selective about when to cross over and where to go: they can and do more easily avoid visiting East Jerusalem during periods of unrest, and while there they generally follow well-defined and more "secure" itineraries.

This asymmetry is well illustrated in the bus transportation choices open to Arabs and Jews. Arabs who travel from East to West Jerusalem by bus must ride on a Jewish bus. There simply are no other alternatives. Since they have become accustomed to traveling on Jewish buses, Arabs also will not hesitate to travel on a Jewish rather than an Arab bus within East Jerusalem itself; their choice is purely practical, based on which bus comes first. Jews, on the other hand, who always have the choice of a Jewish bus for their travel needs, will rarely ride on an Arab bus even on those occasions when this might represent the most practical choice. Few Jews have had the experience of riding on an Arab bus; for them it is like entering alien territory, and is thus generally avoided.

The analysis presented thus far suggests a further range of topics. If segregation is so deep and crossing over so selective, to what extent do Arabs and Jews have accurate information regarding spatial or other features on the other side? In seeking to clarify this issue, a special survey was conducted in 1982 among several hundred high school students in a dozen schools in various sections of West and East Jerusalem.[5] The Jewish and Arab students—all of whom grew up after 1967 and had only experienced a united Jerusalem—were presented with identical questionnaires and asked to identify and locate a number of major sites and landmarks in both sides of the city. Well-known neighborhoods, streets, and public and business institutions of a parallel kind and importance (such as the central bus stations or the main post offices in both parts of the city) were selected for each of the two sectors.

As was expected, both Jewish and Arab students were found to be

[5] See Romann 1984.

much more familiar with, and better able to identify, sites on "their own side" (see tab. 2.3). Overall, the ability of both Jewish and Arab students to identify the location of places on "their side" correctly or even approximately was on the average more than three times greater than the respective ability of the other group. The existence of a kind of sectoral dividing line was further demonstrated by the fact that selective perception was not related to geographic proximity or membership in a given subgroup. For example, it was found that Jewish and Arab students attending two nearby schools—at eyesight across the ethnic border—knew no more about the other side than the general school population. Jewish students residing in the new neighborhoods in East Jerusalem and attending schools there were only slightly better able to locate sites in adjacent Arab areas than Jewish students who lived in more distant neighborhoods well within West Jerusalem. Similarly, even the students in the non-Arab Armenian Quarter, just opposite the western sector of the city, were no better acquainted with the Jewish areas than Muslim students residing in the most remote suburbs on the periphery of East Jerusalem.

Familiarity with the "other side" was generally selective. Only about 5 percent or less of the students could locate one of the "other side's" well-known high schools, while about 80 percent could do so with regard to their "own side." Familiarity with cinemas, football fields, and two major residential neighborhoods across the dividing line was only slightly better. Arabs and Jews were best acquainted, in relative terms, with main streets in the central business districts and major public institutions and buildings such as hotels, museums, and central post offices which serve as highly visible landmarks; yet in those cases as well they scored substantially lower with respect to locations on "the other side." The vague awareness and often distorted mental map of "the other side" was also revealed in the students' inability to correctly locate many of the sites due to the lack of acquaintance with the Hebrew and Arabic names or sufficient points of reference. To cite one example, many Jewish students located Salah-al-Din Street—the major commercial street in East Jerusalem—opposite the Damascus Gate, although it is, in fact, facing Herod's Gate. More significantly, a number of Jewish students perceived the distinction between West and East Jerusalem as pertaining only to the Jewish section; they practically ignored the existence of the Arab section of the city.

Significantly, when we compare each group's degree of familiarity with the space of "the other," it becomes clear that the Arab students are generally better acquainted with the Jewish sections of the city than vice versa. Not only did the Arab students score higher in this respect on an overall average, but they also were better able to correctly identify a larger range of sites in the Jewish sector. While Jewish students were

TABLE 2.3
Familiarity of Jewish and Arab Secondary School Students
with Sites in Jerusalem

Sites in Jewish Area	Jews (% identifying)[a]	Arabs	Sites in Arab Area	Arabs (% identifying)	Jews
NEIGHBORHOODS AND STREETS					
Beit ha-Kerem	89.7	14.4	Sheikh Jarrah	82.4	21.4
Me'a she'arim	83.5	10.5	Ras al-'Amud	82.3	7.9
Ramat Eshkol	86.6	32.0	Wadi Joz	73.2	50.0
King George Street	96.9	41.8	Salah-al-din Street	83.1	51.9
Ben-Yehuda Street	93.3	34.6	al-Zahra Street	64.7	3.0
Gaza Street	67.1	5.2	al-Rashid Street	32.0	2.4
PUBLIC INSTITUTIONS AND BUILDINGS					
W. J'lem central post office	63.4	43.8	E. J'lem central post office	78.5	41.4
W. J'lem central bus terminal	79.3	39.9	E. J'lem central bus terminal	60.8	39.6
Rehavia High School	77.4	4.0	al-Rashidiyya High School	81.7	4.8
Sha'arei Tzedek Hospital	92.7	19.0	al-Maqased Hospital	83.7	2.4
King David Hotel	90.0	36.6	Intercontinental Hotel	64.7	39.6
Kings Hotel	81.7	19.6	Ambassador Hotel	41.2	12.8
ENTERTAINMENT AND BUSINESS LOCATIONS					
W. J'lem main football field	60.3	20.3	E. J'lem main football field	53.6	9.1
Israel Museum	95.7	32.1	Rockefeller Museum	38.0	54.8
Orion Cinema	92.7	19.7	al-Hamra Cinema	80.4	15.9
Mahaneh Yehuda Market	86.5	38.6	Khan al-Zeit Market	72.6	3.7
Ha-Mashbir Department Store	97.0	48.4	Naser al-din Supermarket	53.0	0.6
Atara Cafe	76.2	7.9	al-Sha'b Cafe	43.1	0.0
TOTAL (average)	83.9	26.0		64.9	20.1
Weighted average[b]		40.1			24.0

Source: Survey of eleventh-grade students in West and East Jerusalem schools, May 1982 (Romann 1984).

[a] Ability to identify sites was determined on the basis of students' answers to questions about site location. Students who cited where a given site was located—even if this description was inaccurate—were classified as having been able to identify it. Those not so classified were students who did not note a given site's location, who reported not knowing its location, or who recorded an explicitly incorrect answer.

[b] Each group's average ability to identify sites on the "other side" of Jerusalem was divided by that group's ability to identify sites on its "own side."

often unfamiliar with several locations in the Arab sector, such as a major hospital or even some important streets and neighborhoods, many Arabs did identify corresponding locations in West Jerusalem. This is not surprising when we consider how Arabs and Jews use the other side's space.

Our findings also provide additional supporting evidence regarding the practice and attitudes involved in crossing to "the other side" (see tab. 2.4). Both Jewish and Arab students visited the other side on a relatively frequent basis; about two-thirds of the Jewish students and over one-half of the Arab students reported having visited East and West Jerusalem, respectively, during the month preceding the survey. On the other hand, whereas all the Jewish students have been to the Arab section of the city, over 10 percent of the Arab school boys and even a higher percentage of Arab school girls claimed never to have visited the Jewish side. A significant proportion of students on both sides reported feeling a certain unease when crossing over. The degree of unease, however, was found to be significantly higher for the Arab male students; more than one-third reported feeling "very uncomfortable" while visiting West Jerusalem, compared to one percent of the Jewish students. On the other hand, the Arab students displayed a far greater interest than the Jews in getting to know the other side better. These markedly different experiences and attitudes undoubtedly reflect the broader pattern of majority-minority relations.

THE STRUGGLE FOR SPACE AND TERRITORIAL CONTROL

In Jerusalem, just as elsewhere in Israel and the West Bank, the struggle for space has been a constant feature of the ongoing conflict between Arabs and Jews. Territory is typically perceived by both parties not merely in terms of urban development or land use, but rather in regard to physical control and national symbolic value. It is particularly in this respect that the emerging spatial patterns in post-1967 Jerusalem reflect the overall political conflict and existing power relations. Simply put, since 1967 there has been unequal access to urban space for Arabs and Jews. As a consequence of its overall political control and greater economic resources, the Jewish sector has been able to pursue its territorial goals at the expense of the Arab sector.

Israel's territorial goals with regard to the Jerusalem area were explicitly spelled out soon after the city's reunification. They reflected both the Jewish historical attachment to the Holy City, as well as Israel's experience in the two wars (1948 and 1967) fought in and around Jerusalem. The overall policy had as its main axiom the prevention of any possible future attempt to again divide the city or to cut off the occupied East Jerusalem territory from sovereign Israeli control.

TABLE 2.4
Visits of Jewish and Arab Secondary School Students
to the "Other Side"

| | Jews in Arab Sector | | Arabs in Jewish Sector | |
	Male	Female	Male	Female
		(% out of total)		
Most Recent Visit				
Last month	67.1	66.0	56.6	49.1
From one month to one year ago	28.6	30.9	13.1	15.1
More than one year ago	2.9	3.1	17.2	11.3
Never visited	—	—	12.1	17.0
No answer	1.4	—	1.0	7.5
Feeling of Comfort				
Totally at ease	21.4	12.8	20.2	26.4
Reasonably at ease	48.6	48.9	16.2	32.1
Somewhat uncomfortable	28.6	37.2	25.3	13.2
Very uncomfortable	1.4	1.1	35.4	17.0
No Answer	—	—	3.0	11.3
Accompaniment				
Always go alone	1.4	—	10.1	5.7
Usually go alone	11.4	2.1	24.2	9.4
Seldom go alone	44.3	23.4	36.4	26.4
Never go alone	41.4	14.5	21.2	43.4
No answer	1.5	—	8.1	15.1
Interest in Getting to Know "the Other Side"				
Interested in knowing it much better	25.7	36.2	67.6	79.2
Interested in knowing it a little better	31.4	37.2	12.1	7.5
Satisfied with present level of knowledge	31.4	24.5	8.1	3.8
No interest	11.5	2.1	11.2	1.9
No answer	—	—	1.0	7.5

Source: Survey of eleventh-grade students in West and East Jerusalem schools, May 1982 (Romann 1984).

Note: The above figures represent the percentage of all those questioned.

These objectives were given expression in various ways. When deciding what to include within the boundaries of East Jerusalem, strategic rather than purely urban considerations served as the principal guidelines. For this reason the boundaries were extended beyond the former Jordanian municipal limits of East Jerusalem to include all of the dominating ridges overlooking the city; similarly, the new boundaries were stretched far to the north to encompass the East Jerusalem airport. On the other hand, several nearby Arab suburbs were wholly or partially excluded—in spite of the fact that they constituted an integral part of East Jerusalem's peripheral urban area. In effect, the inclusion of maximum territory and minimum Arab population presented two oftentimes conflicting sides of the same formula, namely, to secure Jewish spatial and demographic control of Jerusalem.

Israeli settlement policy within East Jerusalem itself was also politically oriented. Decisions regarding the scope and nature of the various building projects were always taken at the highest Israeli government level, rather than by officials or planners in the Jerusalem Municipality. These decisions were at times made hastily and under great pressure, mainly in response to external international pressures. For example, the Israeli decision to expand a number of Jewish housing projects on the periphery of the annexed area, first in 1970 and again in 1980, were taken practically overnight in response to the 1969 Rogers Plan and later to the UN resolution calling for Israeli withdrawal from East Jerusalem. In both instances the expanded projects were actually opposed by the local Jerusalem authorities; they argued against the creation of new, comparatively far-off suburbs which contradicted Jerusalem's approved master plan. Objections such as these were, however, always overruled by political considerations.

The choice of specific locations for Jewish settlement projects in East Jerusalem was also and mainly dictated by strategic considerations. The overall planning concept was based upon several principles. Chief among these was the occupation of large sections of land that physically dominated both the urban basin and the surrounding Arab-inhabited areas beyond the actual municipal boundary. In addition, the development patterns were meant to physically link the new Jewish residential zones with the older, settled areas of Jewish West Jerusalem in a continuous fashion, and at the same time also to "breach" the spatial continuity of the Arab built-up areas. When this could not be accomplished, new "strategic motorways" were constructed, designed to bypass or transverse the Arab zones and thus permit a direct approach or link between the Jewish zones. The very terminology involved in these planning strategies commonly made use of military terms such as "engulf," "breaching," "penetration," and "territorial domination and control."

A complementary feature of these policies consisted of various restrictive measures designed to limit Arab access to urban territory under Jewish control. East Jerusalem Arabs were in fact—although not officially—prevented from settling in West Jerusalem; they also could not regain control of their property in this section of the city that had been abandoned during the 1948 war. Within East Jerusalem itself, the possibilities for Arab spatial expansion became in turn limited due to the massive expropriation of land for Israeli development, plus the aforementioned zoning regulations and the necessity to receive building permits from Israeli officials. Moreover, the Israeli authorities restricted the permanent settling of West Bank Arabs within East Jerusalem, since this implied granting these Arabs the status of "resident" and an Israeli identity card. Permission to settle permanently in Jerusalem was normally given only in instances of so-called family reunions. Thus, as can readily be seen, the desire to control Arab population expansion was closely linked with plans to preserve a Jewish population majority and Israeli territorial control.

Nevertheless, in this continuous struggle for space the Arab side was by no means without its own strategies and, for that matter, accomplishments. The Arab refusal to sell land or real estate to Jews was one effective political tactic. The sale of Arab land to Jews was formally forbidden by the Palestinian national organizations as well as the Jordanian government, and was subject to severe sanctions. In addition, the Arabs would not negotiate any matter regarding land with the Israeli authorities. East Jerusalem Arabs generally refused Israeli offers of compensation for their property in West Jerusalem, or for land expropriated in the eastern section of the city. Moreover, they typically did not appeal to the Israeli courts, as they were entitled to do, in order to legally challenge the expropriations. The Arabs took the position that the transfer or expropriation of land was an illegal act, and since they did not recognize the right of the Israeli authorities over East Jerusalem they refused to deal with Israeli government agencies or appeal to the Israeli courts.[6] The Arab strategy was to raise the "Jerusalem question" as an international political problem, and thereby appeal to the United Nations or to the major world powers in opposition to what they regarded as the illegal Israeli occupation.

Beyond these political tactics, the major Arab response to Jewish territorial advances consisted of their own much-enlarged building activi-

---

[6] It should be noted, however, that Arab refusal of offers of compensation for their lost property in West Jerusalem actually represented a broader attitude of nonrecognition compared to the case of the post-1967 expropriations. Indeed, with respect to assets left behind in 1948 Arabs claimed in more general terms that the loss of homeland territory was not subject to any financial negotiation.

ties. Indeed, since the 1970s Arab housing construction in East Jerusalem has taken place on an unprecedented scale. Due to their rapid population growth and the rise of real income, Arab residents have invested extensively in the construction of private homes throughout the Arab sections of East Jerusalem; the availability of Arab family-owned land, their familiarity with the construction trade, and the practice of mutual aid when building family homes contributed to this rapid, spontaneous development. Motivated by a sense of urgency and not always willing or able to conform to formal procedures, part of this Arab residential development was accomplished without first receiving legal authorization, particularly in the rural periphery of East Jerusalem.[7] But if, generally speaking, Arab urban development was spontaneous in nature and individually initiated, it was also directly encouraged by Arab political organizations seeking to resist the Jewish territorial expansion. In the framework of the policy of "steadfastness" (sumud), the Jordanian government and the Palestinian national organizations made funds available to encourage and assist Arab construction; substantial loans were offered to Arabs who wished to build new houses in or around East Jerusalem. Paradoxically, this practice had the unofficial consent of the Israeli authorities; what is more, in order to prevent abuses, East Jerusalem Arabs had to show the Arab organizations an authorized construction permit issued by the Israeli municipality!

Faced by this extensive, space-consuming pattern of Arab housing construction and the resulting urban sprawl, the Israeli authorities took measures to restrict Arab construction when it appeared to close options for future Jewish growth. In fact, both sides were driven by the same motives and fears—namely, that all of the area not physically occupied by one side would be taken over by the other. This struggle for space also spilled over beyond the Jerusalem municipal boundaries and onto the adjoining West Bank territory. There, in areas within the municipal jurisdiction of various Arab towns and villages that were under Israeli military government rule, many Arabs found cheaper land as well as fewer obstacles to obtaining building permits. It is for these reasons that a substantial amount of Arab suburban development, including both East Jerusalem residents and migrants from the West Bank, has taken place in areas just beyond the Jerusalem city limits. Of course, the Jewish response to this was not long in coming. After the late 1970s, the Israeli authorities began building a new series of Jewish semirural settlements and urban suburbs (Giv'at Ze'ev, Ma'aleh Adumim, Efrata) in areas located just beyond the Arab built-up areas on the periphery of Jerusa-

[7] Regarding the scale, nature, and problems involved in Arab residential building since 1967, see Hyman, Kimhi, and Savitzki 1985; Kroyanker 1985.

lem. These Jewish areas were intended to form a second "security belt" and thereby extend Jewish control over the entire Jerusalem metropolitan area.

However, taking greater Jerusalem as a whole, not only have the Jewish-Arab population ratios been more or less equal, but Israel's ability to control Arab in-migration and territorial expansion was also much more limited in comparison with inside the city's municipal boundaries. Moreover, since most of the Jewish settlers in the new peripheral West Bank suburbs came from the central city, this in turn has contributed to the relative decline of the Jewish population within Jerusalem itself. As can be seen, Israel's preference for extending territorial control contradicted its original goal, as formulated in 1967, of securing the largest possible Jewish majority within the united city. Hence there are, to say the least, certain ironies and paradoxes that have emerged in this ongoing struggle for space.

A comparison of building development within the Arab and Jewish sectors since 1967 underscores the different opportunities open to each group. According to available statistics, between 1967 and 1985 approximately 65,000 dwelling units were built by the Jewish sector, more than doubling West Jerusalem's pre-1967 residential stock.[8] Well over one-half of this total consisted of government-sponsored and -subsidized public housing; this was the case since, as we have seen, attracting Jews to Jerusalem was given high national priority. Moreover, nearly 80 percent of the government-sponsored projects were undertaken in the area of East Jerusalem.

In contrast, the Jerusalem Arab population rarely benefited from Israeli public funds for its housing needs. In the period since the city's reunification only several hundred Arab public housing units have been built at Israeli initiative, and a similar number of Arab-sponsored residential developments were helped by government or municipal funding. Similarly, major urban renewal projects undertaken in Jerusalem were exclusively targeted at various low-income Jewish neighborhoods, and never included the more deprived Arab areas such as the heavily crowded, decaying Muslim Quarter in the Old City.

Due to its less orderly nature and the absence of appropriate statistical data, it is difficult to determine the precise extent of Arab residential development. According to one estimate, between 1967 and 1983 over four thousand new structures were built in the Arab areas of East Jerusalem, representing an increase of about 60 percent in this sector's build-

[8] These statistics are based upon annual issues of the *Statistical Yearbook of Jerusalem*, as well as unpublished data.

ing stock outside the Old City.[9] Compared with its much higher population increase—which almost doubled in the corresponding period—it is fair to conclude that in spite of the post-1967 Arab building boom, its housing requirements could not be fully met within Jerusalem itself. Thus, as we have already seen, many East Jerusalemites have consequently built new homes in areas beyond the city boundaries.[10]

The contrast between the Jewish and Arab sectors' post-1967 development is particularly striking with regard to nonresidential growth. Here again, the total floor space in this category more than doubled during the period under consideration. However, practically all of this development took place in the Jewish sections of West and East Jerusalem. The massive construction of new public institutions (government buildings, hospitals, and higher-educational centers) as well as new office buildings and hotels has effectively transformed the face of Jewish Jerusalem, and, more specifically, that of its main business center.

Almost none of these changes occurred in Arab East Jerusalem. With the exception of a few Muslim and Christian religious and other public institutions which were built or renovated, hardly any significant changes have taken place in the Arab commercial districts. This overall stagnation can be illustrated by the fact that since 1967 no major office building has been built in the Arab central business district; this should be seen in light of the fact that most of the present-day modern Arab business center outside the Old City walls developed while the city was divided and under Jordanian control. As in the case of Arab residential construction, here too many Arab commercial establishments preferred to move from East Jerusalem to areas beyond the city limits or to the nearby Arab towns of Bethlehem and Ramallah. In common with Arab housing, this was because of the more permissive procedures for authorizing construction permits and business licenses in the West Bank zone compared to Israeli Jerusalem. However, unlike the increase in private housing, it appears that the Arab sector had far less opportunity to invest in commercial ventures and public facilities and was much more restricted in undertaking large-scale projects that required access to political, economic, and spatial resources.

Finally, it should be stressed that the Israeli authorities did make substantial investments in Arab East Jerusalem's physical infrastructure. Several major projects were undertaken, particularly with regard to the decaying infrastructure of the Old City where major portions of the water and sewer systems were restored and renovated. Once again, however,

[9] See Hyman, Kimhi, and Savitzki 1985.

[10] It should be noted that this was made possible and was actually encouraged by the fact that East Jerusalem Arabs settling beyond the Jerusalem jurisdiction area in the West Bank territory were allowed to keep their Israeli resident status and related privileges.

when analyzing the total investments made by Israeli-sponsored public funds (ranging from roads to community services) it is fair to conclude that well over 90 percent were allocated to the Jewish sector.[11]

In drawing this chapter to a close, it is useful to add a number of remarks regarding Jerusalem's post-1967 spatial patterns, as well as the policies and patterns of behavior that have been prevalent throughout this period. To begin with, it is important to emphasize that the spatial segregation practiced by Arabs and Jews has a basically voluntary dimension that is shared by members of both communities. This mutual preference can be attributed to both cultural and economic factors. Jews and Arabs prefer to live separately in order to better preserve their own group identity as expressed by religion, language, cultural norms, and lifestyle. In addition, this permits the two communities to conserve and develop their own public institutions and various sector-oriented commercial activities. Voluntary spatial segregation also serves a common desire to prevent interethnic frictions which might otherwise arise from different religious practices or severe national conflicts. In all these respects, the basic aspirations and practices observed in Jerusalem are not unlike those in many other places where different ethnic groups share the same urban space.

What makes the spatial pattern of post-1967 Jerusalem exceptional, however, is the multidimensional and nearly total scope of Jewish Arab segregation. Segregation involves not only residence but also, as we have seen, the location of sectoral economic activities. Spatial segregation is not a matter of degree but is almost complete, with no mixed residential areas or commercial centers and with clearly defined, relatively stable ethnic boundaries. This total, rigid, and persistent pattern is undoubtedly the spatial expression of the continuing political conflict between Jews and Arabs in the reunited city. It is an expression not only of the feeling of insecurity and mutual threat perceived by the two rival communities, but in a deeper sense also indicates their uncompromising desire to control their "own territory" in order to further their conflicting national aspirations.

The emerging patterns are highly asymmetrical, reflecting the existing power relations between the Jewish majority and the Arab minority. As we have seen, this is expressed by both Israel's explicit policies regarding its direct control and overall organization of Jerusalem's urban space, as well as by the more spontaneous patterns of Jewish behavior designed to exclude Arabs from Jewish territory. In pursuing their policies, the Israeli authorities have frequently stressed the voluntary aspects of segregation, arguing that the creation or preservation of homogeneous Jewish

[11] See Benvenisti 1981a.

and Arab zones represents the best possible pattern for daily coexistence between the two antagonistic communities. At the same time, unequal allocation of resources and the imposition of Jewish settlements within Arab territory necessarily imply an even greater mixing of Jewish and Arab zones throughout the entire Jerusalem area. In the end, the goal of spatial control is often judged to be more important than that of mutually desired segregation.

CHAPTER 3

Living along the Ethnic Border

THE PREVIOUS CHAPTER presented an overall view of how Jerusalem's space has been divided between Jews and Arabs. The patterns that were depicted referred mainly to physical features, and to how territory was selectively perceived, used, and contested. In the present chapter we turn to a number of related, yet different, topics. Rather than considering the entire urban area of Jerusalem, attention is concentrated upon two particular residential zones. We wish to understand how, within these small portions of the total Jerusalem world, Arabs and Jews who reside close to each other manage their social relationships. Our focus is, moreover, interactional: what kind of exchanges develop between persons who inhabit the same social space? In a word, we turn from the previous macro-analysis to a more fine-grained micro-perspective on ethnic spatial relationships.

Two Jerusalem neighborhoods were selected for intensive study. Both are situated along the old pre-1967 dividing line. In contrast with the majority of Jerusalem residents who live within ethnically homogeneous areas, in these border zones Arabs and Jews are positioned practically next to each other. They may shop at the same stores, walk along the same paths, wait together for the same bus, and even share a common interest in "their neighborhood." Yet cultural differences, political conflict, and outright antagonism between the two sides may restrict or entirely inhibit them from crossing the border. The goal of this chapter is to describe and explain the patterns of ethnic interaction that have emerged in these interface areas.

WITHIN ABU TUR: DIVISION AND FIRST CONTACTS

Located south of the old walled city of Jerusalem, the Arab village of Abu Tur ranges along one of the city's most splendid heights. At its lower end Abu Tur joins the village of Silwan and then abuts upon Gai Ben-Hinom, the cliff where in ancient times the Canaanites hurled children down to their death as sacrifices to Moloch. As one moves westward up the hill the view becomes even more dramatic. From the crest the lookout peers eastward to the hills over the Dead Sea, while slightly to the north the Temple Mount with its silver and gold domes stands out clearly and majestically. This is certainly one of the most prized panoramas in a city that prides itself on its beauty.

Abu Tur (or Turi, as it is commonly called by the Arabs: the name derives from the fabled eleventh-century Arab warrior, Ahmad al-Turi, who fought the Crusaders with such fervor that he charged them while mounted upon a bull!) is one of Jerusalem's classic divided sections. The division took place as a result of war and conquest. Abu Tur abuts upon the western Jewish section of Jerusalem, and during the 1948 war heavy fighting and shelling broke out there. The Arabs living in the western portion of the neighborhood fled from their homes, and the Israeli forces, moving toward the east, occupied all of this area up to the crest of the hills. The cease-fire line was drawn at the point where the two armies faced each other. The lower eastern sections of Abu Tur were incorporated within Jordan, while the higher western half became a part of Israel; a thin stretch of "no-man's land" was then established between them. On the Israeli side, Jews began moving into the abandoned Arab dwellings. Throughout the nearly two decades that marked Jerusalem's division, the Israeli and Jordanian soldiers stationed there stared and on occasion fired pot-shots at one another, while residents on both sides of the barbed wire learned to live with recurring tensions.

The social composition of the two populations is an important variable for understanding the kinds of social relations that developed later. Many of the Jewish families began as illegal squatters; they moved into the homes the Arabs had fled from and later legalized their presence by signing a contract with the government "Custodian of Abandoned Property." They first advanced into the better houses, particularly those that were far from the border; gradually, however, the squatters pushed farther east and began occupying homes closer to no-man's land. Many were recent immigrants from Middle Eastern and European countries; prominent among them were Iranian and Moroccan Jewish families. They moved into this zone with considerable trepidation; this was, after all, a border area where the sense of danger was never absent. Throughout the 1950s and early 1960s, Abu Tur was thought to be an "undesirable address," and many of the immigrants who came there later left.

Gradually this area began to attract a different population. A number of Israeli artists and intellectuals discovered Abu Tur. What attracted them were homes or rooms larger in size than those available elsewhere in Jerusalem, as well as small garden plots and a certain rustic charm. There was an openness too about this marginal urban zone, and this attracted nonconformists and those seeking a Bohemian lifestyle. Besides, the old Arab homes had a special oriental beauty and the view of the Old City was particularly splendid. Slowly, then, an occasional artist or university lecturer moved into Abu Tur.

Changes in population composition were also taking place in the Arab section. Toward the crest of the hill, where the air and the view were magnificent, a small number of well-established families had built large homes. These merchants and professionals, in some cases members of old Jerusalem families, enjoyed the amenities of middle-class Jerusalem life. However, as one moved down the hill the dwellings became more crowded and shabby. For more than a century Arabs from the Hebron region had been migrating to Jerusalem, and some of these "Haleileh" ("Hebronites" in Arabic) rented rooms in Abu Tur. They mainly came from small villages around Hebron, and in Turi they found the kind of low rents and village ambience that suited them. The Arab population was therefore increasingly divided between the more established Jerusalem familes, near the top of the hill, and the poorer newcomers, mainly from Hebron, who lived farther down the hill.

When, on June 5, 1967, war again broke out, fighting and shelling returned to Abu Tur. Following the lightning-swift Israeli victory, everything was suddenly changed: the barbed wire and mines were removed and Abu Tur became, at least in theory, a single residential area within the newly united Jerusalem. As the walls came down there was almost immediate contact between Jewish and Arab residents. Curiosity overcame apprehension and quickly led to a number of encounters. Two particular events then took place that set the tone for much of what has subsequently followed.

The first event was the spontaneous explosion of curiosity that led hundreds and later thousands of Arabs to cross over and gape at Jewish Jerusalem, while even greater numbers of Jews rushed to look wide-eyed at the wonders of the Old City and the holy places. This initial "crossing over" was briefly mentioned in chapter 1. The encounters in Abu Tur had a more personal aspect to them. When the border opened, dozens of Arabs came across to inspect their former homes; they knocked at the door of the present Jewish residence, introduced themselves as the "previous owners," and asked whether they might come inside for a moment. These were difficult moments for members of both groups—the Jews recall being uncomfortable with the realization that they were living in someone else's home, just as the Arabs report that they had to control their emotions when they stepped inside a home occupied by strangers.

The second event was even more complex. Jews from their side and Arabs from theirs had populated Abu Tur up to the border; but with the walls down and the city united a few dwellings situated within what had been no-man's land were still uninhabited. Although they were practically demolished, these structures were in a prime location and obviously were valuable properties. As soon as the fighting ended a number of Arab families began moving back into these ruins, and when questioned by the Israeli police they explained that the places belonged to them and produced a legal deed of ownership.

At the same time several groups of Israelis had also banded together with an eye toward occupying these same long-empty dwellings. Like others before them, they entered the houses, "established a presence," and began repairing the ruins. This seemed to be a continuation of the same process by which, since 1948, Jews had been settling in abandoned Arab homes. But this time it triggered emotions and set off a minor cause celebre.

The Jewish squatters made a point of being armed, and it seemed too that they were acting with the tacit approval of the Israeli authorities. However, some neighbors on both sides voiced their disapproval. Several of the old-time Jewish residents spoke out against the illegal seizure; the Arabs also protested that the homes being occupied belonged rightfully to them. Tensions quickly mounted. There were several scuffles and at least one bloody nighttime brawl during which a number of Arabs were injured. The next morning a delegation of Arab Abu Tur notables went to the police headquarters and complained formally. They met with the Israeli mayor of Jerusalem, Teddy Kollek, who assured them that those guilty of violence would be punished. The Israeli media quickly picked up the story. Who was responsible, they asked, or was this just the Wild West? Embarrassed, the Israeli housing authority announced that the seizure of homes by Jews had been illegal, and that a lottery would be held to determine who would live in the empty dwellings. The new occupants would be Israelis, but they would gain possession in a fair, orderly fashion. A lottery was duly held and those who won began to make plans for their new property.

Events then began taking a different twist. In late June 1967 the Israeli Knesseth voted to incorporate East Jerusalem within Israel, and Jerusalem Arabs were issued Israeli identity cards and became subject to Israeli law. This had an immediate effect in Abu Tur; several of the Arab residents turned to the Israeli courts with the request that their homes be returned to them. (This was unusual; as noted in the previous chapter, Arabs typically have not appealed to the Israeli courts since this presumably would indicate tacit acceptance of Israeli sovereignty over Jerusalem). The case went to the High Court of Appeals where, following lengthy deliberations, the court decided in favor of the original Arab owners. The Israelis who previously had been awarded the homes were compensated for their expenses, and the homes were returned to their former Arab owners.

While these two events were certainly idiosyncratic, they indicate the kinds of contacts that were becoming established between Jews and Arabs. The Jews held dominant power, the Arabs were subordinate, and this basic structural feature found expression in ways that were complex and often paradoxical. The Jews were embarrassed by the Arabs who knocked at their door and asked to enter *their* home; no sustained, serious relationship could grow on competing claims to a home, and hence these contacts were quickly broken. In the case of the no-man's-land homes, the Arabs saw that the Jews might use force; but they learned too that under certain circumstances they could claim their rights and even win. Some of the Jews living along the border encouraged the Arabs to complain to the Israeli officials, and there were also some discussions and visits between Jews and Arabs. In short, a residential pattern, however tenuous and uncertain, had begun to emerge.

Parameters of Contact and Avoidance

According to the 1983 Israeli census the total population of Abu Tur was about 15,500 persons. Of these 10,000 or so were Arabs, and a little less than 5,500 were Jews. The eastern or Arab section was more densely populated: it had a total of 1,308 dwellings units with 1,606 households. The number of dwellings and households on the western or Jewish side is considerably smaller and the housing density is also lower. Not only is the population composition different, but the trends also contrast sharply. Housing problems on the Arab side are acute; while the population has been growing, few new homes have been built. As a result many Arab families live in extremely crowded conditions. Indeed, this section of the village is considered to be a low-status urban zone. Quite the opposite has been taking place in the Jewish section. Abu Tur has become an attractive high-status location for Israelis. Real estate has grown increasingly valuable—several elegant new apartment houses have been built on the heights overlooking the Old City, and many of the original Jewish residents have sold their homes to middle-class professionals and affluent Western immigrants. Indeed, in addition to the fundamental population shift from Arab to Jewish, the Jewish section has become gentrified as a consequence of internal social and economic trends.

Before we turn to consider Arab-Jewish contacts across the border, there are a number of relevant urban features that need to be pointed out. First, there is no reason to assume that the residents' personal social contacts are limited to the neighborhood level. In common with city dwellers throughout the world, Arabs and Jews who live in Abu Tur are likely to visit friends or family members in other parts of the city. This wide-ranging distribution of social networks may be less valid for Arab residents whose expanded family groups, or *hamulas*, are concentrated within Turi, but what may be termed "urbanite" patterns typically hold for members of both groups.

Second, there is little economic or commercial activity within Abu Tur itself; nearly all of the Arab and Jewish residents are employed outside of the immediate neighborhood. In the western half, commercial activities are limited to a few food and specialty shops on Hebron Road, a hotel, tourist center, and restaurant, several artisan shops, and a small plant nursery; similarly, the eastern half has some grocery stores, two carpenters' shops, a cafe and poolroom, and two or three greengrocers. A small number of Arabs who live in Abu Tur work in the Jewish hotel and shops up the hill, while—in keeping with the overall pattern—none of the Jewish residents are employed by Arabs. In addition, some of the local Arabs are occasionally employed by Jews who live close to them. What this means is that early in the morning most members of both groups leave the immediate area for their workplaces and return later in the afternoon or evening. They are linked together, if at all, by the thin thread of common residence.

The point that is being made is that, on theoretical grounds alone, there is no necessary reason for Arabs and Jews to interact with one another. This conclusion is strengthened when we examine the existing system of local city services.

Jewish and Arab children attend their own schools: there simply are no schools where youngsters from both East and West Jerusalem study together. This pattern is repeated in local health services. Kupath Holim, the largest health program in Israel, maintains a small clinic on the edge of the Jewish zone, and Jews may go there or to Jewish hospitals for their medical needs, while the Arabs normally go to Arab clinics and hospitals located in East Jerusalem for medical treatment. Several Israeli government-sponsored well-baby clinics (*tipat halav*) are located nearby—but in keeping with the overall pattern, one serves the Arab women while the other is used by Jewish women. Similarly, a local community center provides recreation and adult education programs for Jewish residents, but Arabs who live on the other side of the hill rarely make use of these facilities (and when they do, this becomes a source of tension). Community activities have also been organized by local Arab residents, but they never involve Jewish participation. In short, at the neighborhood level practically all forms of social services remain separate and divided between members of the two groups.

Taking these facts into consideration, there seem to be few occasions or incentives for sustained interactions between Arabs and Jews. This is, in fact, the general rule: most of the Jews and Arabs who live in Abu Tur do not maintain social links with persons on "the other side." Indeed, for the majority of residents, both Arabs and Jews, the border can still be said to exist; even though the barbed wire was removed two decades ago, few persons cross over and maintain contact with each other.

In addition to the factors already mentioned, there are a number of other reasons why social interactions are almost exclusively concentrated within one's own ethnic group. One reason is spatial or ecological: although more than 15,000 persons reside in Abu Tur, only a small number actually live close enough to the border to be aware of one another's presence. For example, both the Arabs who live near the bottom of the hill and the Jews whose apartments are situated along the western edge all reside in solidly homogeneous areas, and neither has any sense of living close to a border.

Apprehension is a second constraint. Members of each group are uncertain and fearful about the other. Jews are afraid of Arab terrorism and violence, while Arabs express many of the same fears regarding Jews. Some Jewish residents have a continuing sense of living close to a hostile population; in point of fact, since 1967 terrorist bombs have been found in the Jewish sections of Abu Tur and several have exploded. In a number of cases Arab residents who lived nearby were arrested and later convicted for taking part in terrorist activity. Some of the female residents are particularly wary: women of various ages report that they are apprehensive when alone at home or when they walk through the neighborhood at night. Their fear is not entirely unfounded, there have been instances in which Jewish females were bothered or molested by Arab males. This does not mean that Jewish residents live with a constant sense of tension: on the contrary, the lovely panorama as well as the bucolic village atmosphere typically project a sense of calm. And yet an edge of fear and danger is never far away.

Similar fears are felt by Arab residents. The Arabs who cross through the Jewish sections on their way to work tend to walk quickly in order to avoid encounters; there is a certain nervousness until one passes into more open, "neutral" streets. Arab residents have learned to identify certain Jewish homes or places as particularly hostile, and they tend to avoid them on their way to and from the city. (A large walled home belonging to a Jewish resident who is called "the policeman" is thought to be especially dangerous.) What the Arabs fear in particular is being picked up by the police following some incident; the police routinely round up all Arabs in the vicinity for questioning, and they are apprehensive that if caught in such a situation they will face repeated police interrogation.

The Arabs are also worried about Jewish violence. In recent years a number of Jewish terrorist acts have taken place in Jerusalem. In one well-publicized case, the police uncovered a plot in which a bus parked in Arab Abu Tur had been mined with explosives, and although it did not explode, this incident illustrates the dangers that confront them.

Finally, some Arabs and Jews avoid each other because of their beliefs or ideologies. For example, some Jews report that they "don't like Arabs" or that they "don't trust Arabs"; consequently they tend to avoid social ties or relationships with them. Similarly, some Arabs relate that they consciously avoid personal encounters with Jews. It is not that they are fearful, but rather that they believe that interacting with Jews has negative effects upon Arab life. "What good has come from contact with Jews?" they ask, and argue that Arab society has been weakened morally by its exposure to Israel.

Living Together

On the other hand, some residents have established regular patterns of interaction. To be more specific, there are two micro-zones in which Arabs and Jews enter into close contact: a small area where some Jews reside within the Arab zone, and a larger strip along the old cease-fire line where Jews and Arabs live in close proximity. Even though these two micro-zones include only a small minority of residents, their experience has been especially rich and, at least potentially, significant.

In the previous chapter we saw that shortly after 1967 a number of Jewish families rented rooms and homes in Arab neighborhoods; as was also noted, in practically all of these cases the Jews subsequently moved out of these areas. Abu Tur has been an exception in that a small number of Jews continue to live within the Arab section. At the time of our research in 1982/83, there were between twenty and twenty-five Jews living just across the former border. They were concentrated along two short streets, although not all of them lived next to one another.

These Jewish families were divided between six permanent families who had lived there for ten years or more, and another ten or so temporary persons who rented rooms or small apartments for shorter periods of time. Five of the permanent families rented their apartments, while the sixth had purchased his home from the previous owner; all of the temporary residents rented their rooms or apartments on a monthly basis. Most of them lived together with their Arab landlord. The Jewish tenants rented a self-contained unit or several rooms from the Arab owner who lived in another part of the same dwelling. This relationship differs fundamentally from the common Jerusalem pattern—in this instance the Jews are tenants, the Arabs are landlords, and both reside within the same structure.

What features characterize Jews who choose to live in Arab neighborhoods? The permanent residents in our study were in their late thirties and forties. Three were artists, one was a professional, and the other two were engaged in government work at comparatively high levels. The temporary residents were university students and artists, including both males and females. These residents had been attracted to Abu Tur for a number of reasons. One was the low rent—a two- or three-bedroom Arab-owned apartment cost one-third less than an apartment in Jewish sections of the city. Equally important, these Arab buildings with their high ceilings and lovely arched windows are more attractive than the standard Israeli apartments. Indeed, it is this sense of "something special" that attracted these Jewish families—the feeling that they were living within a distinctive part of Jerusalem. Some were motivated by ideology; they believed in living in peace with Arabs, and sought to realize these ideals by making their home in an ethnically mixed neighborhood.

Why do Arab landlords rent apartments to Jewish tenants? Older men in their fifties or sixties, the Arab landlords are entrepreneurial types who in the past have had commercial dealings with the British or other foreigners. They have, first of all, an economic incentive: the rents received from their Jewish tenants are comparatively low, but the income is nonetheless important. Economic exchanges with Jews are considered to be legitimate, and consequently this relationship could be established. Second, there are occasions during which the Jews play valuable roles as intermediaries or brokers for their Arab landlords as well as for other Arabs living nearby. For example, they have been asked to translate official documents written in Hebrew, or to intervene on behalf of "their family" in negotiations with Israeli government bureaucracy. Finally, the Jewish tenants are acceptable since they are small in number and generally maintain a low profile. The handful of Jews attracted to this corner of Abu Tur tend to be nonaggressive, nonpolitical types who do not pose a challenge to Palestinian nationalists or other political activists.

The interesting question, of course, is how these Jews and Arabs interact. The veteran Jewish families have a wide range of social contacts with both their Arab and Jewish neighbors. During the Sabbath, for example, they often stroll up the hill to drink coffee with Jewish friends or to plan a joint shopping expedition to the Old City market. Social ties of a less intensive kind are also maintained with the neighboring Arab families, particularly with their Arab landlord. Several of the Jewish families were fluent in Arabic before they came to Abu Tur, and the others have learned a sufficient amount of Arabic to be able to converse with their neighbors. In some instances their visiting patterns are close and elaborate; one of the Jewish residents relates that when guests arrived the landlord's young son would appear with a tray carrying cups of coffee, and another of the Jewish residents who grew up in an Arab milieu actively entertained his Arab neighbors. If there was sickness in the family the neighbor was certain to offer help, and on special occasions, such as a birth or a wedding, Jews and Arabs were invited and expected to attend. Although they attend different schools, Arab and Jewish children often play together in the afternoon. The overall mood is relaxed. This handful of Jewish residents has become a familiar, accepted part of the social scene.

In fact, the Jewish residents state that they "feel safe" within this area. The women report that they move freely about the neighborhood after dark, and are relaxed when shopping at a local Arab shop or walking along the paths between the houses. Part of this sense of security rests in the fact that the landlord plays a kind of "patron" or "protector" role: the Jews who rent are under the landlord's protection and this "guarantee" is widely understood and respected. Should there be personal problems—articles stolen from a washline or insults shouted at the Jewish children or their guests—the Jews report this to their Arab landlord who is obliged to take appropriate action. The landlord's honor was also at stake: he feels bound to guarantee his tenants' safety lest his own reputation be damaged. In addition to these everyday matters, during moments of crisis the Arab landlords also make declarations of protection. For example, one of the Jewish residents recalls that during the Yom Kippur War her landlord was concerned for her safety and pointedly offered his personal protection.

These encounters are not, however, free from misunderstandings and tensions. For example, one of the Jewish residents relates an incident in which she began to suspect that Arab children were taking her child's toys. She scolded the Arab youngsters, but when the toys continued to disappear she finally prohibited them from playing with her child. This in turn had a negative effect upon the usually warm relationships between the adults—the Arab neighbors saw this as an insult and for a time they avoided their Jewish neighbor. At another level, political crises have had immediate effects upon personal relationships. Terrorist attacks in Jerusalem or prolonged armed conflict such as the war in Lebanon add layers of tension and uncertainty. Generally speaking, political discussions are avoided. Political events and realities are too harsh and threatening, and consequently the Jews and Arabs focus their discussions on family topics and neighborhood happenings.

There are, moreover, still other levels of tension and ambiguity. An incident in the recent past makes this point dramatically. During the summer of 1983 police were called after an attempt was made to attack one of the places rented to Jews; a Molotov cocktail had been thrown at the apartment in question. Little damage was actually done, but this violent act was out of keeping with the calm atmosphere that normally prevailed.

Following a police investigation some of the facts became clearer. The incident had taken place in the middle of the night and there were no witnesses. The tenants of this particular dwelling were Jewish students who had rented the apartment several months earlier. The owner was a local Arab resident who for years had been renting apartments to Jews. No arrests were made following the investigation.

So much for the facts. But why did it happen? Two different interpretations were offered. The first suggests that the reasons lie in antagonism and jealousies between Arabs in the neighborhood. The Arab owner was disliked by others (in part because he rented rooms to Jews), and the bombing was a "message" warning him against continuing this practice. The cause, in other words, was to be identified in a mixture of personal rivalry and nationalist Arab ideology. The second interpretation is quite different. The apartment in question was occupied by both a male and a female Jewish student; on the night preceding the bombing a number of youngsters of both sexes were seen going to the apartment, and the suspicion arose that immoral activities were taking place there. (The incident was even more bizarre; the students apparently were members of a tiny sect that practiced nighttime rituals, and they had come to take part in a ceremony!) According to this interpretation the bombing was an expression of Arab community morality; this was a "statement" made by Arab residents that they would not tolerate immorality in their neighborhood.

The police did not find the offenders, and the motives for the incident remain unclear. It seems likely, though, that there is some truth in both of the explanations. What is important for our purposes are the uncertainties that are illustrated by this incident. The system of understandings that had developed between these Arabs and Jews was by no means permanent and accepted by all. Crises elsewhere in Jerusalem, or for that matter, in the entire complex of Arab-Jewish relationships, easily upset the quiet patterns of contact that had developed within this small corner of Abu Tur.

We turn next to the second micro-zone. This is the nearby area at the crest of the hill where the pre-1967 border separated the Arab and Jewish sides. This zone ranges from north to south along the length of the old no-man's land and extends back several streets on both sides of the border. Forty to fifty homes are included, twenty to twenty-five on each side, and consequently this location is the "richest" in respect to potential contacts between Arabs and Jews.

In contrast to the micro-zone just described, within this area most families live in their own homes. At certain points these Jewish and Arab dwellings stand only a few yards apart, although in other places they face each other at a distance of from fifteen to twenty yards.

Many of the Arabs who live there belong to established Jerusalem families; they include a number who are comparatively wealthy and well-educated and engaged in professional or business activities. The Jews are more mixed. One segment is made up of Middle Eastern working-class families who moved to Jerusalem following the 1948 war. The second group is composed of middle- or high-income European- and American-origin families who in most cases purchased their home from the previous Jewish owners. They include artists, writers, businessmen, and professionals. As noted earlier, this latter group has been growing in size; the low-income Middle Eastern families have been selling their valuable homes to higher-income, mainly European-origin newcomers.

Generally speaking, a limited range of contacts has developed between Arabs and Jews in this zone. These include two different types of social interactions: exchanges between neighbors and contacts based upon business or instrumental interests.

In a few instances Jews and Arabs who live next to each other have fashioned warm, personal "neighborly ties." They not only greet one another and exchange pleasantries, but they also visit each other, are customarily invited to attend family celebrations, and may also make joint shopping excursions to places like the Arab markets in the Old City. The Jews are mainly from among the original Middle Eastern families; in contrast with the newer middle-income Jewish residents, they are fluent in Arabic and more at ease with their Arab neighbors. The women householders are especially active in initiating these contacts—Arab and Jewish women were the first to venture out and interact with one another. In several instances these contacts began even before 1967. One of the Jewish residents recalls that while the barbed wire was still in place she and some of the Arab women from across the border would exchange greetings and freshly picked flowers; when the border opened their relationship grew, and in several instances what can properly be called "friendships" developed. However, as gentrification spreads in the Israeli section these families are being replaced by others who do not speak Arabic. Some members of this latter group may also wish to initiate relationships with their Arab neighbors, but, as we shall see, their contacts have been more ambiguous and problematic.

The second type of link is instrumental or business-oriented. For example, the Jewish residents occasionally shop at one of the two nearby Arab groceries. These neighborhood stores have a mixed Jewish-Arab clientele; the Arab storekeepers have become fluent in Hebrew, and many of the Jewish residents occasionally shop there. These are the closest, most convenient places to purchase bread or cigarettes, and, equally important, they are open on the Sabbath when the Jewish shops are closed. The Arab storekeepers are well-known neighborhood figures. Indeed, with their wide-ranging information regarding the residents they frequently perform a "broker" or "switchboard" function: a Jew who is interested in locating an Arab artisan, or an Arab who wishes to meet a Jewish resident is likely to turn to one of the storekeepers for information.

In addition, many of the Jewish families are periodically in need of an Arab plumber, electrician, or carpenter to make repairs in their homes. Hana, who has lived in Abu Tur for nearly twenty years, describes her continuing ties with Mustafa, an Arab who tends her small garden:

> He has been working for me and in some other gardens here for many years. He is always in and out of the house when he works. I give him something to drink and eat, not like some of the others around here. I have been close to Arabs for many years. I grew up in Jerusalem before 1948 and I speak Arabic and know their mentality. But our relations go beyond that. When his son was in the hospital with broken bones I went to visit and that made a good impression.

Although the extent of these ties may differ (Hana's links with Mustafa seem to be more active and longer-lasting than is commonly the case), many of the Jewish residents report some contact with Arab workmen. There is a solid basis of mutual interest in these relationships, and exchanges of this kind are common.

Reflecting upon their experience along the border, several of the Jewish residents observed that the Arabs who live nearby seem to know a great deal about them, while they know little about the Arabs. The Arabs, they say, are interested in what takes place in and around the Jewish homes. Dena, who lives in the row of homes close to the Arab streets, puts it this way:

> There often are Arabs passing through on their way to and from work. The truth is that I don't know who they are or even distinguish between them. I suppose I don't pay attention or look carefully at what may be taking place around me. But I do know that they know many things about me and my family. Several times when something happened and I spoke to Arabs who were passing by, or who were just around here, I suddenly discovered that they know who I am, what car I drive, what kinds of fruit trees there are in my garden, who my kids are, and even who comes to visit me. It's not that they sit and watch or that there is a spy system—they simply are much more aware of us than we are of them.

It is not surprising that the local Arabs have such detailed information about the Jews; in hierarchical social situations persons lower in rank and power typically know a great deal about those in superior positions. For members of less powerful groups, personal information regarding the more powerful often has survival value, whereas such information has far less importance for the higher-ranked groups.

Another perception shared by the Jewish residents is that the tone of relationships with neighboring Arabs has been changing. Over time, they say, the Arabs have become more outspoken and at times sharp and aggressive in both conversation and behavior. The critical period of change was the 1973 Yom Kippur War. From 1967 to 1973, Arabs had adopted a more passive, polite attitude in their contacts with the Jews; Israel's military prowess and political control appeared to be firm, and as a result the Arabs behaved in a "humble," restrained fashion. However, say these Jewish residents, the Yom Kippur War produced a shift; the Arab armies were at first successful and consequently the feeling grew that the Arabs, too, had power. This new tone was sensed by the neighboring Jews in a variety of ways. One informant relates the following incident as an illustration:

> After 1973 some Arab kids came up and began to pick fruit from my trees. I came out and yelled at them, but they just stood there and said, "Listen, these are our houses, we used to live here, and this is our fruit." Finally I chased them out, but they had never said anything like that until then. This more aggressive sense continues among them to this day. The way in which we talk to each other has become different.

The perspective presented thus far has been from the point of view of the Jewish residents. Not surprisingly, the attitudes and behavior expressed by the Arabs are often parallel and complementary; they too report a narrow range of encounters with the neighboring Jews.

In common with the Jewish residents, the Arabs who reside near the top of the hill are mindful of the "instrumental" ties that link some members of the two groups. They tend, however, to dismiss these as limited and insignificant. Talal, one of the greengrocers, makes the point candidly:

> There really are no connections between us that amount to anything. Some of the Jews who live here come in from time to time when they need something, when they run out of salt or milk. But you will never find one of them who just comes to visit, to try to get to know us, or to take an interest in what goes on here. Actually, most of the Jews who buy from me don't even live in Abu Tur. They come in to my store while on their way to the Old City.

In the same vein the ties that develop between local Arab artisans and Jewish residents are also not thought to be especially significant. Relations between an Arab gardener or plumber and a Jewish householder are sometimes enlarged into broader-ranging social encounters, but normally they remain what they are meant to be: periodic contractual ties between a workman and an employer. A local Arab carpenter seeks to place neighborhood relations within their broader context:

The truth is that it is almost impossible to have neighborly relationships when there is so much intolerance, when they keep on raising taxes and don't give us building permits, and when they keep on taking land from us. How can one talk about "peaceful coexistence" or "neighborly relations" when they won't let us live in peace and quiet?

It is important to note that the carpenter does not distinguish between the local Jewish residents and the Israeli government or city administration. The "they" whom he refers to can include both the Jewish families twenty yards from his shop and the Israeli mayor and his administration. Both are equally "they," and both share responsibility for what the carpenter sees as intolerance and injustice. This perception was also expressed by other Arabs: they too tended not to distinguish between the acts or policies of the Israeli government and the behavior of local Jewish residents.

Beyond these occasional instrumental ties, the Arabs report an almost total absence of social exchange. As they see it, proximity does not lead to "neighborly" relations, or for that matter, to social relationships of any kind. They have a number of explanations for the lack of contacts. An Arab professional who lives close to the Jewish homes lists four general reasons: there is apathy on both sides, the political climate does not permit real neighborly relations, the authorities and leaders do not do enough to develop further contacts, and the prejudices and stereotypes held by persons on both sides keep them apart. His explanation is detached and analytical; the experience of the past as well as the politics of the present keep persons separate. One of his neighbors takes a more piquant view. He is occasionally employed by Jews who live in Abu Tur (he works as a furniture upholsterer) and he has also established good relations with a family that lives nearby. The only way to establish relationships, he maintains, is to block out all reference to politics:

Everyone should simply worry about his own affairs and not get into political discussions. It is possible to have good neighborly relations without getting into politics. Listen, anyone who wants to get along here must be deaf, blind, and dumb; otherwise he'll never make it.

These are viewpoints expressed by Arab residents who do not seem to have a strong ideological position (in this context the remark that an Arab must be "deaf, blind, and dumb" can be taken as a kind of pragmatic realism). There are, in addition, some who explain the lack of contact in more strongly ideological terms. For example, an engineer employed by the East Jerusalem Electric Company who is required to report daily to the Israeli police, explains the issue in direct political terms:

Jewish-Arab relations simply are not possible while the Jewish occupation continues and the Israeli policy of confiscating land and discriminating against the Palestinian people goes on. Under these conditions there is no basis for coexistence.

Given this context, the experience of the Jewish intellectuals, artists, and "Bohemians" who live at the top of the hill is of particular interest. Many of them have an overall "dovish" or left-leaning political ideology; they tend to favor compromise and reconciliation with the Palestinians and are critical of Israeli nationalist political parties that have an uncompromising ideological position. In matters of personal relations they are not hostile to Arabs, and, in fact, are ideologically interested in cultivating good relations with their Arab neighbors. It is partly for this reason that they may make a point of shopping at the nearby Arab grocer's, or avail themselves of an Arab handyman or artisan who lives in the neighborhood. For them this behavior is not strictly instrumental but also has some symbolic value; it is meant to be a personal statement regarding the possibility of cooperation between Jews and Arabs.

These intentions are frequently confounded by reality, however. There is, to begin with, the language problem. In contrast with the Eastern-origin Jewish families, they generally are not fluent in Arabic and therefore can maintain only limited conversations. Moreover, the Jews' understandings or expectations regarding the Arabs have in the past often led to disappointment. To cite several examples, friendly visiting relations were broken off when the Arab neighbor seemed to be asking too much; and misunderstandings regarding prices or dates of delivery effectively ended the ties between Arab artisans and the Jewish families who employed them. As with language, here too the Jews sensed that they were not communicating effectively with the Arabs, and therefore withdrew from contact. Finally, continuing political conflict also complicates these relationships. It is not only that acts of terrorism or full-scale war between Jews and Arabs widen the gulf between them; it is also the case that the Arabs do not distinguish between these "good Jews" who are sympathetic neighbors and the "evil acts" of the Israeli government. The Jews may suppose that they are making symbolic acts that suggest friendliness and separate them from government policies, but according to the Arabs' perceptions, this distinction has little meaning.

A well-publicized incident illustrates this point. Menahem was one of the early pre-1967 Jewish residents of this zone. He had moved into an abandoned Arab dwelling near the border, and although his political views were close to the radical left he managed to balance his political ideology with the splendid location and romantic setting. An outspoken critic, he was quoted in newspaper interviews as willing to "return his home" if this would advance the cause of peace. Menahem made a point of shopping at the local Arab store and was also well acquainted with various Arab workmen whom he had employed to make repairs. He pursued these contacts actively and was thought to have good ties with the neighboring Arabs. It came as something of a shock, however, when on several occasions Menahem woke to find that the tires of his car had been slashed. The vandalism was duly reported to the police. When the damage continued he decided that things had gone too far. He appeared suddenly one evening in the Arab cafe near the bottom of the hill, revolver in hand, and shouted a warning to the proprietor and all those who were present: if the vandalism did not stop he would know how to take proper action! The damage to his car did in fact stop. But so too, apparently, did Menachem's excursions across the border. Like others, his contacts and exchanges with the neighboring Arabs became more limited.

Another measure of the complexity of living along the border can be seen in the problems of joint use of recreation facilities. Near the top of the hill, well within the Jewish residential zone, an Abu Tur neighborhood community center has been established. Modest in size, the center sponsors after-school recreational activities for youngsters, occasional holiday gatherings, and a variety of sports activities. There is a small playing field next to the building and in the afternoons the neighborhood youngsters play soccer and other games. Although the center's small staff and the youngsters who regularly attend are all Jews, Arab youngsters also gravitate there; they stand along the sides of the field and watch the Jewish youngsters, and then gradually they join in and play alongside the Jewish teams. On some afternoons the teams alternate on the field. The Jewish youngsters play a match and when they tire or finish their game the Arabs play their own game. The teams are rarely mixed, nor do they play with or against each other: in keeping with the general Jerusalem pattern they are either "Jewish" or "Arab."

The fact that the Arab youngsters come to play on the "Jewish" field has become routinized and reluctantly accepted. Indeed, this does not seem to have generated much tension or anxiety among the players. However, some of the adult Jewish residents complain that the Arab youngsters cause problems; the Arabs knock over the garbage cans, they say, and leave the area littered with refuse. This has been a recurrent complaint and they have demanded that "something be done" about the Arab children who cross over and make noise or cause damage.

These complaints were brought before the Jewish Abu Tur neighborhood committee, the *va'ad shehunah*. Neighborhood committees are organized in most Jewish residential areas as a forum for venting complaints and improving local services. At one point the Jerusalem city authorities proposed forming a joint Abu Tur Jewish-Arab committee that would plan and coordinate local activities for members of both groups. This was, of course, a revolutionary proposal. There has been no forum in which Arab and Jewish residents meet together. The suggestion was preliminary and "off the record"—the city officials met separately with some of the Jewish va'ad members and also had conversations with several prominent local Arabs. As an example of the kind of activities that a joint committee might sponsor, the city officials suggested that a large playing field be built that could be used by all of the neighborhood youngsters. This proposal met with little enthusiasm. In fact, one response of the Jews was to suggest that a separate field first be built for the Arab youngsters! The Arabs were also cool to the plan, and the idea of joint activities was soon dropped.

If we pause to briefly consider the findings that have been presented thus far, the bare outline of a pattern begins to emerge. Abu Tur does not seem to be a "hot" border zone; although, there have been recurring tensions and occasional violent incidents between Arabs and Jews, their interactions are typified more by avoidance and indifference than by active conflicts or hostilities. Nor is the border entirely "cold." In several small zones Jews and Arabs interact in ways that are personal and neighborly, and for lengthy periods of time an overall sense of normalcy may prevail. The social exchanges that do take place appear to have a number of characteristic features. First, encounters between Arabs and Jews focus upon limited interests and issues, and rarely include a broad range of topics or involvements. For example, Jews may rent apartments from Arabs and Arab artisans may be employed by Jews, but rarely do these contacts expand to include other forms of mutual interest or activity. Second, the ethnic boundaries that separate Jews and Arabs tend to be firm and unbending. In Abu Tur all of the residents are classified unambiguously as either Jews or Arabs. In addition, it does not appear that one can move or "cross" from one category to the other, or that any broader, more encompassing social identity can be applied. Third, there is some tendency to focus relations across the borders upon "brokers" or other specialists who are able to link persons together; the Arab grocers are an example of this kind of bridging activity. Finally, social relationships seem to be burdened with misunderstandings and misperceptions. Jews who think that they are "signaling" a humane or sympathetic outlook find that Arabs perceive them merely as a part of the occupying power, while Arabs who make requests of "their Jewish friends" are rebuffed by Jews for seeking too much.

All of these points require amplification, and additional elements in the Arab-Jewish pattern need to be examined and clarified. Before turning to these more general issues, however, it is useful to consider the second border area that was studied—the Arab village of Beit Safafa and the nearby Jewish residential neighborhood of Shikun Pat.

THE DIVIDED VILLAGE

Beit Safafa is an especially complicated and fascinating place. For nearly two decades this Arab village was literally divided between Israel and Jordan, while, in addition, new Jewish housing estates were also built nearby. This small arena includes, on the one side, both Israeli Arabs and East Jerusalem Arabs, and on the other, a variety of Jewish residents.

How this interface zone came into being requires a brief explanation. Beit Safafa is located just west of the main road that connects Jerusalem with Bethlehem. This is an area of low hills and ridges interspersed with flat, arable fields; in the early twentieth century Beit Safafa was a fairly prosperous Muslim village whose lands ranged from Bethlehem and Beit Jala in the south to the expanding Arab and Jewish neighborhoods of Jerusalem on the north. The Turks had built a narrow gauge railway linking Jerusalem with the coast, and the tracks were laid through the village; once or twice a day the train noisily made its way across Beit Safafa's lands. This was, in short, a rather bucolic spot—rural, agricultural, and tradition-oriented—far enough from Jerusalem to be removed from the recurring crises of the day.

This quiet was abruptly swept away when, in late 1947, hostilities broke out between Jews and Arabs. Most of the fighting was concentrated farther north; however, following a fierce fight near the Greek Orthodox monastery in Katamon, Israeli army units turned south toward Beit Safafa, and many of the villagers began fleeing in the direction of Bethlehem. When Israeli troops reached the outskirts of the village they were opposed by a mixed band of Arab Legionaires and armed residents; but the shooting was brief and scattered, and within a few hours the Israeli army controlled the area.

The fighting in Jerusalem came to an end in 1948. With the opposed armies occupying different halves of the city, the question was where the exact border would be drawn. In general, both sides took the view that the border was to be set at the point where the fighting had stopped. However, in later negotiations they agreed that the railroad would be incorporated within Israel, and that the armistice line between Jordan and Israel would run two hundred yards to the east of the railway. Everything to the west of the railway belonged to Israel, while everything to the east became Jordan.

The railway, of course, ran straight through Beit Safafa; and hence, in a rude Solomonic fashion, the village was literally divided into two parts.

Those villagers who lived to the east of the railroad became Jordanian citizens, while those to the west found that they were Israelis.

This artificial division came as a shock. The residents could hardly believe that an international border had been drawn through their village, and that henceforth members of the same family would be citizens of two different countries. Fearing spies, saboteurs, and smugglers, the Jordanian and Israeli authorities forbade contact between the two populations. Over the years this division became a painful way of life: the villagers recall how they would at times call out news and gossip to one another across the barbed wire, or how, after receiving special permission a wedding would be held close to the railway line so that family members on both sides could gather together and share in the festivities.

During the next nineteen years the two sides of the village were drawn into the different orbits that they had, willy-nilly, joined. On the eastern side they became part of the socioeconomic life of the broader Arab world. Since most of the agricultural land was on the Israeli side and therefore unavailable to them, many of the men began looking for work outside of the village; some were employed in nearby Bethlehem and Jerusalem, while others migrated to distant places such as the Persian Gulf States. In brief, this half of Beit Safafa became part of the fabric of Palestinian society on the West Bank.

Israeli Beit Safafa followed a different course of development. Not only did the villagers become citizens of Israel, but they were also incorporated within a modern city. Some of the men found work in factories, others became specialized in the building trades, and quite a few others were employed in several of Jerusalem's leading hotels (at the prestigious King David, for example, some of the waiters and the head waiter were Beit Safafans). An Israeli elementary school was built there, and some youngsters continued their secondary education in Israeli high schools. Arabic was spoken at home and throughout the village, but children became fluent in Hebrew as well. In short, those living in the western portion of the village became a part of Israeli Jerusalem's small Arab minority.

Beit Safafa had been a separate village, but Jerusalem spread rapidly in its direction. During the 1950s and 1960s new Israeli housing projects were built nearby; these were public housing estates, often poorly designed and hastily built, but they provided shelter for the Jewish immigrants then pouring into the country from Iraq, Iran, and Morocco in particular. Built in stages, this entire area was named Katamon; it soon became, in effect, the most populous Jewish working-class section of Jerusalem.

Gradually, but with an insistent pace, Jewish Katamon pushed closer to Arab Beit Safafa; by the mid-1960s the village homes were only fifty or sixty yards away from the newly built Jewish apartment blocks. This was becoming a marginal, depressed part of the city; in fact, Katamon later gained a reputation throughout Israel as a slum area. Social ties between Arabs and Jews seem to have been sporadic, reserved, and low-key: some of the youngsters attended the same schools, the boys played soccer together on the streets, and some of the older residents struck up casual relations.

And then, once again, everything changed. War broke out in June 1967, and practically overnight Beit Safafa became united. The barbed wire separating the two sides of the village came down, and family members who had not seen one another for a generation rushed out to embrace.

The reunion between the Israeli and Jordanian Beit Safafans was both emotional and confusing. During the nineteen years of separation the villagers on each side had moved in different cultural directions. These first meetings between long-separated families and friends were strained and frequently uncertain. It was something like a meeting between a husband and wife who have not seen one another for a decade or more: each recognized the other, but each also sensed the subtle changes and the differences that had grown during the years of separation. Following the initial joyful meetings persons from both sides tended to withdraw, uncertain and cautious, trying to understand what had happened to one another in the intervening years.

Notwithstanding this confusion and uncertainty, Beit Safafa was physically reunited. During the next several years major urban changes began to take place. To be more specific, new Jewish housing developments, in most instances built on Beit Safafa's land, sprang up in all directions. Directly south of the village a large urban complex, called Gilo, began to take shape; to the east land was taken over by the city in order to build a new industrial zone and assembly points for municipal buses; to the west a highway was built which linked Gilo to Jerusalem. A large new public housing estate was also planned in an area immediately to the west of the village. This housing project, called Shikun Pat, was begun in 1970 and completed in 1973. Altogether a total of 672 new apartments were built in 27 blocks of flats that were placed cheek-by-jowl with Beit Safafa. In effect, a new Arab-Jewish interface had been created. This border zone was the focus of our study.

Observing this area from a distance, the "invisible borders" that separate Arabs from Jews are stark and plain to see. Most of the Arab homes are older dwellings that cluster together in a typical village residential nucleus. In contrast, the buildings of the Jewish housing estate are massive and tower over the Arab homes. The Pat complex includes six eight-storey apartment buildings plus another twenty-four rectangular four-storey structures. The buildings were prefabricated and then assembled according to modern techniques; they are identical to public housing projects throughout Israel, and similar in appearance to housing developments in many parts of Europe and the United States.

In keeping with the general Jerusalem pattern, there was little coordination in planning between the older Arab and new Jewish zones. Beit Safafa developed without a physical plan or guide. The three main *hamulas* tend to concentrate in different corners of the village. There is a small commercial center that includes some shops and a nearby mosque, and the elementary and new high school are situated in an open area close to what had formerly been the border. In recent years residential development has also taken place outside of the village nucleus; toward the east some families have been building on the slope of the surrounding hills, and their new homes offer splendid views of Jerusalem in the distance. On the western edge several garages and workshops were built, and new homes creep out in the direction of Katamon and in between the massive flats of Shikun Pat.

Pat is an instance of a government-planned housing estate. The apartment blocks are set close to one another, and each is surrounded by an asphalt parking lot and interlocking roads. A small shopping zone is situated in the center, and along the southern edge a community center and well-baby clinic were built. In the space closest to Beit Safafa a playground was laid out, and not far away there is a grocery store and a former police outpost. At this point the distance between Pat and the village is not more than fifty yards.

The social composition of Pat and Beit Safafa are much different. Pat was planned as a low- or middle-income residential area. Preference in allocating apartments was given to three categories of persons: recently married young couples, new immigrants, and low-income families who were then being relocated from older Jerusalem neighborhoods. In fact, most of those who were drawn to Pat were in the young couple category: they were attracted by the comparatively low prices and the in-city location, and as the buildings were completed they rapidly moved into their new apartments.

Pat's demographic composition reflects its attraction for young couples. Of the 2,150 persons who lived there in 1982, less than 4 percent were above the age of 55 (this contrasts with a national average of 12 percent), and fully one-third of the population was under the age of 10 (10 percent higher than the national average). Although occupational statistics are not available, it appears that the Jewish residents were employed in a broad spectrum of occupations, ranging from taxi and truck driver, policeman, and low-echelon civil servant, to university student and shopkeeper. Many of them were at an early stage in their occupational careers. It is for this reason (as well as others) that since its inception Pat has been a neighborhood characterized by high population turnover: aspiring young families often purchase a Pat apartment on good financial terms, and then, as they begin to move up the income ladder, transfer to a "better neighborhood."

These demographic and social features have an important bearing upon the relationships between Arabs and Jews. Before turning to these issues, however, it is important to outline the social profile of neighboring Beit Safafa.

According to the 1983 census the population of Beit Safafa (including both the former Jordanian and Israeli sides) was 3,700. There are a total of about 600 housing units in the village; on the average the homes include about six persons per dwelling. The main occupations continue to be factory work, construction, and services (in particular, work in hotels). Those who live in the former Jordanian section have also entered these occupations, although they tend to hold positions lower down on the work scale. Several local families have had striking economic success as building contractors; in addition, a small number of persons are employed in professional occupations such as medicine, law, and accounting. The latter are mainly concentrated in the western portion of the village. For those in the former Jordanian section remittance funds sent by family members working in the Persian Gulf States continue to be an important economic resource. Generally speaking, while there are significant differences in income and education, the village is not deeply divided between contrasting status or interest groups. Divisions between the Jordanian and Israeli segments certainly persist, but they are expressed subtly and in a variety of contexts.

Finally, it is important to point out the location of urban services. The pattern differs in important ways from Abu Tur. Educational facilities are mainly but not entirely separate. Arabs and Jews attend their own elementary and secondary schools, but a small number of the Israeli Arab youngsters are enrolled in a nearby Israeli high school. In regard to medical services, both the Pat residents and the Arabs from the western part of the village go to the same Kupat Holim clinic. The Arab residents of the eastern part of Beit Safafa who do not belong to Kupat Holim go to clinics in East Jerusalem, or they are attended by private doctors in East Jerusalem or Bethlehem. A government-sponsored well-baby clinic is located in Pat, and it provides regular medical check-ups for both Arab and Jewish mothers and their babies.

Recreational facilities in the two communities are separate. A community center was recently inaugurated in Pat, and the small staff organizes activities that are mainly aimed at the Jewish residents. On the other side, there is a small clubhouse that acts as a kind of center for the Arab youngsters. To sum up briefly, although services tend to be separate there is some overlap between the Pat residents and the Israeli Arabs who live close to them. Some attend the same schools, and they wait together to see a nurse or doctor at the local health clinic.

With these background features in mind, we can now turn to analyzing the relationships between Jews and Arabs. Three main patterns can be identified: avoidance, contact and exchange, and confrontation and conflict.

Living Side-by-Side

Hayim zeh al-yad zeh, or living "side by side," is an expression often used by Pat residents. It is meant to express the distancing or avoidance of contacts that typifies their behavior. These Jewish residents are at times made aware of the fact that they live close to Arabs; they hear the muezzin's call to prayer that issues from the village mosque early in the morning, or wait in line for the bus with Arabs from Beit Safafa. Generally speaking, however, they take little notice of the border dimensions of their lives, and have practically no contacts with the Arabs who live nearby. This includes both the Arab families who live within the village, as well as those whose homes are only twenty or thirty yards away; most Jewish residents report that they have no contacts with them. These residents also do not express hostility or unease regarding the nearby Arabs; theirs is more a sense of indifference than of antagonism or anxious concern. One of them, a policeman by profession, explains this outlook as follows: "There is a kind of cold war between us: you do nothing and I'll do nothing. Except for special cases, relations between us are correct and not much else." Another resident, in this case a person active in local affairs, makes the same point: "We do not initiate cooperation or contacts. Really, there are no contacts between us. We just try to avoid any conflicts or trouble."

This pattern of avoidance or indifference can be explained in several ways. First, distance is a factor. For many the distance to the village is considerable, and consequently they have little sense of living near the border. Moreover, in their daily routines they may rarely or never encounter Beit Safafan Arabs; in this regard they are no different from most of the Jewish residents of Jerusalem. Finally, Pat's social composition may also have a narrowing effect. As was noted, many residents consider their apartment as a "temporary stop," a place to live for a few years while on the way to a better neighborhood, and they take little interest in their neighbors, be they Jews or Arabs. For these families the nearby Arab community is simply not a significant part of their everyday lives.

While their reasons differ, a sense of living side by side also prevails among the Beit Safafans. Many of the Arabs report that they have little or no contact with the Jews living nearby.

Physical distance is, once again, a limiting factor. For example, the Arabs who have built homes along the hills to the east are practically in all ways linked with other Arabs on the West Bank or in East Jerusalem; they think of themselves as Palestinians or Jordanian citizens, and consequently there are substantial gaps between them and the Jews in Pat. However, many of the Arabs who are Israelis and who live close to Pat also have few contacts with Jewish residents. The issue is not so much the physical distance between them as the continuing conflict between Arabs and Jews. This point is expressed in the following comment:

> The truth is that the social and political situation—and especially the Zionist propaganda—doesn't allow for neighborly relations or social contacts that mean anything. We are forced to suffer this situation until Allah will help us to find a solution. I hope that the world and the Great Powers will intervene and help us to solve our problems, and that in the end we will have a Palestinian state just like the Jews have their Jewish state.

Remarks such as these are frequently voiced by villagers in both parts of Beit Safafa. That politics restricts social contact is almost always illustrated by referring to the loss of village land. "How can we have real social contacts, relations between neighbors, with people who are living on our land? What will we talk about?" they say. The issue of confiscated land is a continuing sore point.

There is another layer of meaning implied in these remarks. Not only do some of the Arabs reject contacts on political grounds, they also express a cultural or moral basis for avoidance. Like the Arabs in Abu Tur, they too argue that contacts with Jews have weakened or diminished Arab society, and consequently they do not wish to socialize with their neighbors. "Contacts with Jews only lead to decay in the morals of Arab society and to ruining our sons and youth. We get nothing out of this. I have nothing to look for in such contacts." This ideology is expressed not only by some of the older, more traditional Arabs, but also by the younger newly religious persons in the village. For them too close contacts between Arabs and Jews can only have morally offensive results, and they therefore are rejected.

Whether stemming from indifference or hostility, avoidance is a major pattern governing the interactions between Jews and Arabs. Nonetheless, there are considerable contacts across the border: while limited to a minority of persons, they are meaningful and range widely in scope and intensity.

Not surprisingly, practically all of these personal contacts are between the Israeli Arabs who live on the western edge of the village and Jews who live comparatively close to them. Citizens of Israel for four decades, these Arabs speak Hebrew freely, and there are many similarities in outlook and behavior between them and Israeli Jews. Social exchanges that do take place are therefore almost exclusively concentrated among them.

There are, to begin with, what can be characterized as casual contacts. For example, several Arab women sell flowers or fresh fruit and vegetables to the Pat residents; over the years they have developed a regular clientele. The Arab vendors visit the same buildings, shout out the produce that they are selling, and knock at the doors of families with whom they are familiar. Those families in Pat who are fluent in Arabic (there is a considerable number, since a majority of the Jewish residents have a Middle Eastern background) often joke with the Arab women as they bargain over the price. Another exchange involves women from Pat who frequent an Arab hair stylist in Beit Safafa; he is particularly busy on the Jewish Sabbath when quite a few women cross over to use his services. These market-type encounters are typically free and unencumbered by cultural bias or political argument.

Casual contacts can also be observed at the small grocery store located close to the border. The store is operated by an Israeli family, while the clientele includes both Jews and Arabs. During the day housewives from both sides of the border come there to shop, and the crowd of customers is nearly always mixed. The shopkeeper is fluent in Arabic and maintains good ties with persons from both sides; in fact, he frequently plays a broker role, particularly for Jews who are interested in locating someone in the adjoining community (a plumber or electrician from Beit Safafa, for example). The regular customers from both sides keep accounts there, and at the end of the month when salaries are paid both Arabs and Jews line up to pay their monthly bills. Social interactions are characterized by a kind of local familiarity and exchange of gossip, primarily in Hebrew, in which all of the customers, Arabs and Jews, take an active part.

One of the most interesting mixed arenas is the playground situated close to the grocer's shop. The facilities are simple—a circular row of benches, a large sand box, some swings, and a teeter-totter. During the afternoon hours mothers from both sides spend pleasant hours together while their infants or toddlers play in the sand or on the swings; the same faces can be seen throughout the week, and they include both Jewish and Arab women who live nearby. Their children play separately or together, and the women too sit in mixed groups. The conversations are typically in Hebrew, although at times several of the women from Beit Safafa huddle close to one another and converse in Arabic. In short, this spot is calm and neighborly, similar to play areas in practically any urban area.

Local services provide still another framework for casual social interactions. Jews and Arabs who are members of the Kupath Holim health system wait together at the health center, while mothers from both Pat and Beit Safafa attend the same well-baby clinic. The staff in these medical centers is mainly Jewish (although Arab nurses are also employed at both places), signs are posted in Hebrew, and the language of conversation with the clerks or medical personnel is also Hebrew. Some of the older Arab women come dressed in traditional costume, but there are few if any outward signs that distinguish the Arab from the Jewish patients.

Although criticism is often voiced regarding the clinic's inefficiency, these complaints are voiced equally by Arabs and Jews. More to the point, there are rarely complaints regarding the mixed population: limited as it is, the interaction among the patients is typically free of friction. Both the residents and the medical staff have grown accustomed to dealing with Arabs and Jews together, and the system seems to operate smoothly. The Arab residents do not complain of discrimination in receiving medical treatment. They do complain, however, that the clinic is far from the village, and that during the winter they have to walk a substantial distance in the rain. Some also say that they do not always understand the directions given in Hebrew, and wish that the staff spoke Arabic. These persons maintain that they would prefer that the clinic be located in Beit Safafa, even if this meant that it would no longer serve a mixed population.

Education is generally separate. However, a small number of male and female Arab students attend classes with their Jewish peers at the nearby secondary school. (There are fewer than ten Arab students in each grade.) These students chose to attend the Jewish secondary school since the facilities there are better and the educational level higher, and also since they were attracted by the idea of attending a larger school that was outside of the village. They are, in other words, mainly youngsters who were motivated both academically and socially to attend a mixed Israeli high school.

The Arab youngsters report that they are well accepted and that their daily relations with Jewish students are normal. As members of a tiny minority (there are more than one thousand students in the school), they do not report serious problems of discrimination. Nonetheless, they are in a complex, ambivalent social context, and this often poses dilemmas. For example, one of the Arab students reported that while he felt "accepted" and "one of the gang," discussions of politics often separated him from the Jewish students. He had been active in organizing an informal student group that met to discuss the Israeli-Arab conflict, but after a few meetings and candid discussions the school authorities banned the group's meetings; the issues were considered too sensitive to be discussed in a mixed group under the school's auspices. More generally, the students report that they feel a continuing pressure to "pass" and succeed as Arabs in an Israeli school; they learn to behave in ways that are like other Israeli teenagers. "We pay a price in pride and in being Arabs," is the way one of the students describes his situation. In retrospect several stated that they were not certain that they would wish to repeat their experience. It might be better, they say, to attend their own Arab school and express their own Arab identity.

In addition to these frameworks, one can also point to a range of more intense exchanges. Some are personal and idiosyncratic, while others appear to be more broadly based.

An example of personal contacts involved a resident of Pat who through a series of chance meetings struck up a friendship with members of an Arab family in Beit Safafa. Curious about the neighborhood he had moved to, this young man began to walk his dog in the late afternoon on a path that took him close to the village. The trek was repeated for several weeks, until some of the Arab residents invited him into their homes. He was drawn to one family in particular, and soon thereafter he began visiting them on his daily walk. A young daughter in the family offered to teach him Arabic, and with some enthusiasm he regularly came to be tutored in elementary Arabic.

Both the Arab family and their Jewish neighbor were enjoying these encounters. Later, when the Pat resident was visited by several foreign journalists, he arranged for them to spend a day with his new Arab friends. A critical incident in their developing relationship took place soon thereafter. A political demonstration was held in Beit Safafa, and when the Israeli police arrived some of the local Arab residents were briefly held in custody and others were injured. Hearing this news, the Pat resident rushed over to make certain that his friends were well. This seemed to solidify their relationship even more, and the visits continued.

In later months, though, their contacts cooled. The elder son in the Arab family was out of work, and he often came to visit the Jewish family; for their part, they did not always know how to respond to these frequent, unannounced visits. The ties were frayed even more when the Arab friend made a special request to use their apartment in order to privately meet with his Arab fiancée. After some hesitation, the Jewish couple agreed; this was certainly a sign of trust and friendship, since public knowledge of such a tryst would raise difficulties for the Arab couple. This relationship across the border was becoming strained, however; the Jewish family began to express uncertainty as to "how far this friendship could go," and their contacts subsequently became less frequent.

Social contacts also move in the other direction. In certain circumstances Arabs from Beit Safafa cross over and establish social relations with Jewish residents. For example, a local Arab family enrolled their three-year-old daughter in a private preschool located in Pat. The mother explained that this was the closest nursery school; more importantly, perhaps, she also wanted her child to begin learning Hebrew so that she could later attend Israeli schools. The nursery school teacher accepted the new Arab student although, as she recalls, she was uncertain as to how the Jewish mothers would respond. The Arab youngster rapidly learned Hebrew and was just as quickly accepted by the class.

A second case of an Arab "crossing over" was even more complex. In this instance an Arab family purchased an apartment in the Pat project, and, in effect, moved across the ethnic border. This case is also idiosyncratic: it is the only reported instance of an Arab family living in the Jewish apartment complex and for this reason it is of special interest.

The Arab family that moved to Pat were Israeli Arabs. The wife was from Beit Safafa, while the husband had been reared in the Galilee. Both had wide-ranging experiences within Israeli society: the wife had studied in a Jerusalem high school, and the husband was a graduate of the Hebrew University who later continued his studies in France. Having returned from abroad, they decided to settle in Jerusalem, where both found employment. At first they looked for a place to live in Beit Safafa; however, the housing shortage was so severe that they began to inquire about a place to rent in the nearby Pat project. After a lengthy search they found an apartment there; they made inquiries, and then rented an apartment with no difficulty. Indeed, they were on good terms with their neighbors and they developed close ties with several other families in the building.

Pleased with the new apartment and its location, the Arab family then decided to purchase an apartment. Now the issues became more complicated. They first inquired whether there were any legal obstacles, and were assured that there were no legal problems regarding an Arab buying an apartment in Pat. They found an apartment for sale and offered to buy it. Up to this point the negotiations had been quiet and normal, but now a storm began to develop. News quickly spread that "Arabs were moving into Pat"; several of the immediate neighbors objected to an Arab family living next to them, and they began to agitate against the sale. The neighbors argued that the Arabs "would ruin the building," lower its value, and that "these Arabs are just the first, it's the beginning of an Arab invasion." In the course of the dispute it was rumored that the Jewish apartment owner was on bad terms with others in the building, and that he had once said that he "would show them" by selling his place to Arabs.

The Arab family then took their case to the neighbors, explaining that they were already living in Pat. They described their good relations with Jews, and sought to relieve whatever anxieties existed. These discussions were effective, and soon thereafter the Arab family purchased the apartment and moved in. Their experience has been positive. The original opposition dissolved, and the neighbors report good contacts and normal relations.

There is yet another context in which Arabs and Jews interact: Arab and Jewish youngsters periodically form mixed adolescent groups or gangs. These relationships are particularly intense, and it is valuable to depict them in detail.

These mixed groups typically have a loose, shifting membership. They include both Jewish males and females from Pat, and Arab males from the western Israeli section of Beit Safafa. (Social control in Beit Safafa is too tight for Arab females to take part.) Group members range in age from fifteen or sixteen to their early or mid-twenties, with the males generally older than the females. At the time of our study, there were about fifteen youngsters from Beit Safafa who took part in one such group, and a slightly larger number from Pat. On any given evening only some of the youngsters were present. During the day they were at work, at school, serving in the Israeli army, or resting at home after the night's activities.

The group's regular meeting place was the small shopping center located within the Pat project. Either singly or in small bunches the youngsters gathered there in the evening; they joked with one another, bought soft drinks, smoked cigarettes, or played games in the space in front of the stores. Later, all or some of the group moved to an apartment, or wandered over to the nearby park. Their behavior was friendly, often noisy, and at times boisterous; the group was thoroughly mixed, with Arabs and Jews, boys and girls, relating to one another in a highly stylized Israeli-adolescent manner. Hebrew was typically the language of conversation, although from time to time words and snatches of conversation were in Arabic. Not everyone stayed throughout the evening. Some of the girls in particular might be called home early, while others wandered off after a time. There did not seem to be any special plan or direction to the nightly gatherings.

Some members of the group were at times involved in illegal or delinquent behavior; smoking hashish and drinking liquor was not uncommon. They occasionally also took part in petty thefts from the stores or break-ins into cars; not everyone took part, but members of the group were generally aware of each other's behavior and reputation. In addition, some of the youngsters also paired off romantically—an Arab male and Jewish female, or a Jewish male and female, were attracted to one another and became known as "a couple."

Close friendships developed in these nightly encounters. One of the younger Jewish members of the group makes the point that his best friends were from among the Arab youngsters in Beit Safafa:

> I feel like a member of the family with them; we really are like brothers. I see them during the day as well as at night. I've learned a lot from my friends. They taught me how to work on cars. I can now do simple repairs just from watching them work. I hang around with the Arabs a lot. They call me "Abu Ruhi"—that's my nickname—so we are really close. They've taken me on family trips with them to the Kinnereth, all of us together, and on Yom Kippur some of the boys in the family walked with me to the Kotel (the Western Wall of the temple). We really are very close.

To be sure, not all of the links between group members are as intense as these. Nonetheless, for many of the youngsters the nightly gatherings produced close, continuing friendships.

There are, finally, also a narrow range of Arab-Jewish sexual encounters. In some cases these "affairs" grow out of the adolescent gang experience, although in other cases they involve older adults.

Sexual liaisons involving Arabs and Jews tend to be highly patterned: the males are Arab, the females Jewish, and the meetings between them (which take place in the Jewish space) are hidden from public view. Among the adolescents, what begins as a flirtation between an Arab and a Jew sometimes develops into a more serious romance. As the affair develops their relationship is kept secret, and they meet one another at night or in places far from the neighborhood. When their families become aware of these affairs, they strongly oppose them. The girl is likely to be kept home by her parents; the boy may be threatened by her family; and the boy's family takes steps to end the relationship. Arab-Jewish liaisons are potentially explosive, and, as we will soon see, they may lead to open conflict. In some cases, however, mixed couples do continue to live with or near to one another.

Sexual relations have also been entered into by adults. Some Arab men have regular "arrangements" with Jewish women who live in the area; the women are typically single—either widows or divorcées—and they discreetly maintain ties with an Arab male from across the border. While local gossip may "spread the news," efforts are made to keep these relationships private. These cases appear to raise less tension because the persons involved are mature and their family honor is less at stake. They tend to be gossiped about and, if possible, overlooked.

Conflict in the Interface Zone

The two patterns thus far described—avoidance and social exchange—are each strands in the overall system of relationships between Jews and

Arabs. There is, in addition, a third type of contact: conflict and confrontation. What kinds of issues or situations provoke conflict in this border zone?

Romantic liaisons between adolescent Jewish females and Arab males are explosive and provoke tension. The girl's family and friends may threaten and use violence in order to bring the relationship to an end. A police report describes one such case:

> Upon arriving on the spot I found an incident of assault and armed threat, between several soldiers and an Arab youngster. Mr. O. [an Arab whose home borders on Pat] told me that at 12:30 that night some soldiers came to the house and demanded to see his brother. One of the soldiers threatened O., and they also attacked his brother. The reason for the attack is romantic relations between O.'s brother and a Jewish girl who lives in Pat.

A second case is tersely described as follows:

> While receiving a report of a disturbance in Pat, we heard a shot being fired not far away. Upon arriving on the spot we found that a Jewish girl and her sister had been in the apartment when one of the girl's boyfriends broke in through the window. He found the girls with two Arab men. . . . The Arab men drove him out, and they phoned the police. At the same time a shot was fired and the girl was wounded on the left side.

Sexual mixing is apparently a kind of affront, almost a collective insult that extends to the ethnic group as a whole and triggers aggressive responses. Nonetheless, this periodic violence has in the past been contained and has not escalated into widescale communal conflict.

Disputes regarding land are a second major source of conflict. Since 1948 large portions of land belonging to Beit Safafa have been confiscated by the Israeli state authorities or by the Jerusalem Municipality. This process may have been inevitable once the village was incorporated within Jerusalem; the rapidly growing urban population was in need of open land for new residential construction. Inevitable or not, the Arabs have consistently opposed the expropriation of their land, and this issue is one of the major sources of anger, frustration, and hostility.

A recent land dispute can serve as a case in point. This conflict involved a Jewish religious seminary that adjoins the eastern edge of the village. The seminary is situated on the grounds of what previously, during the Jordanian regime, had been a government hospital and sanatorium. After 1967 the hospital land and building were allocated by the Israeli government to a Jewish religious institution that established its main center there. A number of homes that belonged to the villagers were located nearby, and since several stood empty the directors of the Jewish seminary expressed interest in renting them for their students.

The Arab owners negotiated rental agreements with the head of the seminary, and soon thereafter Jewish students moved into the homes and the rents were paid.

However, when the contracts expired the students refused to move out; they claimed that these buildings belonged to the seminary and that the Arabs had forfeited their right to them. In several instances Arab families managed to move back into their homes, but the Jewish students tried to force them out. There were several violent incidents in which armed persons attempted to remove the Arabs; the police were called, and the issue was then brought to the courts. The Jerusalem Municipality joined the Arab families in insisting that the homes were rightfully theirs and that the seminary had no right to these buildings. This dispute was subsequently argued through the courts; finally, after several years, the court ruled in favor of the Arab owners, and the homes have been returned to them.

The issues of land and land ownership are deeply felt by all Beit Safafans. Land has tangible value; land that was expropriated for building projects has a high market price. Yet Beit Safafans received mere token payments. In addition, as emphasized in the previous chapter, land also has important political and symbolic value—this is "Arab land" that has become "Jewish." Finally, land is also important for the villagers since little space has been left for their own needs. Around them in every direction village lands have been taken and allocated to Jews, and consequently the land reserve for their own use has dwindled precariously. Many of the Beit Safafans have been unable to receive building permits to add rooms to their present homes or to build houses. Some new housing was recently built, but this continues to be a smouldering problem.

Turning now to the broader features suggested by these two cases, it is clear that while Jerusalem has been united and in certain respects functions as one city, at various other levels Jews and Arabs are sharply divided by both old and new boundaries. Separation and division are the main structural features that characterize their residential relationships. Avoidance, as a result either of indifference, fear, or ideological beliefs, is the attitude adopted by many members of both groups. "Living side by side" is one statement of this attitude, and the lack of enthusiasm of both Arabs and Jews for shared recreational facilities is another. Both are expressions of disinterest or opposition to crossing borders. There are few conscious, deliberate attempts at establishing interethnic social contacts, and in both Abu Tur and Beit Safafa–Pat most of the residents typically interact within their own community. On the other hand, there is also little in the way of overt aggression: these are not "hot" border zones where persons are placed in personal danger when they cross to the other

side. While there have been violent incidents, in both of the areas studied these were sporadic rather than continuous and repeated.

When we compare the two neighborhoods, it is apparent that there is
a wider, more complex range of contacts between the residents of Beit
Safafa–Pat than those in Abu Tur. It is striking that in the former interface, some of the urban services are shared by the two populations, residents shop at the same stores, and adolescent gangs include both Arab
and Jewish youngsters. How can this be explained?

The main difference between the two zones lies in the fact that the
Arabs who interact with Jews in Beit Safafa are nearly all Israeli Arabs
who were socialized in Israel, while the Arabs who live in Abu Tur continue to consider themselves as Palestinians and Jordanian citizens. The
Beit Safafa Arabs speak Hebrew fluently, tend to behave in ways that
are similar or identical with those of Israelis, and generally share a great
many cultural features together with their Jewish neighbors. Moreover,
these Arab residents consider themselves to be Israelis—in certain respects their political as well as social identities are like those of Israeli
Jews. It is therefore not surprising that a wider, richer series of contacts
have developed between them and some of the Jews who live nearby.

This should not be interpreted to mean that their political and social
status is clear-cut; if anything, the Israeli Beit Safafan's status and identity
is uncertain and ambiguous. Beit Safafans are Israeli Arabs, a minority
within the Jewish state and a tiny minority in Jerusalem. They also have
many links and allegiances with fellow Arabs in the Jordanian segment of
the village, and more broadly with Arab society on the West Bank and
beyond. Although citizens of Israel, the Beit Safafans also think of themselves as Palestinians, and many identify with the "Palestinian people and
its struggle for independence." They are, in brief, involved in a series of
paradoxes. These Israeli Arabs are caught up in the tensions of marginality: they are not fully accepted or entirely at ease with either their fellow Israeli Jews or their fellow Arabs. As one informant put it, plain-
tively: "When we go to the Old City I can hear them [the other Arabs]
saying about us, 'Well, here come the Jews.' " Theirs is a dilemma that
has only grown more acute over time.

Emphasis has thus far been given to the absence of contacts across the
border. Yet, as we have seen, some Arabs and Jews interact regularly.
Judging from the two areas, most of the Jews who take part in these encounters are persons with Middle Eastern backgrounds; for example, in
Abu Tur the initial contacts were made by Jewish women from Iran and
Morocco, just as in Beit Safafa–Pat many of the adolescents who become
friendly include Jewish youngsters whose cultural heritage is Middle
Eastern. There is a certain logic to this selectivity. These Jewish residents are fluent or knowledgeable in Arabic, and they are able to freely

converse with Arabs who live nearby. Equally important, they share some norms and expectations, and consequently are more at ease when conversing or visiting with each other. This is an important point since it refutes the Israeli accepted wisdom according to which Jews from Middle Eastern countries have particularly strong negative feelings against Arabs. To the contrary, when measured in terms of actual behavior it is precisely Jews in this category who maintain continuing ties with Arabs living nearby.

Earlier in this chapter some of the analytical features of Arab-Jewish social relationships were briefly outlined. It is worthwhile to return to this topic now from the broader vantage point of the two interface areas. The issues are vital ones: what features characterize these cross-ethnic exchanges? What are the likely consequences of Jewish-Arab social contacts?

It will be useful to begin by introducing several general concepts. Two types of social relationships can be distinguished: those that are instrumental and those that are multiplex.[1] Instrumental ties refer to interactions between persons with single interests (for example, a buyer and seller in the market), while multiplex ties involve the same persons playing different roles and having various interests (buyer and seller are also kinsmen and both belong to a religious sect). Instrumental ties are not binding, nor do they have implications of continuing obligation; there is no expectation that they will continue, and they are readily broken. Multiplex ties, on the other hand, tend to be long-lasting since they are based upon varied mutual interests. In addition, multiplex ties are a feature of what have been called cross-cutting allegiances.[2] These refer to networks of social relations that range across group boundaries to link persons, even temporarily, who are otherwise members of different and often opposed groups; such ties moderate or inhibit conflicts since they generate mutual interests that cut across group boundaries.

When considered in these terms, it is apparent that the contacts between Arabs and Jews in Jerusalem's border neighborhoods are typically instrumental rather than multiplex. Nearly all of these contacts are of a contractual kind, and they are entered into for specific purposes. Jews hire Arab artisans, or Arabs and Jews shop at the same neighborhood stores, without these single-interest behaviors expanding into other forms of exchange. Contacts across the border rarely include mutual, long-term participation in various informal settings or events, such as family visits, joint membership in some neighborhood voluntary group, or any other type of local gathering. Moreover, these are narrow, brittle

[1] See Gluckman 1964.
[2] Ibid.

links that can easily be broken: there is little if any sustaining interest that enjoins persons to maintain or expand their contacts.

This latter point—the brittle nature of interethnic relations—is reinforced by the absence of shared cultural understandings and expectations. Thus for Jewish residents a friendship may be expressed by occasional highly patterned visits, while their Arab neighbors may expect friends to engage in more personal sharing behavior. As was pointed out earlier, Jews may believe that they are "making a statement" when they purchase from an Arab tradesman, but they soon find that the latter perceives them to be "a part of the illegal Jewish occupation." A Jewish resident finds that his dovish political philosophy does not stop his car from being vandalized.

There are, moreover, few if any cross-cutting alliances and shared interests between Arabs and Jews. Persons on both sides may have a stake in wishing economic relationships (that is, Arabs working for Jews) to continue, or opposing the escalation of terrorism and communal violence; but these are generalized interests and do not refer to specific persons and particular contexts. At the same time there are no joint local services or local political organizations that persons on both sides of the interface have a strong interest in maintaining. "Living side by side" is a powerful expression of the fact that allegiances are inner-focused and tightly drawn.

There is, finally, yet another dimension to these exchanges. Our analysis suggests that in border residential neighborhoods Arabs and Jews rarely cross over and adopt other identities. This particular social field is clear-cut and unambiguous. All of the residents are defined either as "Jews" or as "Arabs"; the residents themselves sort out and label one another as belonging to one group or the other.

The key point for our purposes is that these ethnic identities are retained in practically all of the encounters that take place. There are no different or broader social categories that members of the two groups can adopt, nor are persons normally able to shift their membership from one group to the other. In the neighborhoods studied, the sole exception arises from the mixed adolescent groups in Beit Safafa–Pat, and the interesting case of Abu Ruhi, the Jewish boy who had fashioned such close ties with his Arab friends that they called him by an Arab name. This youngster did not, of course, cease being a member of one group, but his personal relations were powerful enough for him to easily move from one to the other. This is an unusual case, and as such it reflects tight, almost impermeable ethnic boundaries. In subsequent chapters we will see how these matters unfold in other regularized encounters between Jews and Arabs.

CHAPTER 4

Employment Relations: The Integration of a Divided Labor Market

WE TURN NEXT to the economic dimensions of post-1967 Jerusalem. The contemporary pattern of Jewish-Arab labor relationships must be considered against the background of the different economic conditions existing in the two parts of the divided city prior to reunification. These reflected the substantial disparity between the overall levels of economic development in Israel and Jordan, as well as the divergent growth potential and economic base of the two urban entities on either side of the dividing line. As we saw previously, the population growth and economic development of the Israeli capital were explicitly encouraged by the central government through extensive public investments and other means. A large public service sector along with other industrial activities effectively secured its Jewish inhabitants the kind of expanding, diversified, and high-income employment opportunities typical of many Western urban bureaucratic centers. By contrast, Arab East Jerusalem to a large extent retained the features of a traditional, slow-developing Middle Eastern town. Under Jordanian rule it remained a secondary regional center with a narrow economic base, heavily dependent upon foreign tourism, mainly from Arab and Muslim countries. In common with the West Bank in general, East Jerusalem constantly suffered from an insufficient expansion of the local labor market, high unemployment rates, and a continuing out-migration.

The basic differences in economic scale and structure between the Jewish and Arab sectors were clearly revealed when the entire city came under Israeli control. East Jerusalem Arabs, who then comprised 26 percent of the total urban population, accounted for only 16 percent of the united city's labor force, and, according to rough estimates, commanded barely 6 percent of its aggregated income or purchasing power.[1] This overall disparity reflected, in turn, the relatively low labor participation rates in East Jerusalem, and particularly the substantial gap in average income existing in the two sectors. Whereas close to half of the working-age Jewish population participated in the labor force, the corresponding

---

[1] For a broader comparative analysis of the different economic structures of the two parts of the city and related implications brought about by the reunification of Jerusalem, see Romann 1967.

rate was just over one-third among the Arab population, and was particularly low among Arab women. Average nominal per-capita income was estimated to be four times higher in the Jewish sector. This gap was even higher among the low-income categories of East and West Jerusalem. Compared to the Jewish labor force, the Arab active population was far less qualified in terms of both its level of education and occupational composition. For example, within the male working-age population, about 70 percent of the Arabs had finished only up to eight years of school and no more than 7 percent had completed thirteen years or more, compared with almost 25 percent among Jews. Similarly, whereas the greater part of the Arab active population consisted of semiskilled manual workers or unqualified service employees, in the Jewish sector almost half of the entire labor force could be classified in the white-collar category, which was greatly underrepresented in East Jerusalem. Indeed, by practically any social and economic yardstick, the reunification of Jerusalem represented a case where, almost overnight, a relatively underdeveloped economic entity was integrated into a far more developed and economically dynamic structure.

The direct consequences of the Six-Day War and the changing political and economic conditions associated with reunification at first had diametrically opposed effects on the two labor markets. Within East Jerusalem, economic conditions deteriorated as a result of the considerable out-migration, as well as the severance from traditional sources of demand and supply in Jordan. This led in particular to the cessation of all tourist movements from Arab and Muslim countries and practically froze all local investment initiatives. The abolition by the Israeli authorities of many of the previous Arab government and administrative functions and the political uncertainty which reigned in East Jerusalem further contributed to a general slow-down in local economic activity. According to the Israeli census taken in East Jerusalem in September 1967—four months after reunification—about one-quarter of all men who reported having been employed before the war still remained out of work. In fact, the rate of unemployment reached over one-third of the total labor force, if we include those not employed before the war and others who abstained from looking for new jobs under the prevailing conditions. By contrast, on the Jewish side the 1967 victory plus reunification directly contributed to the emergence of a new era of optimism and rapid economic expansion. This was immediately reflected in the unprecedented increase in the number of foreign and Israeli tourists for whom the united city became a major attraction. This was, in addition, given concrete expression through the major investment projects initiated by the Israeli authorities immediately after the war: their goal was to consolidate and expand the Jewish presence in the united capital.

It can readily be seen that, with the removal of the political barriers, the complementary economic conditions prevailing in the Jewish and Arab sectors necessarily implied and brought about a process of integration and adjustment. In the context of the labor market this was mainly reflected by the increasing flow of Arab workers into the Jewish sector, where the widespread working relationships between Jews and Arabs became the major area of mutual contacts and, presumably, economic integration. At the same time, however, the Jewish and Arab sectors continued to maintain the distinctive economic and institutional features that are typical of a dual labor market. It was the combination of purely economic factors plus the deep and persistent political and ethnic divisions which dictated the emerging patterns of intersectoral labor relations.

The Absorption of Arab Labor in the Jewish Sector

Following the Israeli annexation of East Jerusalem, its Arab inhabitants gained free access to the Jewish labor market. This was publically encouraged by the Israeli authorities who were anxious to demonstrate and justify the advantages of reunification. Israel extended its labor-oriented services to the Arab sector, such as government-operated labor exchanges, as well as the Histadruth, the Jewish Federation of Labor, whose principal task was to facilitate and regulate the movement of Arab labor into the Jewish sector. But it was mainly the severe unemployment situation in East Jerusalem and the wide disparity in wages that encouraged an ever greater number of Arabs to seek the alternative and better paying employment opportunities in nearby West Jerusalem.

The flow of Arab workers began immediately after the 1967 war and continued at a relatively rapid pace. By early 1969 it was estimated that the number of East Jerusalem Arabs employed in West Jerusalem had reached approximately 4,000, rising again to about 5,400 by 1970. This figure represented roughly one-third of the gainfully employed persons residing in East Jerusalem, where unemployment rates correspondingly declined to prewar levels. The absolute and relative number of Jerusalem Arabs working in the Jewish sector gradually increased during the following decade. According to available statistics, by 1980 their total number reached 8,600 (this includes an unspecified number of Arabs residing in West Jerusalem or from other parts of pre-1967 Israel). Compared to the total of 20,000 actively employed Jerusalem Arabs, the share of Arab employment in the Jewish sector was thus stabilized around the 40 percent level, or nearly equal to that in East Jerusalem proper.[2] More signifi-

---

[2] Whereas current statistics continue to indicate the ethnic origin of those participating in the labor force, no such classification exists regarding the Jewish-Arab sectoral affiliation

cantly, the number of Arabs working in the Jewish sector practically equaled the net expansion in the local Arab labor force that has taken place since 1967.

The presence of Arab labor in Jewish Jerusalem expanded even further due to the influx of West Bank commuters from beyond the municipal boundaries of Israeli-administered Jerusalem. Unlike East Jerusalem Arabs, those residing in the West Bank periphery of the city required special working permits in order to be employed in Israel and West Jerusalem. However, these restrictions were not applied to West Bank workers in Arab East Jerusalem, and as a consequence unauthorized employment in the Jewish sector could not be prevented. In practice, the official restrictions were lifted in response to the growing demand for additional labor which could only be satisfied by these Arab workers. As a result the volume of both authorized and unauthorized West Bank residents employed in Jerusalem steadily increased, reaching its peak by the early 1970s. By 1972 the number of West Bank Arabs holding official work permits in the Jewish sector had reached 7,600, and this number remained relatively stable during the following decade. According to Israeli labor force surveys, the total number of West Bank residents employed in Jerusalem was in fact almost double this figure, numbering around 14,000 in the mid-1970s. This included an undefined number (probably several thousands) employed in East Jerusalem, but for the most part it reflected the substantial proportion of unorganized Arab labor employed by the Jewish sector.

Altogether, by the early 1980s the various categories of Arab workers in the Jewish sector could roughly be estimated as ranging between 18,000 and 20,000. When compared with and added to the more than 100,000 Jews employed in Jerusalem, this meant that Arab labor constituted about 15 percent of the entire workforce in the Jewish sector. A significant proportion of Arab employment could be characterized as unorganized labor temporarily engaged by Jewish employers; this is reflected in the seasonal and yearly fluctuation in the total number of Arab workers, particularly from among West Bank commuters. On the other hand, the sheer size and long-term nature of Arab employment testify to the fact that the majority were permanently integrated into the Jewish labor market. By 1982 about three-quarters of the Arab workers could be classified as "organized labor"; this includes the 6,500 East Jerusalem Arabs who became members of the Histadrut, and a similar number of West Bank workers whose employment was officially regularized through the Israeli labor authorities. With the passage of time most of the Arab workers—including many women—who at first were recruited on an occa-

---

of workplaces. Thus, the number of Arabs working in the Jewish sector are a crude estimate based mainly on data related to those working in West Jerusalem.

sional basis, became permanently employed in hundreds of organized workplaces throughout West Jerusalem.

These Arab workers were mainly engaged in manual jobs or similar low-status tasks at the bottom of the occupational ladder. The overall occupational distribution of Jerusalem Arabs employed in the Jewish sector indicates that by 1980 over 60 percent were classified in the blue-collar category, while about 20 percent were unskilled service workers. On the other hand, the absolute and relative numbers of those holding clerical or other white-collar positions remained particularly low, and they were practically unrepresented in the managerial or academic occupations (see tab. 4.1). The related complementary classification by industrial activity also illustrates the fact that Arab employment was largely concentrated in several specific economic areas. This was particularly the case in the

TABLE 4.1
Jerusalem Residents Employed in the Jewish and Arab Sectors
by Ethnic Origin and Occupation, 1979–1981

Occupation	Jewish Sector				Arab Sector	
	Total	Jews	Non-Jews	% Non-Jews	Non-Jews	% of Total Non-Jews
Total Employed (thousands)	106.8	98.9	7.9		11.3	
(percentage)	100.0	100.0	100.0	7.4	100.0	58.9
Scientific and academic professions	13.2	14.2	-	-	3.6	100.0
Liberal and technical professions	16.1	17.1	3.8	1.7	13.6	83.3
Managerial workers	4.5	4.9	..	..	..	
Clerical workers	26.1	27.6	7.7	2.2	10.9	66.7
Salesmen, agents, etc.	5.6	5.8	3.8	5.0	12.7	82.4
Service workers	12.6	11.9	21.8	12.6	17.3	54.0
Agriculture workers	0.6	0.5	1.3	16.7	0.9	50.0
Skilled workers in industry, construction, etc.	17.9	16.2	38.5	16.2	36.4	57.9
Unskilled workers in industry, construction, etc., and unqualified	3.4	1.8	23.1	50.0	4.6	21.7

Source: Israel, CBS, labor force surveys, unpublished data.
Note: - = no cases; .. = statistically insignificant. Since labor force figures are based on a small sample, a yearly average was calculated. The non-Jew category includes for the most part East Jerusalem Arabs, but also non-Jews permanently residing in West Jerusalem. Arab West Bank workers are not included.

construction industry, which accounted for about one-third of the Jerusalem Arabs and almost two-thirds of West Bank workers employed in the Jewish sector (see tabs. 4.2 and 4.3). An additional one-sixth of both Jerusalem and West Bank Arabs were engaged in manufacturing, far exceeding the proportion of Jews employed in this particular branch. In the broad service sector Arab employment was also overrepresented among the least prestigious subcategories, such as commercial and personal services, whereas it was relatively underrepresented in the large-scale public sector and particularly in financial and business services. It is fair to say that, as a general rule, Arab workers filled those employment categories that Jews rejected or avoided; indeed, a wide range of low-income and low-status occupations, ranging from unskilled construction, industrial, or maintenance workers to unqualified positions in sanitary services, garages, or fuel stations, became synonymous with "Arab occupations."

The general pattern of Arab integration into the Jewish labor market

TABLE 4.2
Jerusalem Residents Employed in the Jewish and Arab Sectors
by Ethnic Origin and Industry, 1980–1981

Industry	Jewish Sector				Arab Sector	
	Total	Jews	Non-Jews	% Non-Jews	Non-Jews	% of Total Non-Jews
Total Employed						
(thousands)	109.9	101.3	8.6		11.5	
(percentage)	100.0	100.0	100.0	7.8	100.0	57
Agriculture	0.2	0.2	. .	. .	0.9	100
Manufacturing						
and crafts	11.0	10.5	17.4	12.4	19.7	61
Electricity and water	0.5	0.5	. .	. .	6.1	100
Construction	7.2	5.0	32.6	35.4	7.9	24
Trade and catering	11.8	11.5	16.3	10.8	21.4	63
Transport and						
communications	5.6	5.8	3.5	4.8	6.1	70
Finance and business						
services	9.1	9.9	0.6	0.5	3.5	83
Public services	47.2	49.7	17.4	2.9	29.2	68
Personal services	7.4	6.9	12.2	13.6	5.2	30

Source: Israel, CBS, labor force surveys, unpublished data.
Note: - = no cases; . . = statistically insignificant. Since labor force figures are based on a small sample, a yearly average was calculated. The non-Jew category includes for the most part East Jerusalem Arabs, but also non-Jews permanently residing in West Jerusalem. Arab West Bank workers are not included.

TABLE 4.3
West Bank Arabs Employed in Jerusalem
by Main Industries, 1975–1981

	Total (thousands)	Construction %	Manufacturing %	Services %	Agriculture %
Total Employed					
1975	14.2	57.4	12.9	25.6	4.1
1977	11.2	53.4	12.2	29.8	4.6
1981	13.9	66.8	7.6	25.6	—
Organized Labor					
1970	4.8	83.3	5.0	8.4	3.3
1972	7.6	81.1	9.1	9.5	0.3
1975	6.4	75.0	20.5	4.1	0.4
1977	5.6	61.7	17.2	20.4	0.7
1979	6.7	60.7	16.4	22.4	0.5
1981	7.3	62.4	15.5	21.8	0.3

Sources: Data on total employed—Israel, CBS, unpublished data. Data are based on labor force surveys conducted in the West Bank during April–June in corresponding years. Data relate to all West Bank workers in Jerusalem, including East Jerusalem. Data on organized labor—Israel, Ministry of Works, Labor Exchange Services, internal reports. Yearly averages relate to West Bank registered workers in the Jewish sector only.

can best be illustrated by analyzing the construction industry. The large-scale Arab entry into this type of work was greatly facilitated by the fact that during the mid-1960s—on the eve of the 1967 war—many Jewish construction workers had been laid off, and some had entirely abandoned the building trade because of a major recession. When, after reunification the new large-scale Jewish construction plans began to be implemented, the readily available Arab workforce was recruited. This applied in particular to unskilled workers typical of this industry, but it also included skilled workers such as stone cutters and masons, trades traditionally followed by Arabs from Jerusalem and its environs. Over the years the presence of Arab workers on Jewish construction sites became predominant. They gradually occupied an ever-wider range of skilled and responsible tasks, in which Arab foremen or working groups often took charge of entire building projects. At the same time, the number of Jewish construction workers continued to decline, so that by the early 1980s Arabs accounted for over 70 percent of total employed persons in the Jewish construction industry and constituted the overwhelming majority of workers at actual construction sites. The overall dependence on the Arab labor force is best seen by the fact that during Muslim holidays, Jewish construction sites in Jerusalem practically close down due to the absence of workers.

With the passage of time Arab employment became more diversified, testifying to its horizontal and vertical integration in the Jewish labor market. This was expressed in the relative decline in the proportion of Arab workers in construction, and their wider distribution throughout the industrial spectrum. This was particularly the case in the Jewish manufacturing industry, which by 1980 had recruited about one-quarter of its total workforce from among East Jerusalem and West Bank Arabs. Arab workers became particularly prominent in the various labor-intensive industries, such as textiles, stone, wood, and metal, and in some of the larger plants hundreds of Arabs constituted the majority of the local workforce. An additional important outlet for Arab employment was the expanding tourist industry. In several West Jerusalem hotels Arabs (including males and females) accounted for about half of the entire personnel; kitchen workers, waiters, and maintenance personnel were largely Arab. Significant numbers of Arabs were also employed in other major Jewish commercial establishments and public institutions, ranging from department stores and transportation companies to hospitals and government agencies such as the postal delivery service and even the Israeli police force.[3]

As might be expected, in the course of the long years of permanent employment in Jewish workplaces many Arab workers became fluent in Hebrew, acquired "on-the-job" and formal training, and consequently reached higher occupational positions. This is well illustrated by the fact that in the early 1980s the overall proportion of Arabs classified as skilled construction, industrial, or transportation workers exceeded those defined as unqualified manual workers. In several manufacturing plants and workshops Arab employees gradually assumed more responsible tasks; Arab foremen were even placed in charge of entire working teams, including Jews. A similar process could be observed in certain categories within the service sector, which also offered promotion possibilities for the more educated workforce, and in nonmanual occupations. This was particularly the case in the Jewish hotel industry, where Arabs entered the whole range of positions, such as head waiters, telephone operators, reception clerks, or took charge of entire maintenance facilities. Another illustration is those Jewish medical institutions where many Arabs have been engaged as nurses, ambulance drivers, laboratory workers, or similar paramedical and qualified technical positions.

At the same time, however, Arabs moving up the professional hierarchy faced significant constraints. Specifically, they were largely denied access to white-collar occupations. Arabs with high school diplomas or

[3] For a more detailed survey of Arab employment outlets in the Jewish sector, see Romann 1984.

university degrees could hardly compete, even on objective terms, with the by far greater number and generally better qualified Jewish candidates for desired clerical or professional positions. Both East Jerusalem and West Bank Arabs continued to follow the Jordanian educational curriculum and attended non-Israeli institutions of higher learning (mostly in Arab countries). This represented a long-term handicap in those occupations where a knowledge of Hebrew and formal Israeli professional certificates were required. The fact that Jerusalem Arabs maintained their Jordanian citizenship further excluded them from administrative positions in the government sector where Israeli citizenship was required. This formal requirement was at times disregarded, especially in those cases where the extension of Israeli administrative functions to East Jerusalem implied the incorporation of former or new Arab employees in related government services. The fact that Arab citizens of Jordan—with which Israel remained officially at a state of war—continued to serve in the Israeli police force is but one example. Most Arab white-collar workers employed in the Jewish public institutions provided services exclusively designated for the Arab population. Those clerical or professional workers directly integrated into the Jewish sector were primarily Israeli Arabs who had graduated from the Hebrew University or other Israeli educational institutions. Several Arab physicians were employed in West Jerusalem clinics and hospitals, but only in one known case did an East Jerusalem Arab specialist find an appropriate position in a major Jewish hospital. Moreover, highly trained East Jerusalem residents were in competition not only with Jews but also with Israeli Arabs for the few available white-collar positions open to Arabs in the Jewish sector.

The selective opportunities offered to Arabs in the Jewish public sector can best be illustrated when considering the ethnic occupational distribution of Jerusalem Municipality employees. The Israeli municipal administration represented one of the few important cases where all of the former Jordanian city employees were fully integrated and allowed to keep their respective positions. Nevertheless, over the years many of the veteran Arab white-collar and higher-echelon employees retired, and only on rare occasions were they replaced by other East Jerusalem Arab clerks or professionals. By 1982, out of a total of 6,200 municipal employees close to 1,100, or 17 percent, were Arabs, which roughly corresponded to their overall share in the Jerusalem labor force.[4] However, of this total, close to two-thirds were manual laborers mostly concentrated in the public works or sanitation departments. Arabs were greatly underrepresented in the administrative, financial, and city planning divisions, as well as in related clerical or professional occupations. To illustrate the

---

[4] Data are based on internal unpublished records of the Jerusalem Municipality.

disparities, out of the total number of city employees holding an academic or professional degree other than teachers (such as engineers, physicians, social workers, and the like) only about 3 percent were Arabs, and this ratio has declined over the years. These employees mainly served the East Jerusalem Arab sector; significantly, only one among them has attained the position of deputy head of the department.

Arab workers were in principle entitled to wages and social benefits in accordance with Israeli labor legislation. The rule of identical working conditions for Jews and Arabs was adopted by the Israeli authorities and the Jewish Labor Federation in order to avoid the exploitation of the Arab labor force by Jewish employers, and more particularly, in an attempt to prevent the potential competition of cheap Arab labor. For the same reason this general rule applied to both East Jerusalem and West Bank Arab workers, in spite of the fact that in several respects their legal working status was different. As Israeli residents, East Jerusalem Arabs benefited fully from all the direct and indirect payments and rights associated with employment and most notably from those related to the Israeli social security system. This did not apply to Arabs living in the nearby West Bank territories. Nevertheless, when employing West Bank workers, Jewish employers had to pay their share of social benefits to a special fund, so that from their point of view the actual cost of employing Jews or the different categories of Arabs was practically the same. In addition, Arab workers indirectly benefited from the protection of the Jewish Labor Federation and were generally represented in local work committees. In fact, in organized workplaces it was hardly conceivable that Jews and Arabs working side by side for many years would receive different pay for identical work.

However, the practice of implicit discrimination was not entirely absent. Preferential hiring, allocation of tasks, and offers of advancement were practiced by Jewish employers. Most importantly, Arabs were commonly underpaid in the unorganized labor market. In many small businesses, the hiring of Arab workers was often associated with employer cost-saving incentives, particularly those concerning contributions of social benefits and compensatory rights. By the same token, whenever the choice had to be made between hiring occasional Jewish or Arab workers for odd tasks such as house renovations or repairs, the latter would be offered the job only on condition that they would accept lower pay.

The general pattern of Arab labor integration in the Jewish sector was in many ways similar to those economies in which foreign workers were absorbed in a domestic labor market. In purely economic terms, this was made possible by the expanding demand for particular categories of unskilled or semiskilled labor which could readily be met by Arab workers on a complementary, noncompeting basis. In other words, the absorption of Arab labor was largely facilitated by the fact that it generally replaced rather than displaced the Jewish workforce.

At the same time, however, for analogical economic reasons the Arab absorption in the Jewish labor market faced serious limitations. The overall size of Arab employment remained largely dependent on changing economic conditions, and was also a function of the industrial composition and long-term structural changes within the Jewish sector. For example, the periodic contraction in building activities mainly affected the employment opportunities for Arabs, as reflected by the fact that the total number of West Bank workers ceased to grow after the mid-1970s. The long-term relative increase of Jewish employment in the public, financial, and business services, from which Arabs were largely excluded, had similar effects. Significantly, the share of Arab employment in the Jewish sector, which reached roughly 20 percent in the early 1970s, gradually decreased in relative terms during the following decade. In addition, the limited access of Arabs to particular economic activities can also be explained in large measure by objective reasons, particularly their lower level of educational and professional qualifications. Arabs faced ever-greater difficulties in climbing the professional ladder whenever this involved direct competition with Jews. Such constraints could be observed even with regard to certain mid-echelon employment categories, where professional certificates were acquired by successfully completing standard courses conducted exclusively in Hebrew. For example, in spite of the overwhelming presence of Arabs in the Jewish construction industry, they were practically excluded from certain specific occupations, such as the highly skilled and better paid heavy equipment operators.

The limits imposed on the integration of Arab labor cannot, of course, be dissociated from the broader political context and ongoing national conflicts. The Israeli authorities were primarily concerned with securing the economic expansion of the Jewish sector. Labor requirements by Jewish employers were always first referred to the labor exchanges located in West Jerusalem, and only if these could not be satisfied were they then transferred to the separate, parallel agencies in East Jerusalem or the West Bank. Jewish administrators and employers alike were also concerned about the ever-increasing dependence on Arab labor in specific key industries and essential services; these might, after all, be crucial in the event of political conflict. The Jewish majority sought to maintain maximum control over its sectoral economy in other ways as well. This was strongly expressed by the fact that East Jerusalem Arabs could never attain or establish positions of self-employment within the Jewish sector. It should be recalled that in various small workshops or retail businesses, Arab employees increasingly assumed major responsibilities, and on various occasions practically ran the shop on behalf of their Jewish owners. As a general rule, however, East Jerusalem Arabs never became full partners nor were allowed to formally rent the location and operate such establishments on their own account. Even though this was not legally prohibited or codified in explicit government policy, it nevertheless reflected the practical limits imposed by the Jewish population. East Jerusalem residents working in the Jewish sector had to accept the status of "guest workers" or that of salaried employees working for Jewish employers.

ARAB SELF-EMPLOYMENT IN EAST JERUSALEM

Most Jerusalem Arabs continued to be employed in their own economic sector located within pre-1967 East Jerusalem and its immediate periphery. This applied to the various Arab-owned business establishments as well as to those public institutions which as a general rule exclusively relied on the local workforce and mainly served the Arab population. The Arab section of the Jerusalem labor market thereby preserved several distinct features when compared to the Jewish sector, mostly related to the ethnic identity of employers and employees, as well as to various other structural and institutional features.

The extent and development of Arab self-employment in East Jerusalem since 1967 cannot be precisely determined; comprehensive, comparative data were not systematically collected. According to the Israeli census records of September 1967, the number of male Arabs gainfully employed before the war was 11,500. This figure did not include the relatively small number of women who participated in the labor force, those East Jerusalem residents who had left the city in the wake of the 1967 war, or others living beyond the municipal boundaries who were formerly employed in the central city. By 1981, the total number of Arab Jerusalem residents, women included, who were employed in the city's eastern sector was once again estimated at no more than 11,500—the same figure recorded fourteen years earlier. This includes, however, those employed in several public services which were taken over by the Israeli administration and thus cannot be regarded as self-employment in the strictest sense of the term. On the other hand, when evaluating the actual size of the Arab labor market one must also take into consideration an unrecorded number of West Bank commuters, who, according to unofficial rough estimates, account for between one-quarter and one-third of the local wage earners. Indirect indications further suggest that their absolute and relative number probably increased slightly over the years, particularly among Arabs from Hebron, who have for several decades been migrating to Jerusalem and constituted a significant component among both unskilled workers and local entrepreneurs. In any event, self-employment in East Jerusalem remained rather limited and stagnant, or at best, hardly expanded following reunification.

The industrial and occupational character of Arab self-employment did remain relatively diverse, particularly when compared to employment in the Jewish sector. By 1981, close to 30 percent were engaged in public services, about 20 percent in commercial services, and a similar proportion in manufacturing and crafts. In these and various other economic branches, such as transportation and finance, the scope of Arab self-employment significantly exceeded that in the Jewish labor market both in absolute and relative terms. While the greater part, or nearly 60 percent, were menial or simple service workers, over one-quarter were classified as holding academic, liberal, or clerical occupations and about one-eighth as salesmen, commercial agents, and related workers (see tabs. 4.1 and 4.2). Thus, it was mainly in East Jerusalem proper that Arabs could maintain higher-level professional positions or otherwise be engaged in self-enterprise in the business sector. This was particularly true of lawyers, physicians, teachers, and similar liberal professionals. In a broader sense this was mostly due to the maintenance of a whole range of separate educational, religious, medical, and other public services, ranging from local Arab newspapers to the East Jerusalem Electric Company. Nevertheless, the access to white-collar or professional positions also remained rather limited within the Arab sector. Even more significantly, when compared to the pre-1967 occupational structure, available data indicate that within this broad category the absolute and relative numbers of clerical and managerial workers probably decreased following reunification.

The scope and nature of Arab self-employment can essentially be attributed to the traditional structure of the East Jerusalem economy which hardly changed after 1967.[5] In the local business sector numerous small establishments continued to rely on family enterprise, low capital investment, and traditional modes of production. In 1981, out of 3,200 registered businesses in East Jerusalem, close to one-half were classified in the retail trade category; over one-quarter were workshops such as garages, carpentry shops, metal workshops, and the like; others were also for the most part engaged in traditional activities in transportation, tourist, or personal services (see tab. 4.4). Only a small number of East Jerusalem firms could be classified in the financial or business service category typical of a modern economic structure. Within the entire Arab sector one could find no more than half a dozen banking, insurance, or accounting offices, and only one publicity or real estate agency. The number of registered building contractors, engineers, architects, and the like were equally underrepresented and for the most part consisted of

[5] See Romann 1984.

TABLE 4.4
Commercial Business Units in the Jewish and Arab Sectors
of Jerusalem by Taxation Categories, 1981/82

	Jewish Sector	Arab Sector
Major Categories		
Total	7,634	3194
Retail trade	2,431	1545
Wholesale trade	199	60
Business and personal services	3,344	753
Manufacturing and crafts	1,660	863
Selected Categories		
Banking branches	110	6
Insurance agencies	186	7
Tax consultants	41	1
Publicity offices	45	1
Real estate offices	116	1
Engineering/architectural firms	167	9
Law firms	300	25
Money changers	—	18
Travel agents	153	41
Airline offices	11	5
Haulage and trucking	279	649
Taxis	295	219
Car repairs	109	65
Metal workshops	91	79

Source: Based on Jerusalem Municipality tax files, unpublished data.

self-employed entrepreneurs or professionals. The underdeveloped features of the Arab business community can be further illustrated when
considering its fragmented structure and modes of small-scale operation.
In a local industrial survey conducted in 1978, it was found that only 180
establishments employed more than three salaried workers, their average size hardly exceeding that figure. The few mid-sized Arab manufacturing plants that do exist were located in the West Bank periphery. Similar features also characterize the service sector. East Jerusalem did not
have a single department store, and the public transportation system consisted of several privately owned companies, each operating a small number of passenger buses.

It can therefore be seen that internal structural patterns limited the
possibilities for regular salaried employment opportunities in the industrial and commercial sectors, particularly with respect to professional and
other white-collar workers. The number of such positions was further

limited in the local public sector, since these could only be found in non-government functions exclusively serving the Arab population. The only private corporation offering a large number of clerical and managerial positions was the East Jerusalem regional electric company. By the same token, the single largest and expanding subgroup in the liberal occupation category consisted of Arab teachers employed in East Jerusalem's separate elementary and secondary school system.

The trend of limiting employment opportunities within the Arab labor market was also reinforced by Israeli administration over East Jerusalem, as well as by the presence of a dominant Jewish sector. As a direct consequence of Israeli hegemony, several functions related to Arab self-rule were formally abolished or otherwise ceased to operate following reunification. This applied primarily to regional offices and functions of the former Jordanian administration, as well as the local consulates and other agencies representing the Arab and Muslim countries. But this also referred to a number of purely commercial functions, the most notable case being the East Jerusalem Arab banks which have been closed since 1967. This was brought about by the Jordanian authorities, who during the war froze all the accounts of the nine local bank branches that were deposited in Amman, and who have since refused to allow the Arab banks to reopen so long as they are under direct Israeli control. As a result, Israeli banks have opened branches in East Jerusalem which have replaced the former Arab-owned establishments. Similar developments can be seen in other economic activities, although they are more indirect. For example, since they were effectively cut off from Jordan and the Arab countries, about half of the East Jerusalem travel agencies ceased to operate after 1967, as did several import and wholesale companies. Many foreign commercial agencies, such as airline representatives or car importers, which formerly had parallel representatives in the divided city, have also closed their offices in East Jerusalem or gradually concentrated their operation in West Jerusalem. Overall, as a result of reunification the possibilities for Arab self-enterprise and commercial activities were greatly reduced whenever this depended on Israeli sources of supply, or Arab enterprises were otherwise exposed to direct competition with the better placed Jewish business community.

On the other hand, the proximity of the Jewish sector also offered new employment opportunities to the Arab sector. Various tourist-oriented activities expanded greatly due to the increased volume of foreign and Israeli visits to East Jerusalem. In addition, Arab workshops or transportation facilities were mainly engaged by Jewish firms and private customers. Following reunification many East Jerusalem establishments changed their function in order to meet the particular demands of the Jewish sector. To cite several examples, between 1967 and 1981 the number of Arab souvenir shops, taxis, trucks, and garages practically doubled, while the number of small workshops engaged in shoe production multiplied nearly fivefold.

In this fashion Arab self-employment became basically restricted to provision of their own needs or to a limited number of economic niches where they could successfully compete with the parallel Jewish sector. In both respects this depended not only on purely economic factors but also on Israeli policies. This, in turn, hinged on whether the Jewish authorities would permit the functioning of autonomous Arab public institutions or the operation of Arab businesses and professionals according to their own pre-1967 norms. Arab physicians, lawyers, and money changers were allowed to operate in East Jerusalem after 1967, while retaining their Jordanian certificates, or according to standards not authorized in West Jerusalem and Israel. But this effectively limited their activity to the Arab sector, and also exposed them to competition from Jewish professionals and businesses. Where Israeli regulations were strictly imposed on the Arab sector, opportunities were even further restricted; although East Jerusalem veteran tourist guides were permitted to practice their trade, after 1967 new candidates were required to complete Israeli courses in order to receive authorized certificates. Since such courses were conducted exclusively in Hebrew, this in effect excluded new Arab guides from this profession. By contrast, Arabs could more easily meet Israeli requirements for operating tourist buses, and consequently their numbers greatly expanded in East Jerusalem, many of them being employed by Jewish travel agencies. As in similar cases, this successful Arab competition with Jewish enterprises was possible since it involved restricted capital investment and cheaper labor costs.

The existence of a separate labor market in East Jerusalem is primarily exemplified by the persistence of different labor conditions in the Arab and Jewish sectors. Here again, in spite of the formal application of Israeli law to East Jerusalem, the Israeli authorities did not impose the same labor regulations that were in effect in the Jewish sector upon the Arab self-employed. As in other cases, Israel's policies in this regard were due to a mixture of political and economic reasons, and mainly reflected Israeli willingness to allow the Arab sector to continue to conduct its own activities according to previous norms. The Histadrut, which became active in East Jerusalem after 1967, restricted its activities to organizing that portion of the Arab labor force that crossed over to work in the Jewish sector, and rarely attempted to organize Arabs working in Arab-owned workplaces. Indeed, in spite of initial attempts in this respect, the Jewish Labor Federation refrained altogether from intervening in East Jerusalem labor relations. In one of the few cases where it supported a local strike in Arab hotels this did not succeed, mainly since it

lacked the support of the Israeli authorities who did not wish to antago-
nize the Arab employers. For their part Arab employers never made use
of the Israeli labor exchange office or other related services located in
East Jerusalem; instead, the Arab professionals and worker unions sought
to organize themselves in order to resist Israeli intervention and influence.

Work conditions in East Jerusalem have changed little since 1967, remaining much the same as in the Jordanian period and similar to those of
the West Bank. In most places no formal legislation applied to child labor, maximum working hours, minimum wages, paid vacations, and a
host of other social regulations that were in effect in the Jewish sector.
To be sure, in a few large Arab public institutions and commercial establishments, work conditions were negotiated with local unions and the
workers joined certain pension programs or medical care funds. The only
significant exception in this respect is the Israeli government's social security program, which, since 1967, has been applied to all Arab East Jerusalem residents who thereby became entitled to social benefits regulated by Israeli law. This was also the only case where the Israeli
authorities gradually imposed the Israeli system on East Jerusalem employers: they were compelled to pay their respective contribution to the
social security funds for their workers, in order to permit the latter to
exercise their rights in case of need.

These substantial differences in employment terms between the Jewish and Arab sectors were also reflected in the persistent gap in the actual
wage scale practiced on either side of the ethnic boundary. In East Jerusalem and the West Bank periphery, wages varied greatly according to
specific workplace and occupation. In the absence of official labor regulations the wages earned by Arab women, children, and unskilled workers in the textile or shoe industries remained far below the minimum
wage requirements imposed in West Jerusalem manufacturing plants.
This was the case despite the longer working hours and the lack of social
benefits. Nominal wages were more favorable in the larger Arab institutions and commercial establishments, although in these cases too average
wages barely equaled those earned by Jewish and Arab unskilled workers
in Jewish-owned or -organized places of employment. According to Histadrut sources, monthly salaries earned by Arabs in East Jerusalem were,
on the average, 40 percent lower than those received by Arabs in the
Jewish sector who held the same or similar occupations. A case in point
is the remuneration for Arab waiters or drivers working respectively in
East and West Jerusalem hotels or engaged in parallel public transportation companies. This gap would be even greater for more qualified personnel in the hotel industry who were much in demand in the Jewish
sector. However, an essential wage gap persisted even with respect to

the most mobile unskilled and unorganized Arab daily workers. Arab workers who crowded daily near the Damascus Gate waiting to be hired for occasional jobs could expect a different daily remuneration depending upon whether they worked in West or East Jerusalem.

In effect, the persistence of a dual labor market not only applies to the two distinct ethnic sectors but also to the Arab workforce itself, and further testifies to the imperfect mobility of Arab labor across the ethnic boundary. The maintenance of different institutional and normative frameworks constituted one relevant factor in this regard. Several other socially related factors were also important. Arab employees holding permanent jobs in East Jerusalem were often reluctant to leave them even for better opportunities in the Jewish sector since this involved giving up tenure and seniority compensation. Those working in family enterprises would also maintain their positions due to various nonmaterial benefits and social constraints. Interestingly, the reverse was also true: some Arabs preferred working for Jews rather than in their own sector. The reasons given emphasized the more open and egalitarian employer-employee relationships in Jewish places of work, compared to the more stringent environment in class-structured or family enterprises typical of working relations in the Arab sector.

Nevertheless, the persistence of a dual wage scale in general, and for the most mobile categories of Arab labor in particular, clearly illustrates that selecting between Jewish or Arab employers continued to involve a host of noneconomic considerations. In the same way that Jews were willing to employ Arabs so long as they received lower wages, so too Arab workers needed an extra premium in order to accept employment in the Jewish sector, or were satisfied with lower pay when employed within their own sector.

THE EFFECTS OF INTEGRATION ON JEWISH AND ARAB EMPLOYMENT OPPORTUNITIES

The overall picture of Jewish-Arab labor relations can be properly evaluated by considering the differential employment opportunities and related changes in the economic status of the two ethnic groups after 1967. The integration of the two distinct economic systems necessarily implied some broader processes of adjustment and structural change within each sector and across the entire labor market. To what extent and in which respects have each of the two sectors benefited from the renewal of employment relations both in the short and long run?

There can be little doubt that East Jerusalem Arabs benefited greatly from their access to the more developed Jewish sector. This is reflected primarily in the substantial improvement in their overall employment situation when compared to the pre-1967 period. It will be recalled that, since reunification, the net increase in the number of gainfully employed Jerusalem Arabs can be entirely attributed to new opportunities found in West Jerusalem, while, at the same time, unemployment rates in East Jerusalem drastically declined as did out-migration for work purposes across the Jordan River.

The opening of the Jewish labor market also substantially improved the general income level of Arab households in both nominal and real terms. The income of Arab wage earners practically trebled immediately following reunification, as soon as they gained access to the Jewish sector. According to rough estimates, by the end of the 1970s the average income of East Jerusalem Arabs as a whole had more or less doubled in real terms.[6] Once again this is directly related to the general improvement in employment opportunities, higher wage levels, and the additional transfer payments from Israeli social security sources. The rise in the purchasing power of the Arab population becomes apparent when considering various related economic indicators, such as private consumption levels of durable goods and dwelling amenities. As pointed out in chapter 2, in the longer term this was mainly reflected in the extensive expansion of new housing in East Jerusalem and its immediate periphery, representing a major outlet for private investments made possible by increasing disposable income.

In a certain sense, Arab gains in employment opportunities even surpassed those experienced by the Jewish population. In fact, one of the most noticeable outcomes of the renewed labor relationships was that in the reunited city Arab total employment figures grew even faster than Jewish labor expansion. Between 1968 and 1983 the number of both Jewish and Arab Jerusalem residents gainfully employed increased substantially, and in general at a similar rate: Arabs slightly increased their share in the local workforce from roughly 17 percent to 18 percent.[7] However, the growing Arab share in the total Jerusalem labor market is most obvious when we consider, in addition to Jerusalem Arabs, the thousands of West Bank workers who also found employment in the city after 1967.

The selective expansion of Jewish and Arab employment opportunities was expressed, in turn, by the differential population growth trends of the two communities. During the period between 1968 and 1983, the Arab population of Jerusalem increased from 70,000 to 120,000, and

[6] Comparing the real disparities between the Jewish and Arab sectors of Jerusalem before 1967 and the changes brought about after reunification is obviously problematic. The main reasons are that these involved differences and changes in currencies, purchasing power, relative prices, wage structures, and other features. For some general estimates in this regard, see Romann 1967; Amir 1969; Benvenisti 1982.

[7] See *Statistical Yearbook of Jerusalem.*

more significantly, it increased its relative share in the entire city population from 26 percent to nearly 29 percent. The differential demographic growth trends basically reflected the substantial gap in natural growth rates (those of the Arabs being practically double those of the Jews) as well as the selective migration patterns to and from the city. It is in this latter respect that the diminishing of the pre-1967 out-migration of East Jerusalem residents, and the parallel migration trends of Arabs from the surrounding region toward the city's periphery, can be directly attributed to the general improvement in their employment situation. Yet, paradoxically, Arab population growth was also indirectly caused by the Jewish development policies in Jerusalem aimed at securing a Jewish majority in the united city. As mentioned earlier, in order to attract additional Jewish settlers to Jerusalem the Israeli authorities invested extensively in the construction of new residences and public facilities, as well as the creation of needed employment opportunities, particularly in the manufacturing and tourist industries. It was precisely the expansion of these activities that offered new employment opportunities to local Arabs, as well as attracting additional Arabs from the periphery to Jerusalem. This can be illustrated when examining the available data regarding the expansion of employment in the manufacturing branch of the Jewish sector. Between 1968 and 1982 the net addition of Jewish employment did not exceed a few hundred, compared to approximately 1,500 East Jerusalem Arabs and a similar number of West Bank workers employed in Jewish-owned industry by the end of this period.

In most respects, however, it was mainly the Jewish population that benefited from labor market integration and the emerging patterns of economic relations. This can clearly be demonstrated when comparing the development of overall employment opportunities within each of the two economic sectors, as distinguished by the ethnic identity of employers rather than employed persons. Looked at from this angle, total employment in the Jewish sector more than doubled after 1967, if we add the various categories of Arab labor integrated in this sector to the expansion of Jewish employment proper. By contrast, as already observed, Arab self-employment in East Jerusalem in effect stagnated, its relative share of the entire labor market declining from 16 percent in 1967 to less than 10 percent by the early 1980s. The reunification of Jerusalem therefore had two major and complementary outcomes: on the one hand, from an individual perspective, Arabs greatly gained from the presence of the Jewish sector, while on the other hand, from a sectoral perspective Arab self-development has been severely restricted as a result of the same processes.

These unequal opportunities for sectoral development reflected the nature of relationships between a politically and economically dominant

Jewish sector and a less-developed, subordinate Arab sector. In united Jerusalem, Jewish enterprises not only had far greater economic resources at their disposal, but they also benefited greatly from Israeli government funds and support. The Israeli authorities invested exclusively in Jewish development projects, while in no known case did they directly assist the creation of new factors of production in East Jerusalem. Moreover, the dependency of Arab enterprise on the Israeli administration further limited local initiatives whenever this involved large-scale projects which always implied access to and approval by the Israeli bureaucracy. In more general terms, the imposition of Israeli laws on Arab businesses (regarding licensing regulations or municipal and state taxes, for example) had similar restrictive effects. In the course of the years following 1967, many East Jerusalem Arab businesses preferred to relocate or develop outside of Jerusalem's municipal boundaries, within the jurisdiction of nearby Arab towns and suburbs in the West Bank, where development norms and constraints were more relaxed.

These selectively different opportunities for Jewish and Arab development can best be seen when considering the growth patterns of the tourist industry in united Jerusalem. This was the major activity in which the Arab sector maintained a relative advantage when the city was divided. In 1967 the number of rooms in hotels recommended for tourists was just over one thousand in West Jerusalem, compared to almost double this figure in East Jerusalem. However, between 1967 and 1980 the number grew fourfold in the Jewish sector, whereas in the Arab sector only a marginal addition was recorded. Hence, fifteen years following reunification the proportion of tourist accommodation facilities had been practically reversed—the Jewish sector now accommodated 80 percent of the total visitors staying in the city.[8] As was previously observed, the Arab sector was able to expand only in those marginal tourist-related activities which did not require high investment or access to Israeli authorization and public funding. In more general terms, this testifies to the fact that even where the Arab sector enjoyed certain advantages when the two city sections were separated, under the new conditions of unification it was primarily the dominant Jewish sector that benefited from economic integration.

The integration of the two economic systems also involved significant changes in the industrial and occupational structure of the Jewish and Arab labor forces. Among Jews, these were expressed by a constant rise in the percentage of those engaged in public, financial, and business services as well as in the broad category of white-collar occupations; the relative share of those employed in manufacturing, personal services, or

[8] See Kimhi and Hyman 1978; Hyman, Kimhi, and Savitzki 1985.

manual labor correspondingly declined (see tabs. 4.5 and 4.6). Although these trends can for the most part be attributed to long-term structural changes in the Jewish sector already observed before 1967, they were accelerated following reunification in ways not unrelated to the patterns of integration of Arab labor. This is illustrated by the fact that while the rates of Jewish employment in construction continuously decreased, from 9.4 percent in 1968 to 5.5 percent in 1983, respective rates among the Arab active population increased dramatically, from less than 7 percent upon reunification to a record level approaching 20 percent in 1972, declining again to about 10 percent toward the early 1980s. The distribution of Arab labor across the various economic branches fluctuated considerably over the years, depending to a large extent on the selective and changing opportunities offered by the Jewish sector, especially in construction. By the same token, it was mainly the Arab labor force that had to adjust to the new economic circumstances during the initial transitional period; available data shows that even when compared to the occupational characteristics of East Jerusalem Arab men employed before 1967, by 1972 the proportion of all non-Jewish residents of the city clas-

TABLE 4.5
Jerusalem Residents Employed by Ethnic Origin and Industry, 1968–1981

	Jews			Non-Jews		
Industry	1968	1972	1983	1968[a]	1972[b]	1983[b]
Total						
(thousands)	63.2	71.2	101.1	11.7	17.6	22.7
(percentage)	100.0	100.0	100.0	100.0	100.0	100.0
Agriculture	1.3	0.3	0.4	2.6	1.1	. .
Manufacturing	15.8	12.4	9.1	19.7	18.3	15.9
Electricity and water	1.5	0.9	0.7	3.4	0.6	1.8
Construction	9.4	7.3	5.5	6.8	19.4	10.5
Commerce and catering	12.0	10.9	11.8	21.3	23.4	22.7
Transport and communications	7.0	6.0	6.8	9.4	12.6	11.8
Finance and business services[c]	—	7.9	10.5	—	. .	3.2
Public services	42.6	46.6	48.9	19.7	18.3	25.9
Personal services	10.4	7.7	6.3	17.1	6.3	8.3

Source: Jerusalem Municipality and the Jerusalem Institute for Israel Studies, *Statistical Yearbook of Jerusalem*, various years. Based on Israel, CBS, labor force surveys for corresponding years.

Note: - = no cases; . . = insignificant. Since data are based on a small sample, specific rates are subject to yearly fluctuations—particularly when few persons are involved.

[a] East Jerusalem residents only.

[b] All residents, including those in West Jerusalem.

[c] The category of finance and business services was introduced after the 1970s. Those employed in this category in 1968 were mostly included in commercial and public services.

TABLE 4.6
Jerusalem Residents Employed by Ethnic Origin and Occupation, 1967–1983

Occupation	Jews		Non-Jews		
	1972	1983	1967[a]	1972[b]	1983[c]
Total Employed					
(thousands)	68.5	120.0	11.5	17.0	23.6
(percentage)	100.0	100.0	100.0	100.0	100.0
Scientific and academic professions	13.2	13.8 ⎫	6.2	2.1	5.0
Liberal and technical professions	15.7	19.4 ⎭		10.6	12.9
Managerial workers	0.7	0.5 ⎫	13.4	0.7	0.0
Clerical workers	25.4	23.5 ⎭		7.1	8.5
Salesmen, agents, etc.	6.6	7.2	18.7	14.2	10.9
Service workers	12.1	12.5	15.2	17.7	17.8
Agriculture workers	0.8	0.7	1.8	2.1	1.7
Skilled workers in industry, construction, etc.	19.7	15.0 ⎫	44.6	33.3	34.1
Other workers in industry, construction, etc., and unqualified	2.8	1.4 ⎭		12.1	8.2

Sources: Israel, CBS, East Jerusalem: Census of Population and Housing 1967, pt. 1; Israel, CBS, Census of Population and Housing, 1972, unpublished data; Israel, CBS, Census of Population and Housing, 1983, pub. no. 13.

Note: Due to differences in resources and methods of data collection, total employment figures also differ when compared to tab. 4.5. There is only one figure for combined categories for non-Jews in 1967.

[a] Reported occupations of East Jerusalem males before the 1967 war.
[b] All residents of East Jerusalem.
[c] All non-Jews, including those residing in West Jerusalem.

sified as skilled and unskilled workers had apparently risen, while that of managerial, clerical workers, salesmen, and others had substantially declined. Precisely opposite trends can be seen in the occupational structure of the Jewish labor force during the same five-year period. In the following decade a certain increase in the percentage of Arabs employed in white-collar occupations did take place, and general trends among Arabs more closely followed those observed in the Jerusalem labor market as a whole. Nevertheless, occupational disparities between Jews and Arabs in some of the more professional categories remained constant and, indeed, may have grown. This growing ethnic differentiation can best be appreciated when considering the two extremes of the occupational hierarchy: Jerusalem Arabs, who in 1983 accounted for one-sixth of all the local residents gainfully employed, were hardly represented in the managerial occupations while they constituted over half of the total number of unskilled workers! Thus, generally speaking, the process of integration was equally associated with a growing proletarization of the Arab labor force, and the parallel upward mobility of the entire structure of Jewish employment.

Considerable disparities between Jews and Arabs were also maintained in average income and the related parameters of economic well-being. Here again a distinction should be made between the initial effects brought about by the integration of the two economic sectors in 1967 and long-term trends. In the first phase, there is no doubt that the substantial income differences which had existed in the two parts of the divided city before 1967 significantly narrowed as a result of reunification and the subsequent adjustment of wages, commodity prices, and the like. In addition, due to the more equalized income structure in the Jewish sector and the greater accessibility of Arab manual workers to alternative and better paid employment opportunities there, it was mainly the lower income groups among the Arab population that improved their economic situation in relation to both the higher-income groups and the pre-1967 period. However, the income gap between Jews and Arabs remained substantial and hardly changed during the following years. This can be seen when comparing available data on the average income of Jerusalem households whose head was a salaried employee (see tab. 4.7). Average family income remained about twice as high among Jews compared to non-Jews, in spite of the fact that in 1972 the data referred to gross revenues before taxes, whereas in 1983 it concerned net disposable income. The disparity in per-capita income was even higher taking into account the marked differences in the average household size between the two population groups. In addition, the overall income gap was even higher considering the fact that reported revenues of the self-employed were on the average significantly higher than those of salaried employees in the Jewish sector and respectively lower in the Arab sector.

Similar disparities and trends can be found when examining selected indicators of living standards, such as housing density or private car ownership, among Jewish and Arab households. The wide disparities in the percentage of families who owned a car in 1972 were apparently reduced in the following decade, but this should be mainly attributed to the particularly low consumption levels in the Arab sector at the beginning of the period. Of course, comparative data can be interpreted in different ways depending on the angle of observation. Thus, for example, between 1972 and 1983 the proportion of car ownership among Jews doubled,

TABLE 4.7
Level of Well-Being of Jerusalem Residents
by Ethnic Origin (Selected Indicators), 1972, 1983

	1972		1983	
	Jews	Non-Jews	Jews	Non-Jews
% of Households Possessing:				
A private car	22.9	6.3	44.8	21.8
A telephone	51.3	7.5	87.8	22.9
Household Residential Density:				
Persons per room	1.4	2.7	1.1	2.3
Less than one person per room (%)	24.6	6.1	39.0	10.5
Average Income of employee households[a]:				
Per household (index)	100	47	100	54
Per person (index)[b]	100	29	100	36

Sources: Israel, CBS, *Census of Population and Housing*, 1972, pub. nos. 13 and 15; Israel, CBS, *Census of Population and Housing*, 1983, pub. no. 5 and unpublished data.

[a] 1972—gross annual income; 1983—net monthly income.

[b] 1972—per average person; 1983—per "standard person," i.e., using a decreasing weight for additional household members.

while the relative growth among Arabs was over threefold. On the other hand, when comparing the increase in the percentage of households that became first-time owners of a private car during the same period, respective ratios were 22 percent among Jews and only about 15 percent among non-Jews. In other words, it can be shown that the previous gap in this particular category of private consumption increased rather than declined over the years. This was even more pronounced with reference to such matters as telephone ownership or housing conditions. In general, the relative improvement in the consumption levels of the Jewish as compared with the Arab population was most significant in those categories which more directly depended on public sector allocation.

In summary, in spite of significant improvements in Arab employment level and standard of living since reunification, in most regards the direct correspondence between national-ethnic affiliation and the socioeconomic status of Jews and Arabs was basically maintained and in several respects even grew over the years. What is more, in the dichotomous environment of Jerusalem, ethnic identity, political antagonism, and divergent social norms also remained highly relevant for the patterns of economic integration and intersectoral labor relations.

The willingness of Jews and Arabs to work together could be basically attributed to sheer economic necessity and complementary opportunities. As we have seen, for the Jewish sector the availability of an Arab workforce enabled it to carry out major development projects and meet the labor demands of an expanding economy. For Jerusalem Arabs access to the Jewish sector also represented a timely response to chronic employment problems. However, even under these circumstances mutual relations and dependency remained essentially asymmetrical. Whereas Arab motives were mostly dictated by necessity, those of Jews were more generally responses to opportunity. To put it in broader economic terms, for Arab labor the alternative to employment in the Jewish sector was either unemployment or emigration. By contrast, for the Jewish employers the alternatives to Arab workers were more diversified and far less severe: Arab workers could be replaced, at least in the long term, by introducing more capital-intensive and labor saving-methods, as was indeed done in several manufacturing plants and even in certain service industries.

These underlying conditions help explain the basically asymmetrical employment relations emerging between Jews and Arabs. Generally the Arabs were willing to work with Jews. Jews, on their part, were more reluctant to engage Arabs, and generally avoided Arab employment whenever possible. Moreover, by virtue of their dominant position the Jewish sector could also dictate the modes and terms when in need of Arab labor. Jewish entrepreneurs could choose whether to employ Arabs in the framework of the organized labor market and on a permanent basis, or instead, hire occasional unorganized Arab labor on an ad hoc basis. Subcontracting to Arab workshops in East Jerusalem was another way to save on capital investment or social payments and benefit from cheap Arab labor.

In spite of the extensive mutual employment relationships, ethnic identity and social and national barriers continued to play a crucial and essentially restrictive role. Jewish employers generally preferred to hire Jewish labor, while the hiring of Arabs often had to be justified by the nonavailability of Jewish workers for tasks involving low pay or stigmatized as "Arab work." Jewish employees in mixed places of employment might also resent the presence of Arab workers, particularly when this reached large proportions. In those cases where Arabs did attain leadership positions or were elected to local work committees, this was tolerated by Jews due to the overall Jewish character of the workplace. In a similar vein, one of the most revealing observations is that no Jews were reported to be salaried employees in Arab-owned establishments in East Jerusalem; in those few cases where Jewish employees were engaged in the Arab sector as teachers, doctors, nurses, or bank employees, this always concerned public and commercial institutions under direct or indirect Jewish control. Many Jewish professionals also worked for Arab firms, but here again, this was exclusively as self-employed persons offering their services: Jews have been willing to work *for* Arabs, but not *under* Arabs.

Finally, the pattern of mutual relationships and behavior in the employment market cannot be dissociated from the political context. It is mostly in this regard that the Israeli authorities faced dual, contradictory goals. On the one hand, by virtue of their responsibility for the Arab population they felt obliged to provide Arabs with sufficient labor opportunities, judging that in an environment of political conflict economic stability would help avoid political unrest. On the other hand, they were also concerned about growing Jewish dependence on Arab labor. But it was mainly the Arabs who had to compromise and cooperate with Jews in economic terms in spite of their political antagonism. The necessity for economic survival under Jewish hegemony was formalized in political terms in the Arab policy of *sumud* ("steadfastness"), which justified Arab employment in the Jewish sector. Indeed, it even permitted taking almost any job offered by Jews, even in the Israeli police, or providing Arab labor for the construction of Jewish settlements in East Jerusalem. The essential Arab obligation was to work in order to remain steadfast, and ultimately, to prevail.

CHAPTER 5

Working Together

JERUSALEM IS, as we have been emphasizing, a deeply divided city. Boundaries of various kinds continue to separate Jews and Arabs. However, as demonstrated in the previous chapter, if there is one single realm in which they intersect actively with one another, it is in the context of work. In contrast with Jerusalem's residential areas, where comparatively few persons from both sides maintain ongoing social relations, within the workplace literally thousands of Jews and Arabs have daily contacts. The realities are such that, in effect, workplaces are the most active arenas of ethnic social interaction.

This poses some intriguing questions. What happens when Arabs and Jews work together for extended periods of time? What rules govern their repeated social encounters? Does working side by side lessen the animosity or tension between them, or, on the contrary, actually reinforce the suspicion and misunderstandings that divide Arabs and Jews?

These are among the principal concerns of this chapter. A Jerusalem factory was selected for intensive study of the broad trends identified in the previous chapter. Later, in chapter 7, we will also consider how Jews and Arabs interact in a second setting—namely, within a major hospital. In both places members of the two groups enter into active social exchanges, and their experience provides the basis for our examination of ethnic relations in the workplace.

BAKING BREAD TOGETHER

Nimrod is a large Jerusalem bakery. It is one of several baking plants located in the city, and it employs close to three hundred persons. Nimrod was chosen for study since the factory employs both Jews and Arabs, and also since, based upon a preliminary survey, the patterns of contacts appeared to be similar to those in other moderate- and large-sized industrial firms.

The factory is owned and managed by members of the Nimrod family, who have been in the baking business for several generations. It is one of the main suppliers of bread to Jerusalem and surrounding communities (since 1967 this also includes parts of the West Bank), and it also supplies substantial quantities of bread to major consumers such as the Israeli army. The plant itself is located on the western edge of Jerusalem in an industrial zone surrounded by several residential neighborhoods (a second bakery is located nearby). The plant covers several acres and includes baking and bread production sections, administrative offices, a garage for maintaining a fleet of delivery trucks, and shipping and receiving areas. The factory complex is modern in appearance and well maintained; the large warehousing zone was recently covered by an aluminum roof. The production and management areas are also clean and well tended.

The production of bread is standardized and relatively simple. There are four major operations: preparing the loaves, baking them, packaging the loaves for shipment, and shipping. Two standard types of bread are produced: a long, flat white bread (*lehem lavan*) and a dark-grained thicker bread (*lehem ahid* or *lehem shahor*). These two breads are the factory's staple product, and during an average week tens of thousands of loaves are produced and sold. In addition, the factory also produces a special white bread for the Sabbath and Jewish holiday consumption (*halah*). These *halah* are small and square in shape; a special braided *halah* is also made for Sabbath use. The standard breads are entirely produced by machine, while the braided *halah* is made by hand. At the time of the study Nimrod did not make any other kinds of bread or bread products.

Bread production takes place in two daily shifts. The first shift begins at 8:00 P.M. and continues until 5:00 A.M.; the second shift starts at 7:00 A.M. and finishes at 4:00 P.M. Both shifts follow the same procedures. The breads are prepared by work crews and placed in large ovens where they remain until properly baked. They are then removed and packaged in paper wrapping; finally, the loaves are packed in cartons and shipped by truck to market. Organizationally, the work is done by three separate departments: preparing the dough and baking the bread is done in the production department, packaging in the packaging department, and shipping in the warehouse department. Crews of workers are trained to perform each of these three main tasks. The work crews vary in size from thirty or so in each of the production shifts to fifteen workers in the packaging department. The work in each of these departments is highly standardized; in the baking or production section the workers work on-line seeing that the dough is prepared into proper-sized loaves, and then they transfer the loaves to the ovens. In the packaging department workers operate machines that place the bread in paper bags or within cartons. In the warehouse they load the bread into trucks for delivery to supermarkets and retail shops.

Taken as a whole, the bakers are the most skilled workers. They are responsible for preparing the dough and tending the ovens. In contrast, the work in the warehouse consists of unskilled physical labor in packing and loading the bread for shipment. Since much of the work is mechanical the actual specialization is limited; in most cases the tasks are categorized as "semiskilled" or "unskilled," and the specialization requires only a limited amount of prior preparation. There are exceptions (the factory employs several electricians and other technical workers who maintain the machinery) but, in general, the degree of training or special knowledge required is minimal. With the exception of several secretaries and telephone operators, all of the workers are men.

Each of the work functions is directed by a shift foreman who is directly responsible for his section. For example, there are two shift foremen responsible for production during the night and day shifts, just as there are two shift foremen in the packaging section. The foreman is responsible for organizing the work in his section. He assigns particular tasks, makes certain that work discipline is maintained, and sees to it that there are no errors or problems in production. These shift foremen are, in turn, responsible to a general production manager who oversees the entire work schedule. The production manager is responsible to the plant management, and ultimately, to the owners of the factory. In this particular factory the owners and the managers are one and the same: the work is directly managed by members of the Nimrod family.

The worker's salary depends upon the type of work that is being done and relative seniority. For example, since work in production is more skilled than in shipping, bakers tend to receive higher salaries. Because the turnover rate in unskilled jobs such as packaging tends to be high, this too affects salaries (the less time worked the lower the job status and salary). As is generally the case in Israel, workers are awarded job tenure (Heb. *kvi'ut*) after an initial work period of a year or more; those who receive *kvi'ut* cannot be laid off or fired unless they receive severance or compensation payment based upon the length of time employed. In addition, since many of the workers are members of the Histadrut, specific work grievances or salary issues are negotiated with the local work committee (*va'ad ovdim*), the Histadrut officials, and the bakery owners. Wages in food production plants such as bakeries tend to be low, and in the late 1970s the Histadrut negotiated a more favorable contract after lengthy negotiation and occasional work stoppages.

The bakery's workforce has, over time, gone through major changes. Indeed, the history of employment at Nimrod follows the broad trends of Palestinian and Israeli social stratification during the past fifty or more years. When the factory was originally established, nearly all of the workers were Jews. During the 1930s and 1940s they were mainly recent immigrants from European and Middle Eastern countries, although some were also veteran Jerusalemites; jobs were hard to come by, and even though the pay was low and the work unskilled, it attracted members of the then Jewish working class. Later, following the establishment of Israel and the resultant mass immigration, the workforce was largely composed of recent immigrants from Middle Eastern countries as well as a small number of Jerusalem Arabs (several of whom were residents of Beit Safafa). The major change took place following 1967; Arabs from East Jerusalem and the West Bank were hired by the bakery. Since then to an increasing extent the workforce has become mixed between Arabs and Jews. As table 5.1 indicates, in 1983 the majority of workers were Jews, while Arabs were a large minority.

With the exception of management, both Arabs and Jews are employed in each of the departments. There are, however, differences within each of these categories. The Arab workers include both Jerusalem residents and those who live on the West Bank; this is an important distinction since, among other things, while the West Bank Arabs receive identical pay they are always in the category of "temporary workers" and have no permanent work security. The Jewish workers are also a mixed group. Some of the Jews working in production are veteran Europeans in their late fifties or sixties; in effect, they are the last remnant of the Jewish working class. Most of the other Jewish workers are younger men, the majority of them Middle Eastern in background. Many of those employed in the warehouse are younger men who are temporarily employed until they find other work.

The bakery management is exclusively Jewish: all of the clerks, telephone operators, and higher-level managers and executives are Jews. This conforms with an important feature of the bakery's organization and self-image: Nimrod presents itself as a Jewish firm that employs both Jewish and Arab workers. This is a critical point, and we will return to it later in this chapter.

EVERYDAY WORK SITUATIONS

We now turn to questions of Arab-Jewish relationships. How do Arab and Jewish workers relate to one another on a day-to-day basis? A good way

TABLE 5.1
Nimrod Employees by Ethnic Group and Department

Department	Arab Workers	Jewish Workers
Production	56	64
Packaging	19	18
Warehouse and shipping	26	62
Garage and maintenance	5	18
Management	—	19
TOTAL	106	181

to begin this analysis is to briefly depict a common or everyday series of events. Drawn from our field notes, the following brief description indicates the tone and texture of everyday exchanges between Jews and Arabs. In this miniature Ahmad, Youseff, and Baker are Arabs, while Moshe, Shimon, Krankie, and Shimie are Jews.

> The second-shift workers have been at it since 7:00 A.M. Ahmad is the foreman, and he works closely with all of the others. Everyone is gathered around the mixing machine. The pressure of work is off now, since almost all of the loaves have been prepared and are being stoked in the ovens. Moshe and Shimon, two of the older workers, are resting on the side, chatting quietly. Ahmad helps Shimie clean the mixing machine and sort out the rest of the loaves. As usual, Arab workers are close to one another on the line, and so are the Jews. Earlier there had been a problem with the flour mix, but now it seems to be working well. Shimie whistles a tune, and the others look out of the window to see if it is still raining. David, the production manager, comes into the room and asks Ahmad for the next day's work schedule. He jokes with Baker and Krankie. Ahmad replies that he has not made it up yet; he has to hear first from Shimon. Shimon retorts that he must go to see the doctor tomorrow and won't be around. Ahmad grumbles, as do some of the others. He asks Youseff if he can work overtime and mumbles that it will all somehow work out. David leaves, and everyone relaxes. Ahmad tells Moshe to help him get the loaves into the oven, and he asks the others to begin to clean up. Almost all of the discussion is in Hebrew; occasionally the Arabs speak among themselves in Arabic, and some Jews in Yiddish. The tone is easy and tired; everyone is waiting for the shift to end.

Moments such as these are commonplace at Nimrod. As in this particular depiction, the work teams typically are mixed: Jews and Arabs work together in each of the three departments. In many instances they perform the same tasks, doing the same kind of work together for eight hours or longer each day. Indeed, an outside observer would be hard-pressed to distinguish between Jews and Arabs; they commonly wear the same factory-issue grey clothing, are often the same age, and in many instances speak in either Arabic or Hebrew, or in a kind of "patter" that includes both languages. Conversations are open, free, and "normal"; these workers have come to know one another after weeks, months, and sometimes years of working side by side, and have developed norms of conduct that are personal, direct, and typically unencumbered by ethnic prejudice or hostility. The workers themselves observe that "we spend most of our lives here working together, and the question of who is a Jew or who is an Arab does not get in the way."

Moreover, as was indicated in the description of everyday interaction, in some situations Arabs have authority over Jewish workers; Ahmad, who is an Arab, is the shift foreman, and the Jewish workers take their orders from him. This is the case in several of the departments, and in the various work shifts as well. To some extent Arab workers are able to move up in the bakery work system, and the Jewish workers must therefore become accustomed to a situation in which an Arab is in a higher-status position.

Outsiders may not be able to immediately distinguish between Arabs and Jews. But the "insiders," the workers themselves, do identify one another in these terms. Although work relationships seem to be uninhibited by stigma or tension, being a Jew or an Arab is a fundamental feature of the social structure of work relationships. A careful observer will note, for example, that small work teams generally form along ethnic lines. Similarly, while all of the workers on a particular shift eat together, it is often the case that Jews will sit next to one another during their lunch break, while the Arab workers do the same. Given the choice, the workers apparently feel more comfortable with those who are like themselves. This is by no means always the case, nor are sanctions applied against members of one group who work or eat regularly with the other. Nonetheless, the common pattern is for there to be an informal social separation between them.

In addition, the ethnic composition of the two shifts varies. Most of those who work during the day are Jews, while a majority of the night shift workers are Arabs. This is not a total division, however, and each shift has a significant proportion of persons from both groups. The Jews who manage the bakery explain that the Arabs prefer to work at night; many of the night shift workers live on the West Bank, and by working at night they can spend part of the day tending crops that they have planted or performing other chores.

The experience of working together has been shared by the veteran Arab and Jewish workers for more than a decade. Many have the same evaluation of their experience. Arabs make the point that the bakery is a good place to work; the owner is said to be fair and working conditions are better than in many other places. All of the workers who are at the same work level and who have the same years of seniority receive equal pay, whether they are Arabs or Jews. This measure of equality in the workplace is important to the Arabs and it provides a framework of proper working conditions. The actual pay may be low, and everyone complains—but these are complaints voiced by all of the workers. In addition, one of the veteran Arab workers made the point that working at the bakery is tolerable "when they need you; when management knows that they really need you, and that without you the work shift won't go well, then you're in a strong position. It doesn't make any difference whether you are a Jew or an Arab; the important thing is that they can't get along without you." Some also note that it is better to work for a Jewish employer than for an Arab:

> In the past I worked for both Arab and Jewish employers. Some years ago I quit working for Jews—I really was fed up—and worked for an Arab. There, though, the pay was terrible, much lower than here, and the working conditions also were bad. So I decided again to work for a Jew. To tell you the truth, at the moment at least I prefer working in a Jewish company.

While they share the view that the bakery is a good place to work, the Arab workers also express considerable ambivalence and uncertainty. Together with the Jews, they are "workers" in the factory. But they are also, at the same time, "Arab workers," and this places them in a different category. As was noted, not all of the Arab workers have *kvi'ut*, and this by definition limits their chances for advancement. With a few exceptions, all of those who live on the West Bank do not have tenure, and this places them in a particularly vulnerable position. One of the veteran Arab workers sums up his situation as follows:

> When any Jewish worker starts out he can get *kvi'ut* within a half-year or so. The boss will raise any of the Jews quickly, no matter how they work. But with us, with any Arab, it will always take longer, two years, three years, and no one cares. What can you do? Complain? Who will listen, who cares? And all of the time you can't really lift your head up; you have to be nice and do whatever they tell you to do, because otherwise they can fire you in a minute. If you say no to something, say that you won't do some kind of work, then they can just fire you.

Moreover, the Arab workers make the point that they move up the factory grade and pay scale much more slowly in comparison with their Jewish colleagues. They complain that if a Jew is promoted to a higher grade after two years, in their case it will always take much longer. Even when they perform well and everyone knows that they are good, reliable workers, the rewards always come slower, if at all. Neither the local work committee (*va'ad ovdim*) nor the Histadrut is really interested in the work conditions of Arabs. Thus, they complain, it may be true that everyone at the same rank gets the same pay, but the Arab workers do not reach the same rank as the Jews, and even when they do it takes them a longer time to get there.

Take the case of the young Arab worker who, like Ahmad in the miniature, had reached the rank of shift foreman. Energetic and increasingly skilled at his task, he wished to move ahead in the business of baking. Vocational courses for middle-level managers leading to promotion were organized by the Histadrut, and he enrolled in one of these courses. However, the classes were held in the early evenings in Tel Aviv, and

the course was also taught entirely in Hebrew. Although he struggled
with the course for several months (the bakery helped him by translating
some of the material into Arabic) in the end he dropped out. The effort
was simply too great, he felt, and he became resigned to remaining at
the same low-level position in the factory.

These issues of relative status (what might be termed "effective inequality") in the bakery work system are one dimension of the Arab
workers' ambivalence. A second dimension stems from the everyday
work relationships between Jews and Arabs. As is normally the case in
workplaces, personal relations vary among the workers; the Arabs find
that some of the Jews are better, more sympathetic work partners, and
they naturally gravitate to them. They avoid others whom they sense are
more remote or hostile. During the work day it is common for persons to
converse, carry on a bantering, light series of exchanges, joke with one
another, or exchange mild insults and curses. "We talk to keep things
moving, to pass the time more quickly," the workers explain. Indeed, in
some exceptional cases personal friendships have developed between
Arab and Jewish workers who become, they say, "like brothers" on the
work line.

But the relationships are not always so free and easy going. For example, the Arab bakers complain that following the baking they are always
expected to clean the machines; the Jewish workers have come to expect
that the Arabs will perform such menial cleaning chores. It places a strain
upon them and they are displeased with it, but most accept this additional task. Similarly, they also complain that frequently Arabs are required to work overtime hours. While they are paid for the work, in some
instances it is inconvenient for them to do so, and the pay increment is
not necessarily attractive enough for them to volunteer for overtime.
They are annoyed that it has become expected that they will always agree
to perform additional work. To cite yet another example, Arab workers
who have become shift foremen also relate that they often have problems
with the Jewish workers. "They don't like taking orders or directions
from us, and some of the Jews give us problems; they say, 'I won't take
orders from an Arab,' and then what am I supposed to do? I always have
to be careful when I tell one of them to do something, and many times I
just end up doing it myself. It's simpler that way."

Beyond these particular problems, the Arab workers are also confronted with the persistent dilemma arising from the fact that they are
"Arabs" working for a "Jewish" firm. That the Nimrod Bakery is "Jewish"
and "Israeli" is made manifest in a variety of ways. The owners are Jews,
the management is exclusively Jewish, and the normal language of discussion is Hebrew (even though at the entrance to the factory instructions to workers are also printed and prominently displayed in Arabic).

In effect, the bakery "belongs" to the Jewish owners, managers, and workers, while the Arabs come each day to work there. As outsiders, the Arab workers must always be careful and on their guard; they need to behave in ways that are considered proper and take care not to voice words or vent opinions that will offend their Jewish hosts or be resented by them. Arab workers must also learn how to react to Jews; they need to control their reactions when, for example, someone makes derogatory statements about Arabs, or when they believe themselves to be affronted or insulted. In short, the Arabs feel themselves to be in a vulnerable social position.

It is within this context that the Arab workers often complain that they suffer from being "shamed" or "offended" (Heb. *mushpal*). They complain, sometimes bitterly, that their "proper manhood" suffers from these encounters.

> Our real problem is that we must be quiet and simply take all of the nasty, mean things that we hear. I understand Hebrew, and I hear the Jews talking about Arabs—"Dirty Arab" I hear them say, or even worse. I am often ashamed of myself, but what can I do? I can never say to them what I really think. I must be quiet and just listen, not say anything in return. Look, the pay here is alright, and the *ba'al habayit* [owner] is also alright. But when you work in a place like this you face insults all of the time. That's the real problem.

Comments such as these are voiced by many of the Arab workers. The problem—and it is not unique to the bakery—is how to adjust to working within the other's territory.

The Jews' perceptions of their relations with the Arab workers are, as one would expect, quite different. They too have learned to work side by side with Arabs, and to a considerable degree they share the same views as their Arab colleagues. "Relations between us are good," many say. "There really are no problems in working together. We come here to work, not to argue about politics. So there are no problems." Such remarks are typically voiced by Jewish workers in all of the departments, and by the management as well. To illustrate, the Jews often describe incidents or situations involving Arabs that are light-hearted and sociable:

> We always joke together when we are working. One fellow says this, another says the opposite, and there is a lot of kidding. Like the other day I said, "Well, Arafat is in a lot of trouble; he'll come out of Beirut in a box," and all of us laughed, Arabs and Jews. Salim (an Arab) said, "Yes, he'll come out in a broken box," and we all laughed some more. That's the way it is with us, that's how it goes here; we are all one big family while we're here.

From the point of view of the Jewish workers these "jokes" are legitimate—particularly when they are at the expense of the Arabs. Joking behavior among the workers lightens the atmosphere and provides common topics of conversation. These jokes also indicate, as they are meant to, that the bakery is a part of the Jewish territory, and that statements that conform with Israeli political attitudes are acceptable. (It is hard to imagine, for example, that jokes could be told about Israeli politicians in a mixed group.)

The Jewish workers rarely voice disapproval of the behavior or the work performance of their Arab workmates. This does not seem to be a topic of discussion or a source of complaint. On the other hand, they frequently complain about the bakery management's attitudes toward Arab workers. This is an interesting and perhaps paradoxical point: the Jewish workers consistently claim that the Nimrod management favors the Arabs, and that the owners of the factory will go out of their way to help Arabs while they rarely do the same for Jews. The following is an example of the Jewish workers' complaint:

> When one of the Arabs asks the boss for a loan, he'll always get it. Let's say that it's a few days before payday, and the Arab comes along and says that he has a big payment that he must make now. The boss will say, "How much do you need?" and he'll give him an advance on his salary. And then let's say that a Jew comes along and asks for the same thing. The Jew will be refused. He'll tell him that he must learn to live within his means, has to budget his money, and all of that. That's the way he is, I'm telling you. He helps Arabs, but not the Jews.

This purported favoritism perplexes the Jewish workers. Why would a Jewish owner or manager favor Arab workers over Jews? Several explanations are offered. Some argue that the Arab workers are more skillful and polite when asking for favors. Others, however, have a more Machiavellian explanation: favoring the Arab workers has the effect of weakening the workers' unity, and divides them between Arabs and Jews. Management will favor the Arabs, some Jews argue, since this divides the workforce in negotiations or confrontations with the factory owners.

TENSIONS AROUND THE OVENS

This chapter has mainly been concerned with what can be called "everyday events"—the patterns of daily social relationships. These are the normal patterns of conduct, the attitudes and expressions that are typically expressed. However, in addition to these regular events there are also more unusual moments or situations that occasionally take place. Not surprisingly, these special moments and unusual situations are typically provoked by political events and issues. In a word, the patterns of Jewish-Arab relationships in the factory are influenced not only by internal factory issues, but also by events that take place in Jerusalem, within Israel, or, more broadly, throughout the Middle East.

The management and the workers, both Arabs and Jews, make a conscious effort to dissociate the bakery from the outside world. They are well aware that as Arabs and Jews they are likely to have different, contrasting, and probably even antagonistic political ideas and viewpoints. The workforce, after all, includes Arabs who are Palestinian nationalists working with Jews who are Israeli nationalists. Some of the West Bank Arabs are Palestinian refugees who fled from Israel during the 1948 war, and the Jews include some who privately say that they are supporters of extreme right-wing Israeli political groups. Confrontations in the factory are, therefore, potentially explosive. Simply put, for the bakery to successfully produce bread there must be cooperation among the workers, and revealing political attitudes would only damage or destroy this cooperation.

It is for this reason that the bakery workers, both Jews and Arabs, generally refrain from discussing politics. At all work levels they take care not to enter into political discussions or to raise issues or statements that are likely to provoke strong emotional responses. "We come here to work, not to talk politics," is the oft-repeated slogan voiced by both Jewish and Arab workers. Should a political discussion or debate begin, the workers are usually careful to moderate their views so as not to insult or anger the others. Politics is dangerous, and since many of the workers understand both Hebrew and Arabic even stray phrases can trigger strong responses. "We came here to work, not to talk politics" has become a kind of ideology of the workplace. It is, in effect, a strategy of avoidance.

The norm at the factory is not to raise political issues and provoke heated discussion. The exchange of mild political jokes or brief comments that presumably will not offend others are acceptable. However, while efforts are made to maintain this norm, it is not always possible in practice. From time to time outside events or internal conflicts become too powerful to insulate the bakery from the Arab-Israeli conflict.

An explosion on an Israeli bus in Jerusalem or an attack on the Muslim shrines on the Temple Mount, are examples of events that raise the level of tension on the bakery's production line. In fact, in the years following 1967 Arab workers typically would remain at home following an Arab terrorist attack in Jerusalem; they feared being picked up by the Israeli police in a roundup of suspects, or even worse, that there would be retaliation against Arabs. However, in recent years the Arabs generally have come to work even when tensions in the city are high; experience has shown them that there are few personal dangers, and besides, workers on the night shift are brought directly to the factory by special transportation. In quiet conversation with Jewish workers they are also likely to express their personal sorrow and anger against indiscriminate terrorist attacks. Nonetheless, some of the Jewish workers may make strong statements or insulting remarks against Arabs, and this leads to mutual anger and heightened tension. Typically this charged situation persists for a short time and then begins to fade; it has become an almost commonplace feature of life in united Jerusalem.

More complex, longer-lasting conflicts were generated by the Israeli invasion of Lebanon. Ethnic identifications and emotions were seriously strained by the war. On the one hand, the Jewish workers applauded the swift move of the Israeli army into Lebanon and northward toward Beirut; on the other hand, the Arab workers worried about members of their families who lived in the Palestinian refugee camps that were being attacked. The tensions between workers were serious and prolonged. The bakery was a major supplier of bread for the Israeli army, and during this period some of the Arabs were upset by the fact that they were baking bread for an army that was, in effect, attacking their fellow Palestinians. In addition, some of the Jewish workers were called into their army reserve units, and the work pressures consequently grew for the Arabs who were working longer shifts. As is typically the case, the Arabs were mainly silent about their feelings, but some of the Jews suspected that they were purposefully working more slowly or causing problems on the production line. To add to this already tense situation, the Israeli army drivers who daily picked up loads of bread often cursed or spoke disparagingly about Arabs while they waited for their trucks to be loaded. In some instances the drivers may not have realized that many of the bakery workers were Arabs—but whatever the reason, their comments only increased the Arabs' anger. The Jewish shift foreman recalls that

> it was the worst time here that I can remember. The tension was absolutely thick. The Arabs said that this was a defense factory, and that their families were being killed, and how could they work like this? Some even stopped coming to work. Those that did come were reading Arab newspapers, and you could see that they were angry. They even told me how they felt. I'm happy now that it is all finished. It was just awful working here then.

In addition, interethnic conflicts also explode as the result of anger or quarrels among the workers. Some persons irritate one another, or they compete for authority and prestige within a particular work group. Issues may finally be settled violently. One such instance occurred several years earlier, and it was unusual enough to be remembered by many. Two workers in the shipping department, one a Jew and the other an Arab, began quarreling with one another. The Jewish worker made insulting remarks about Arabs, and the Arab answered back in kind. Finally, a fist fight broke out between them. The other workers stepped in and stopped the fighting. In the excitement the owner was called. He asked them what had happened; why were they fighting? The Jewish worker's reply was evasive, but the Arab made it clear that he and "his religion" had been insulted by the Jew. The owner promptly fired the latter: he loudly announced that he would not permit prejudice against *any* worker in his bakery, and that a Jew who insulted an Arab because he was an Arab would immediately be fired. The incident made a deep impression upon all the workers. They interpreted it as a firm statement of equality and fairness on the part of the bakery management.

In these and other instances of conflict the initiating actors are Jews. Since this is a "Jewish factory" the Jewish workers feel strong and secure enough to express their superior position. Squabbles and fights are rarely provoked by the Arab workers, who generally are content to maintain a "low profile"; for the Arabs in particular, the expression "we have come here to work, not to talk politics" is especially appropriate. Nevertheless, in the past some of the Arab workers have engaged in political activities. A case in point can illustrate the dynamics as well as the dilemmas of their position.

It will be recalled that Arabs who reside in Jerusalem are eligible to become members of the Histadrut, the Jewish Federation of Labor, while those who live on the West Bank are not Histadrut members and instead are organized through government labor exchanges. In the late 1970s some Arabs on the West Bank and in Jerusalem began to organize their own all-Arab union. Although this new organization described its objectives in terms of protecting and advancing the rights of Arab workers—that is, in traditional union terms—it was apparently sponsored by Palestinian nationalist political groups, including the PLO, who saw it as a means for expanding their political activities and influence. Workers in this new union were to be organized along craft or industry lines. Separate groups were formed for Arabs working in construction, automobile garages, the food industries, transportation, and so forth. They established a "club center" in East Jerusalem, began to hold meetings and other activities, and invited Arab workers to join them.

'Ali, one of the veteran Arab workers, became active in this union. He quietly discussed the new organization with his fellow Arab workers and urged them to join. 'Ali described their grievances—they were not promoted as rapidly as the Jewish workers and did not receive adequate benefits—and promised that the new Arab union would take a tough, aggressive stand in protecting their rights. Some of the Arab workers agreed to join and began paying membership dues; others were reluctant or uncertain. As a consequence the question of joining the new union became a divisive issue among the Arab workers. It was apparently at this point that the Nimrod management became aware that an attempt was being made to organize a separate Arab union. The factory owners immediately contacted the Israeli authorities, including the police, and consulted with them: was an Arab organization, perhaps sponsored by Arab nationalists, organizing within their own factory? The police investigated, and shortly thereafter 'Ali was called into the owners' office; the police were present, and he was questioned about his activities. Later that day he was taken to police headquarters for additional questioning, and several weeks later he was fired from his job at Nimrod. In effect, this ended the attempt to organize a separate union among the Arab bakery workers.

This incident expresses some of the facets of Arab-Jewish relationships in the factory context. It is, in fact, richly suggestive. The Arab workers' vulnerability is well illustrated; this attempt on the part of some of them to organize separately was quickly beaten down. It may be, as one of the Arab workers remarked, that "you have power when the owners need you," but this refers to particular work roles in baking bread rather than to organized political power. In effect, the Arab workers are not permitted to organize politically. This fact, in turn, reinforces one of the major structural features of the workplace—namely, that the bakery is a Jewish firm where Arabs may take part in the work process. According to this design the unions must also be Jewish; Arabs can be minority members within Jewish-controlled unions, whereas organizing separately is not acceptable.

What is more, the incident also has important implications for power relationships within the factory itself. Specifically, it bears upon the relative power of management and workers. Management's view was that the PLO was organizing within the bakery; this could not be tolerated by them, and the Israeli police were called in. Labeling the attempt to organize and those who supported it as "PLO" had the effect of discrediting 'Ali and others who had joined him. From management's point of view this was entirely in accord with the ideology of keeping politics out of the workplace; after all, the new Arab union was at least in part a maneuver to expand the influence of Palestinian nationalist groups. In addition, a separate Arab union would have complicated the relationships between workers and management. Management might, for example, have had to negotiate with both groups, and this would have led to results that could not always be anticipated. PLO or not, it was in management's interest to oppose a union representing the Arab workers. The owners of the factory had nothing to gain from changing the pattern of worker-management relations.

Some of these same features are emphasized in the internal organization of the work committee and its relations with the factory's executives.

The *va'ad* is the elected committee that represents the workers in their negotiations with the bakery management. Organized within the framework of the Histadrut, the *va'ad*'s general purpose is to protect and advance the bakery workers' rights and benefits. Problems raised by the workers—for example, in regard to their meal arrangements or salary scale—are discussed in meetings between the work committee and management, and specific grievances expressed by a particular worker or by those working together on one of the shifts are also brought before the bakery management by the *va'ad* members.

Elections to the *va'ad* are held periodically. The committee is composed of three members, one of whom is selected to be chairman. At the time of the study the *va'ad* included two Jewish and one Arab member. The Jewish members were veteran factory activists (one of them, the chairman, had been a member of the *va'ad* for almost fifteen years), and the Arab who was elected was also a veteran worker who had moved up to the position of shift foreman. The fact that an Arab had been elected to the committee was unusual but not exceptional; in the past Arabs had also been elected to the *va'ad*, although at other times all of the representatives were Jews. The committee tended to meet irregularly. The chairman convened a meeting when a particular problem arose; the committee members first met separately to decide their own policy and later met with management when, for example, a worker complained that he had not received his severance pay, or when workers on a particular shift claimed that they were being underpaid.

The *va'ad*'s internal dynamics are particularly interesting. The fact that the committee included both Arab and Jewish members seems, on the face of it, to indicate a positive pattern of relationships among the workers. Not only were Jews and Arabs elected as equals to the workers' major negotiating body, but within the *va'ad* itself the three elected members were charged with implementing policies beneficial to all of the members, both Jews and Arabs. The reality, however, was considerably more complex. Although he had been elected to the committee, the Arab representative typically was a passive participant in *va'ad* meetings, and rarely took part in negotiations with the factory management. This lack of activity was deliberate, a kind of tactical choice: his analysis of factory politics led him to conclude that the Arab workers were better served when they negotiated privately with management. As he put it,

> I prefer to talk quietly with the owner about my own problems and those of the other Arabs. It works better than going through the *va'ad* with all of the noise that the *va'ad* makes. I have been working here for a long time, and from my experience it is best to go directly to him and talk, let him know what is bothering you. He's usually fair, and if he can he'll help.

These comments are clear enough. Separate, private discussions with the owner were thought to be the most effective way for the Arabs to successfully negotiate. In effect, they preferred a more personal patron-client tie rather than the more bureaucratic politics of the Jewish-dominated work committee.

Nonetheless, even though the Arab representative was inactive the other two Jewish committee members met periodically with the factory executives. However, they recognized that without the active participation of the Arab workers their own influence was weakened. The Jewish head of the committee made this point clearly:

> When we arrange a meeting and go to talk to the owner he will usually listen to us. But I don't know who we represent. All of the workers? Just the Jewish workers? The Arabs don't always want to come along. They prefer to keep their heads down and to talk directly with the owner. I don't really blame them— they have their own problems. There are two different kinds of Arabs working here: those who live in Jerusalem and belong to the Histadrut, and those who don't. Each has different problems and different interests, and this too makes it hard to act together.

What this suggests is that while the work committee is an important forum for Arab-Jewish contact and interaction, the different statuses and interests of the workers make it difficult for them to effectively coordinate their negotiating position. At certain times they may join together as "workers," but at many other moments they appear as "Jewish" or "Arab" workers without a solid, long-term basis for cooperation.

CONTACTS AFTER WORK

Working together around the ovens or chatting during a break, many workers establish personal ties that extend over comparatively long periods of time. This poses the question of their contacts outside of the workplace. To what degree and in what contexts do Arabs and Jews who work together also interact with one another outside of the bakery?

Generally speaking, persons who work closely with one another during the day do not necessarily seek one another out after work hours. At Nimrod this applies equally to both the Jewish and the Arab workers. Members of both groups relate that they have their own friends and families, and that they see their workmates infrequently outside of the factory. There are many reasons for this. The workers are of different ages, they reside in various parts of Jerusalem and its environs, and besides, as many say, "isn't it enough that we *have* to see one another at work!" In addition, acquaintances or friendships formed at work do not always or easily continue after work hours; those who enjoy working together may find that they prefer socializing with different persons in the evening or on their day off.

Still, there are some events and occasions when workmates do gather together outside of the factory. Both Arabs and Jews invite their fellows to small gatherings. For example, when one of the Jewish workers is married, or when there is a birth in an Arab worker's family, close friends and workmates are invited to take part in the celebration. Not everyone who is invited actually attends, but at least some of the Arabs and Jews who work together are likely to take part. Gifts are presented, a meal is served, and the workers also have an opportunity to meet or see one another's wives and children. While they are infrequent, these festive events lend a feeling of fellowship to all of those who take part. Of course, there is also a kind of contingent reciprocal promise involved in attending: a worker who is invited and attends is bound to also invite his host when he later has his own celebration. This pattern of visiting at special family occasions may consequently continue over the years.

In addition, the Nimrod management or the factory work committee also sponsors occasional social activities outside of the factory. Each year there is likely to be one or more large-scale social events organized for the workers by or through the factory. Not all of them will necessarily attend, but these too are gatherings during which Jews and Arabs interact informally.

One such occasion was a well-remembered bus excursion sponsored by the work committee. Trips of this kind are traditionally organized by the Histadrut, and the Nimrod workers were pleased to learn that such an outing was planned for them. The trip was scheduled for the Passover holiday, a time during which the bakery itself is closed. (Bread is not baked then since according to religious tradition Jews eat only unleavened bread, or *matzot*, during this festive period.) The day-long trip was an excursion to the north of Israel, with a stop at the Sea of Galilee and a guided explanation along the way.

Many of the workers, both Arabs and Jews, signed up to attend. Along the way they sang songs, joked with one another, and generally enjoyed the outing. There was a sense of relaxing together and comraderie. However, an incident took place during lunch that jarred this atmosphere. Everyone had been told to bring their own lunch, and they joined one another in a shady spot to eat. The Jews, of course, took out their *matzot*, while the Arabs began eating sandwiches made from bread. The presence of bread in this common meal offended some of the Jewish workers; they were certain that the Arabs had purposely brought bread since they knew that it was prohibited and offensive to religious Jews during Passover. Although tempers later calmed and the trip continued, some of the Jewish workers were upset. Once again, the incident signaled the differences and boundaries between them.

The occasions that have thus far been described are sponsored events of one form or another. There are, in addition, a variety of more informal situations during which Arab and Jewish workers interact outside of the factory. Some of the workers stated, for example, that from time to time they meet others in chance encounters. Jerusalem is a small city, and it is not uncommon for persons to meet one another in a bus, at a cafe, or while strolling through some part of the city. Interestingly, the meeting point most often mentioned was the Old City; both Arabs and Jews reported that they occasionally met one another while shopping in the Old City markets, or during a leisurely walk through its narrow streets. If they were walking together with a group of persons—family members or friends—they might acknowledge each other and exchange a brief greeting; or, if they were alone they paused to chat, invited one another for a cup of coffee, and remained to talk and gossip for a pleasant half-hour or more.

Finally, even though the workers do not normally form friendships that extend beyond the workplace, in some instances Arab and Jewish workers have entered into closer relations. Rare as these may be, on such occasions they establish visiting relations outside of the factory. The usual pattern is for the Arab to invite his Jewish friend to visit him on the Sabbath or during a work holiday; the visits of Arab families to the homes of Jewish workers may raise questions on the part of the Jewish worker's family and neighbors, whereas the reverse is apparently more acceptable. If he is married, the Jewish worker arrives with his wife and children, and the two families may spend several hours in conversation between cups of coffee or tea, cold drinks, and an elaborate meal. According to one informant these visits can sometimes end in disaster; he described an occasion in which the wife of a Jewish worker was reluctant to eat any of the food that was being served by her husband's Arab friend. "She couldn't get it out of her head that Arab food is unclean and that she would get sick from eating it," and consequently her husband was distraught while her Arab hosts were nonplussed and, finally, insulted. In this case at least friendship in the workplace was not easily transferred to another context.

There have also been occasions in which contacts in the factory have blossomed into long-lasting personal ties. These are spontaneous friendships, the kind of personal attraction that can successfully move across ethnic boundaries. The friendship between Shuli and Micha is a case in point. Shuli (whose name in Arabic is Suleiman) is a young Arab who lives in the Old City, and Micha is a young Jew who began working at the bakery following his Israeli army service. They first met while working in the shipping department, and soon found that they shared something in common and enjoyed each other's company. Shuli describes these relationships in the following terms:

> There is just something about him that I like. We joke a lot together, horse around, work well together, and so we just began to see each other after work. I am married and Micha is not, but that does not stop us from being friends. They joke about us here at the factory, about the two of us being friends. But why not? Why shouldn't we go out together like other friends?

Micha and Shuli visit one another at their homes; Shuli has visited Micha at his parents' home, and Micha has become a kind of *ben bayit* (literally, "son of the home" or frequent visitor) at Shuli's rooms in the Old City. Micha's parents opposed their son's friendship with an Arab, and placed pressure upon him to end the relationship. But Micha was able to withstand these pressures, and their friendship continued. Typically they would meet in a cafe in the Old City, and later return to their respective families.

PATTERNS OF COOPERATION, PATTERNS OF CONFLICT

A variety of situations and encounters have thus far been described. Reflecting upon these contexts, it seems clear that they are typified by a fundamental dialectic or tension: are those who interact with one another around the ovens "workers," or are they inevitably "Jewish workers" and "Arab workers"? To what degree do all of those who report to work in the morning and evening equally belong to the category of "worker"—or are their contacts in the workplace always shaped and influenced by their belonging to different ethnic groups in conflict?

Previous studies of multiethnic work situations in different countries demonstrate that ethnic-group membership is not a key factor in the organization or execution of work tasks. For example, in the United States whites and blacks have worked together in factories without recurrent frictions, just as African ethnic or tribal group membership (even in the case of traditionally hostile tribes) does not negatively influence the workplace.[1] The same conclusion applies to the Nimrod factory: the evidence suggests that, by and large, Jews and Arabs are able to bake bread together in a broadly cooperative fashion. To put it plainly, whether one is a Jew or an Arab is simply not relevant to the workplace encounter itself. Ability and performance are more significant than the group to which one belongs. What is more, these contacts are personal, direct, and repeated, rather than mediated through brokers or other kinds of social go-be-

[1] See Blumer 1965; Epstein 1958; Izraeli 1979; Kapferer 1969.

tweens: Jews and Arabs who work together gain immediate, first-hand knowledge of each other.

The reasons for this can be adduced and briefly explained. First, work relationships are instrumental contacts par excellence. They are encounters of limited duration in which the participants are primarily focused upon performing a task and receiving remuneration. Factory workers or office staffs are not usually interested in contemplating or exploring one another's personalities—they are mainly concerned with completing a task and receiving their rewards. Since bread can be baked and packed equally by both Jews and Arabs, ethnic group membership has little effect upon many of these and other facets of the production process. Moreover, the ideology of avoiding political discussions while at work ("we come here to work, not to talk politics") is eminently functional: talking politics would expose the antagonistic views held by members of both groups, and it would make working together extremely difficult. Finally, the factory's stated policy of equal treatment also strengthens the common "worker" features of their encounters. The Jews and Arabs who work at the Nimrod factory *all* wear the same factory-issue clothing, clock in at the same time, receive identical pay for the same work and seniority, and, what is more, can expect equal treatment from management if there are conflicts between them. Taken together, these features of the work process strengthen the common bonds and identities of all of the workers.

At the same time, however, in a variety of ways the workers are also regularly separated into those who are Jews and those who are Arabs. Ethnic affiliations do not disappear, but instead find expression in many minor and several major ways. The Arab workers are never freed from the sense that they are "outsiders" who daily come to work in a setting that they cannot control. As we have seen, the periodic political crises between Jews and Arabs magnify their sense of difference and alienation. What is more, the Arabs' divided political status, plus management's tactic of "helping the Arab workers," has also served to separate the Arab and Jewish workers.

The most complex and perhaps crucial problem is that of power and authority. Plainly put, to what level of authority can an Arab worker aspire within this Jewish firm? Will Jewish employees work under the direction of Arabs at all levels of authority? The facts in this regard seem clear; a number of Arab workers have risen to the rank of shift foreman, and they have regular supervision and direction over Jewish workers. This appears to be acceptable, even though some of the Jewish workers are said to "cause trouble" when they are directed by Arabs. On the other hand, all of the management roles are filled by Jews; the factory's executives, bookkeepers, marketing and production officials, secretaries, and telephone operators are exclusively Jews. The ethnic boundaries in this regard are firm and clear.

The question therefore is whether Arab workers can move to higher positions. This involves not only technical skill and leadership abilities, but also trust and confidence on the part of the Jewish management. It is relevant in this regard to relate the experience of an Arab worker who did move higher in the system. One of the veteran Arab workers, Ahmad, was promoted to the position of work manager; this is a key position, since it involves coordinating the work process and work schedules throughout the entire bakery. An Israeli Arab, Ahmad was promoted to work manager after he had worked successfully in a number of lower-level positions; he had gained the trust and confidence of the owners, and appeared to be performing his duties with success. Indeed, the workers had nicknamed him "Ahmad Nimrod"—it seemed that he had become so close to the Nimrod's that he was "one of the family." However, this experiment ended in failure. It was discovered that "Ahmad Nimrod" had been falsifying records to obtain bakery money that was improperly being paid to him. Shortly thereafter he was fired from his post and left the factory.

Did Ahmad actually falsify the records and illegally pocket the money—or was this charge contrived by others in order to force him from his position as manager? Does the promotion of an Arab to a high management post provoke such jealousies and tensions among Jewish subordinates that efforts are made to sabotage him? The facts are not entirely clear. What is clear, however, is that in this instance "Ahmad Nimrod" returned to his previous role of being "Ahmad," the Arab.

CHAPTER 6

Public Functions and Private Businesses

THE NATURE of daily coexistence between Jews and Arabs in Jerusalem can be further illustrated by examining the patterns of public service distribution and economic interaction in the marketplace. To what extent do the two communities, living within a common urban space, share the same public facilities and exchange goods and services? While the question is easy to formulate, in practical terms no simple and straightforward answer can be provided. In common with other spheres of intersectional relationships the picture which emerges is diversified, ambiguous, and complex, reflecting once again the unique reality of a united yet polarized urban environment.

In contemporary Jerusalem, as in any other ethnically mixed city, aside from the workplace it is mainly in the marketplace that Jews and Arabs regularly meet and interact. A great number of Jews and Arabs commonly shop at each others' commercial centers or frequently intermingle in workshop areas, public offices, and the like, while pursuing their everyday needs. In a similar fashion, since 1967 extensive interactions also developed between the two sectors' business firms involving a broad range of economic transactions. On the other hand, many indications of ongoing segregation are no less common or significant. Most apparent and striking are the various areas in which Jews and Arabs retain separate public institutions and even parallel economic functions. Moreover, where transactions do take place between members of the two groups, certain distinct rules of behavior typically mark these exchanges. Ethnic identity plus underlying cultural, institutional, and political differences continue to play a crucial role in producing patterns of both segregation and integration.

THE DISTRIBUTION OF PUBLIC SERVICES

The pattern of public service distribution among the Jewish and Arab populations of Jerusalem is closely linked to the legal and institutional frameworks that were applied to the two city sectors following reunification. The extension of Israeli law, jurisdiction, and administration to East Jerusalem reflected Israel's original intention to fully integrate the Arab sector into the state in conformity with the principles and practices applied to the Arab minority living within Israel's pre-1967 boundaries. According to this model the only legal and administrative authority for providing public services is the central government or other national Jewish public institutions; where necessary, due to specific cultural and economic needs, separate administrative departments for Arabs were also established within this framework.

In the case of East Jerusalem, however, the application of this model to the local Arab population immediately faced serious political difficulties. These mainly involved the Arab community's opposition to recognizing Israel's unilateral act of annexation, as expressed in its refusal to cooperate with the newly imposed Israeli administration. In addition, unlike the Arab minority in Israel, the East Jerusalem population already possessed a full range of independent public and semipublic institutions and was determined to maintain them wherever possible. For their part, the Israeli authorities in several instances refrained from directly imposing Jewish control on an unwilling Arab population that was intent on preserving its own distinct political and cultural identity. From a purely legal point of view this meant that Israel did not fully apply its legal and administrative system to East Jerusalem. In effect, this produced a complex situation in which public service integration remained only partial and often reflected the different statuses of Jewish and Arab individuals and institutions.

Public service integration does exist, at least in principle, only in those areas in which immediately following reunification Israel imposed its administrative system and Arab self-rule was abolished. These include the various functions directly provided by the central government and the Jerusalem Municipality in which, since 1967, authority, management, and budgetary control rest with the Jewish administration. In all of these cases, ranging from law enforcement functions to local social services, the relevant Israeli administrative bodies have become directly responsible for providing the Arab population with the same public services as those available to the Jewish sector. Full and complete integration also implies that Jews and Arabs apply to the same administrative offices and are served by the same personnel according to identical procedures. As we have seen, this is true in various cases, such as the civil law courts and the vehicle licensing authority, each of which has only one local office, thereby serving the entire Jerusalem population irrespective of ethnic membership.

Yet in many other cases public service delivery continues to be separate. These services cover a whole range of basic functions, including income tax collection, the distribution of national insurance allowances, and building licensing. In all of these areas the Israeli authorities established separate administrative units for the Arabs of East Jerusalem. This practice was introduced primarily in response to the specific requirements of the large Arab population, and these departments were typically staffed by Arabic-speaking personnel. To a certain extent, this practice also conformed to previously established patterns of governing the Arab minority in Israel; for example, just as the Israeli prime minister's office engaged a special advisor on Arab affairs, a similar position was established in 1967 by the mayor of Jerusalem. In addition, the pattern of separate public service delivery reflects the underlying differences in the personal legal status of Jews and Arabs. East Jerusalem Arabs, although granted the status of Israeli residents, have not become citizens of Israel and continue to retain their Jordanian citizenship. Jerusalem Arabs are therefore subject to certain administrative norms which are different from those applied to Israeli Arab citizens. In practical terms this can be illustrated by the fact that following reunification the Arab inhabitants of East Jerusalem were provided with Israeli identity cards bearing special serial numbers denoting their particular status as "Arab Jerusalem residents," distinguished from both Jews and Israeli Arabs living in the city. As a consequence, all matters involving the personal status of East Jerusalem Arabs—such as the issuing of identity cards, registration of births and marriages, granting of permits for travel abroad, and the settlement of Arab relatives from the administered territories or abroad in East Jerusalem—are handled by a separate department in the Israeli Ministry of the Interior.

As a general rule, wherever Israel directly applied its administrative system to the Arab population, this has entailed the Arabs' becoming directly dependent on Jewish institutions. Dependence is manifested particularly in those areas where they are obliged to apply to government or municipal offices located in West Jerusalem, deal with Jewish clerks (most of whom are not Arabic-speaking), and abide by Israeli-Jewish administrative rules. The Israeli bureaucracy has done little to accommodate Arab Jerusalemites, who are often at a loss when confronted with unfamiliar administrative procedures. For example, only in rare cases have signs in Arabic been posted in government offices and other Jewish public institutions for the convenience of Arab clients. Although Arabic is Israel's second official language, government and other documents normally are written only in Hebrew. The Jerusalem Municipality, which is more conscious of this problem, has made some effort in this direction by including Arabic translations in various forms and notices, particularly those addressed to East Jerusalem businesses and households, but even then Arabic is not consistently given a status equal to Hebrew. Perhaps the most striking example is the fact that the official Jerusalem telephone directory is issued only in Hebrew and not in Arabic as well (even though an English version is available upon request). While since 1967 all East

Jerusalem Arab telephone subscribers have been included in this directory, few Arabs could easily utilize this official publication, even to communicate among themselves. Consequently, in response to a pressing local need a telephone book in Arabic was published and distributed annually as a commercial venture by a private Arab entrepreneur. However, unlike the official directory, it lists only the Arab subscribers; apart from a handful of Jewish public institutions such as the Jerusalem Municipality and a few major hospitals in West Jerusalem, Jewish subscribers are entirely excluded.

Indeed, the fact that in the same city two telephone directories appear which differ not only in language but also in origin and content is one of the major indicators of deep, persistent segregation. But it equally reflects the divergent attitudes of Jews and Arabs regarding unification. For the Israeli authorities, Jewish rule over the Arab population is frequently interpreted as simply the technical extension of their own norms of public service delivery to the subordinate minority; Arab dependence is taken for granted. Arabs, in contrast, strive to fill in the gaps as much as possible, ignoring, in turn, the Jewish presence altogether.

The major exception to this general rule has been the special case of electricity supply. It will be recalled that since the Arab electric company was permitted to continue operating within its pre-1967 East Jerusalem concession area, Jewish residential neighborhoods, industrial zones, and even military installations established beyond the former dividing line became directly dependent upon an Arab-owned facility for the provision of this essential public service. This represents the only case where Jewish customers were compelled to approach Arab offices and be served by Arab clerks and technical personnel on a regular, involuntary basis. The exceptional nature of this case is reflected in the fact that the problem of the East Jerusalem Electric Corporation has been a subject of constant contention. The Arab company insisted on retaining its concession rights, even though growing demand for electricity required it to purchase most of the needed supply from the Israeli national electric company; moreover, it operated at a loss, thus indirectly subsidizing its Jewish customers. Nevertheless, it is mainly the Jews who have objected to this situation; they considered their reliance on Arab electricity to be intolerable and have constantly pressed for change. The Israeli government for years sought to nationalize the East Jerusalem Electric Company or, alternatively, to confine its operation to Arab areas.

This continued existence of two separate ethnic-based institutional systems within the united city is even more evident wherever the authorities have refrained from directly or fully applying Israeli law and administration to East Jerusalem. The most obvious example is that of religious institutions and their various activities. Christian and Muslim communities in East Jerusalem still supervise their own holy places, with little intervention from the Israeli authorities. Besides the fact that religious autonomy is a long-respected tradition in Jerusalem, the enforcement of direct Jewish control over the historic Muslim and Christian sacred sites in the Holy City is unprecedented and a highly delicate matter. Furthermore, in Israel itself the religious autonomy of the Arab minorities is largely respected and in fact incorporated into the administrative and legal system. In the case of Muslim Arabs, Shari'a laws (the Islamic religious code) were slightly amended to conform to the Israeli law in such matters as marriage age and polygamy. Yet Muslim judges are nominated by the president of Israel, Shari'a courts are administered by the Ministry of Religious Affairs, and verdicts are enforced by the civil authorities.

Israeli attempts to apply the same legal structure to the Jerusalem Muslim population never materialized in light of the adamant opposition of the local religious and political establishment. The highest religious authority in East Jerusalem is the Supreme Muslim Council, a body which neither recognizes the legal authority of Israel nor is recognized as a legal entity by the state. It derives its authority and funding from Jordan; it was, in fact, established after the Six-Day War in order to oversee all Muslim assets and to handle religious matters in East Jerusalem and the West Bank.[1] More significantly, it appoints its own religious judges and courts, which continue to operate according to laws and procedures that are different from those observed in Israel. Needless to say, this de facto dual system under formal Israeli jurisdiction creates various complications and legal abnormalities in everyday life. The Israeli authorities would not recognize or enforce rulings of an East Jerusalem Shari'a court, nor would Arabs request the assistance of Israeli civil courts. Even simple marriage and divorce certificates or uncontested wills issued in East Jerusalem have to be nominally approved by an Israeli-appointed Shari'a court located outside the city in order to be registered by the official authorities. These complicated procedures must be employed in order to circumvent the obstacle of mutual nonrecognition.

Public education represents yet another case in which a completely segregated system reflects both cultural and political motivations. Jewish and Arab pupils not only continue to study at separate schools in their respective languages, but even more significantly, they also follow a totally different curriculum.

In Jerusalem, as elsewhere in Israel, the administrative and pedagogical supervision of Jewish and Arab public schools is shared by the Min-

[1] During the Jordanian period all Muslim religious affairs and assets were under the direct responsibility of a special government ministry. Thus, the formation of the Supreme Muslim Council in Jerusalem actually meant the reestablishment of a body dissolved upon the termination of the British Mandate in Palestine. For more details, see Benvenisti 1976.

istry of Education and the local municipality. Consequently, since 1967 all East Jerusalem public schools have come under the direct control of the respective Israeli authorities. This covers approximately half of the Arab pupil population; the other half are enrolled in private schools operated by various Christian and Muslim institutions or by the United Nations Relief and Work Agency (UNRWA). In both public and private schools, one of the first acts undertaken by Israel was to abolish a number of highly nationalistic anti-Israeli and anti-Jewish textbooks which were part of the Jordanian curriculum. But the government's decision to replace the entire curriculum in East Jerusalem municipal schools with the program of studies followed in Israeli-Arab schools was strongly opposed by the Arab community. Again, this controversy involved not only purely educational-cultural issues but also—and primarily—legal and political principles. For the Jewish authorities, such an act involved the principle of sovereignty and their desire to formally integrate East Jerusalem public schools into the Israeli system—the very concepts the Arabs opposed. Their objections were also motivated by more culturally related considerations. Arab educators claimed that the Israeli curriculum largely ignored Arab Palestinian national history and values, and they were equally concerned that graduates with Israeli diplomas would be denied access to higher learning institutions in other countries in the Middle East and thus be culturally and economically cut off from the Arab world.

This Arab opposition undermined Israel's ability to institute its original plan. A major reason was that enrollment in East Jerusalem municipal schools sharply declined; parents transferred their children to private schools, and even to West Bank public schools, where the pre-1967 curriculum had for the most part been retained. The Israeli authorities eventually yielded, and the Jordanian curriculum, slightly amended, was reintroduced in Jewish-administered Arab public schools. In fact, a unique pattern of shared responsibilities has emerged: while the Israeli authorities continue to appoint teachers and maintain budgetary control, matriculation examinations are provided and supervised by Jordanian inspectors.

This structural separation between the Jewish and Arab educational systems clearly perpetuates segregation and is further expressed in everyday life. In the first years following reunification, on various occasions the Jerusalem Municipality attempted to bring Arab and Jewish pupils together for extracurricular activities or sports events, but these efforts became less frequent with the passage of time. In effect, the two educational systems do little to help the new generation overcome the language barrier. Hebrew language courses have been introduced in East Jerusalem public schools, but only to a limited extent; similarly, Jewish pupils are in principle encouraged to study Arabic, but Arabic language courses remain optional. Significantly, in contrast with the growing numbers of Israeli Arabs who attend Israeli universities, only a handful of East Jerusalem Arabs have enrolled at the Hebrew University, even though it is located in the midst of East Jerusalem. They generally choose—as their studies have prepared them—to pursue their higher education at West Bank colleges, in Arab countries, or in other locales outside of Israel.

Within the complex social and political reality of Jerusalem even public medical services remain segregated. With regard to the institutional framework, the Jewish and Arab sectors maintain the full range of separate and parallel medical facilities that were developed before 1967. A public system of medical care exists within the Jewish sector, managed by various national health insurance programs and largely subsidized by the state. Medical treatment is provided by a network of clinics and West Jerusalem's sizable modern Jewish hospitals. In East Jerusalem, by contrast, since no overall health insurance system existed under Jordanian rule, basic medical services as well as hospitals were and still are administered by private or semipublic institutions—Christian and Muslim charitable foundations and agencies of the United Nations. East Jerusalem health organizations continue to operate as autonomous entities with respect to financing, management, and staff, and function according to their pre-1967 norms and practices. Since the Arab institutions are insistent upon maintaining their independence, the Israeli government and municipal health authorities rarely intervene in their daily activities and even general supervision and inspection remain limited.

This absence of city-wide integration of medical systems is reflected in the fact that Jewish and Arab hospitals maintain their own unrelated emergency systems or fee schedules and generally adhere to different standards of medical care. This dual system also continues to exist with respect to various other medical services, where the Israeli authorities did try to incorporate Arab facilities into the more developed Jewish structure, but were unable to overcome Arab opposition. Perhaps the most striking example of this dualism is the fact that in united Jerusalem two separate blood banks continue to operate, one Jewish and the other Arab. Similarly, and no less symbolically, the two sectors maintain parallel emergency ambulance services—the Jewish "Red Shield of David" and the Arab "Red Crescent."

It is, therefore, hardly surprising that, in daily practice as well, the ethnic identity of patients continues to play a crucial role. Generally speaking, Jews are never hospitalized in an Arab institution, even in those urgent or emergency cases where this might appear to be the best option. Should a Jew be injured in an accident in the Arab section of the city, a Jewish ambulance service will invariably be called in, and it will take him to the nearest Jewish hospital. The scenario might be different only on those rare occasions when a passing Arab car takes the injured Jew to a nearby Arab hospital for first aid; but even in such a case, the patient will promptly be transferred to a Jewish hospital. The Jewish ambulatory and emergency services regularly provide assistance to the entire Jerusalem population, including Jews and Arabs, in all parts of the city. Nevertheless, in nonemergency cases as well, the hospitalization of Arab patients from East Jerusalem is often different from that of Jewish patients.

In other important respects, however, medical care integration can be observed. This relates to the fact that following reunification, the medical facilities of the Jewish sector became generally accessible to the Arab population. Jewish medical insurance programs operating in West Jerusalem extended their services and established a number of clinics in the Arab sections of the city. Most active in this area is the health fund of the Jewish Federation of Labor, which serves mainly the families of unionized Arab workers who are regularly employed in the Jewish sector. Also available to Arab residents are low-level medical services provided by the Jerusalem Municipality, such as mother and child care centers. In addition, the Israel national insurance system covers basic medical treatment and welfare assistance for needy Arab residents. Altogether, according to rough estimates Jewish-sponsored public medical services reach one-third of the entire East Jerusalem Arab population. Yet in this case, too, daily service delivery functions remain essentially separate: Jewish-sponsored clinics operating in East Jerusalem are generally designed to serve the local Arab population exclusively, because of the need to staff them with Arabic-speaking personnel and locate them in Arab residential areas. Only in a few cases do Jewish facilities located near Arab sections of the city serve members of both communities.[2]

It is primarily in the higher-level medical facilities of the Jewish sector that integration is best manifested. Large numbers of Arab patients are treated in various Jewish hospitals, particularly the Hadassah Medical Center located on Mount Scopus in East Jerusalem, and consequently the most accessible to the Arab population. The main category of Arabs utilizing these facilities are those covered by the Jewish health care plans and consequently entitled to the full range of medical care. A second category comprises those cases in which Arabs choose to be hospitalized in Jewish institutions or have to do so for specialized treatment which cannot be provided in East Jerusalem. Moreover, since East Jerusalem hospitals lack various specialized wards and up-to-date facilities (such as

<hr>

[2] Regarding the particular problems involved in providing municipal day care services to the Arab sector as well as the more general framework of health services in the two city sectors, see Yuval 1988.

those providing coronary care or handling complicated surgery) they are compelled to transfer some of their own patients to Jewish hospitals. In this context as well, however, a combination of practical and ethnic considerations prevails. For example, most Arab women prefer to give birth in Arab hospitals, even though they are entitled to choose any Jerusalem hospital since hospital costs are covered by the Israeli national insurance program. Jewish medical insurance plans often agree to hospitalize their Arab patients in East Jerusalem hospitals, mainly because the hospitalization fees charged in the Arab sector are considerably lower than in the Jewish sector. The East Jerusalem medical institutions occasionally make use of West Jerusalem laboratories or, in cases of urgent need, utilize the Jewish blood bank. They are, however, generally reluctant to call in Jewish specialists from nearby hospitals for consultation.

Just as we previously saw in regard to education and electricity, the organization and distribution of public health services largely reflect the underlying political realities and the two sides' divergent motives and attitudes. The Arab community perceives the preservation of an independent structure of medical care largely in national, symbolic terms. Purely functional considerations proposed by the Israeli authorities have generally been rejected, even if they entailed the provision of better services to the Arab population. For instance, when the Jerusalem Municipality built a new central day care facility in East Jerusalem, Arab leaders and organizations refused to take part in the funding, since they considered the center to be a Jewish institution. These contrasting positions can also be illustrated in the case of the East Jerusalem Arab government hospital. This small hospital, located within the Old City walls in a nineteenth-century structure known as the Austrian Hospice, initially became a medical facility as a temporary measure undertaken by the Jordanian authorities. Inasmuch as it was the only government hospital in East Jerusalem at the time of reunification, it was the sole Arab medical institution which came under the formal responsibility of the Israeli Ministry of Health, even though it continued to be staffed exclusively by Arab personnel and served a small number of needy East Jerusalem residents. Since the Israeli authorities judged this hospital to be unfit for its purpose (due to its inaccessibility, lack of basic facilities, and low standards of medical care), they argued that it should be closed and its function filled by the nearby modern Hadassah Hospital or other better equipped institutions. However, such practical arguments were not accepted by the Arab public. When, following years of negotiations, the hospital was closed in the mid-1980s, vehement Arab protests broke out. East Jerusalem residents interpreted this act as yet another proof that the Jewish authorities wished to deprive the Arab population of needed medical services, provided by what was considered by them to be an Arab institution.

This persistent pattern of institutional separation can be found in practically all of Jerusalem's voluntary public organizations and professional associations. The Jewish and Arab sectors have, since 1967, maintained separate Chambers of Commerce and continue to operate dozens of parallel public bodies, ranging from hoteliers' and cinema owners' associations to those representing teachers, lawyers, pharmacists, and even taxi drivers. Here again, the merger proposals advanced by the Jewish associations after 1967 in the "spirit of unification" were categorically rejected by all of the Arab organizations. For them acceptance implied the formal recognition of East Jerusalem's annexation to Israel. Since similar outlooks are also held by foreign countries and international organizations, as a general rule they too continued to regard Jerusalem as a divided city. This is the case with respect to United Nations organizations, Christian institutions, and particularly diplomatic representations of countries such as the United States, Great Britain, and France, each of which retains parallel consulates in West and East Jerusalem. In all these cases, Israel has tolerated this de facto situation even when it encroached upon its own political goals or formal jurisdiction.

The intricate way in which legal formalities and opposing political stances were sorted out by practical compromise can be illustrated in the case of East Jerusalem lawyers. According to Israeli law, lawyers must be members of the Israel Bar in order to practice. However, since Arab lawyers would not apply for membership on their own, the Israeli authorities went ahead and nominally registered them. In practice, however, since 1967 East Jerusalem's Arab attorneys have boycotted the Israeli courts. They retain their own separate organization, and formal contacts with the Jewish association are virtually nonexistent. This does not mean that in other, less extreme cases, practical cooperation between Arab and Jewish professional organizations is totally absent. But this cooperation has always involved purely technical matters which do not imply formal recognition, and official contacts have also not developed over the years. Significantly, in all areas of cultural, professional, and economic activity, with the passage of time the number of independent Arab public bodies in East Jerusalem has continuously increased, largely with the support of Jordanian and Palestinian national organizations. This form of organization has been the Arab community's major strategy for consolidating its own institutional structure in the face of Jewish economic hegemony and political control.

COMMERCIAL SERVICES AND BUSINESS RELATIONS

The economic integration of the Jewish and Arab sectors of Jerusalem has necessarily led to the development of extensive relationships between the two business communities on an entrepreneurial level. These connections were encouraged by such major factors as the possibility of free movement of goods and services, complementary economic opportunities, and geographic proximity. However, as in the case of public services, sectoral divisions remained a dominant feature and often reflected the institutional organization of Jerusalem's commercial market as well as particular patterns of exchange across the ethnic dividing line.

The scope and nature of exchange between Jewish and Arab business firms in Jerusalem generally reflect the differences in scale and industrial structure between the Israeli economy and that of the West Bank. Following the city's reunification, the Arab sector of East Jerusalem became largely dependent on the Jewish sector for the supply of a full range of manufactured goods and specialized commercial services which could not be provided from its own sources. This situation is most apparent with regard to East Jerusalem retail markets, where, since 1967, most of the consumer goods, ranging from agricultural produce (including vegetables, fruit, and milk) to nearly all manufactured items, originate in the Jewish sector. The same applies to many basic materials and imported goods, such as fuel, cement, and vehicles, for which Arab entrepreneurs and merchants have been obliged to turn to Jewish wholesalers, importers, and distributors in order to carry out their regular economic functions.

Similarly, East Jerusalem businesses have to engage Jewish firms for most tasks requiring specific technical know-how or professional qualifications. The installation and maintenance of air conditioning and elevator systems in East Jerusalem hotels, for example, are generally assigned to West Jerusalem branches of Israeli firms. Jewish consultants are also regularly called in for the installation and servicing of computer equipment and similar facilities in Arab businesses and institutions. In fact, quite a few Jewish professionals, such as engineers, architects, lawyers, and accountants, specialize in serving the Arab sector or have East Jerusalem firms and public institutions among their regular customers.

Jewish firms also engage many Arab enterprises but, as we have seen previously, only under certain conditions and terms. These entail the employment of simple and relatively cheap factors of production, based on unorganized labor, lower overheads, and narrower profit margins. The three major areas in which business relations can be found are the construction, manufacturing, and transportation industries. The Jewish construction industry has become almost completely dependent on the supply of stone—the essential building material in Jerusalem—from Arab quarries located on the West Bank in the vicinity of East Jerusalem. In addition, Jewish construction companies regularly subcontract with Arab entrepreneurs and workshops for a broad range of assignments such as masonry, ironwork, and carpentry. Subcontracting to East Jerusalem workshops is also widely practiced by Jewish manufacturers, particularly in the clothing and shoe industries, as well as with other simple, labor-intensive activities. The hiring of Arab trucks and taxis by Jewish firms has also become a common practice.

Jewish-Arab business ties have developed in many other areas in which mutual interests and complementary opportunities have emerged. In the tourist industry, Jewish travel agents occasionally direct organized groups under their charge to East Jerusalem hotels, particularly during peak seasons when West Jerusalem hotels are fully booked, or in response to more advantageous price offers. They also engage the services of East Jerusalem tour bus companies since the latter normally charge less than their Jewish competitors. Although Arab travel agents tend to rely on their own section of the Jerusalem tourist market and facilities (which are more oriented toward Christian pilgrims or tourists entering the country via the Jordan River bridges), they occasionally turn to the Jewish sector when in need of special tour guides, package tours, or airline services offered only by West Jerusalem agencies. To cite yet another example, intersectoral transactions are widely conducted even in the meat market, where a particular kind of complementarity has emerged, mainly related to the contrasting ritual prohibitions followed by the Jewish, Muslim, and Christian communities. Arab butchers regularly purchase nonkosher meats from Jewish wholesalers; these transactions usually take place in Jerusalem's joint municipal slaughterhouse. Indeed, it is fair to conclude that business associations between Jews and Arabs have become far more frequent than is generally believed or publically disclosed. Numerous undocumented joint ventures range from a variety of financial transactions to what are rumored to be underworld criminal associations.

Although these intersectoral relationships are generally occasioned by purely economic motives, the emerging patterns also reveal asymmetrical elements which reflect the dominant position of the Jewish sector. As observed, Jewish firms are prepared to engage Arab entrepreneurs only under the implicit condition that the latter will accept less favorable terms than those normally prevailing in the Jewish sector. Moreover, Arab firms are often obliged to associate with Jewish firms rather than apply directly for contracts. The Jewish construction industry can once again serve as an example. It is always Jewish construction firms which sign major contracts involving public and private housing projects, even when substantial parts of the job are subsequently handed over to Arab subcontractors. This practice can be explained, in part, by an objective fact: the absence of large-scale Arab building companies with sufficient resources. But even in small-scale ventures, Arab entrepreneurs are hindered from directly signing contracts whenever these require officially submitting their bids in accordance with procedures and legal formalities imposed by the Israeli administration. East Jerusalem business establishments frequently associate with Jewish firms even when operating in their own sector; a typical case is that of East Jerusalem lawyers who normally transfer some of their cases to Jewish law firms because they are unwilling to plead directly before Israeli courts. In many other instances Arab firms and institutions prefer to engage Jewish lawyers, architects, or accountants, believing that they are in a better position to represent their interests in matters involving building licensing, taxation, and the like, with government and municipal authorities.

While the different characteristics of the Jewish and Arab business communities often encourage interaction, the very persistence of basic distinctions along ethnic-sectoral lines testifies to ongoing divisions in the overall commercial market. As in the case of public institutions, this mainly involves the different legal statuses and modes of operation of business functions in the two sectors. When Israel applied its laws to East Jerusalem in 1967, the problem of legalizing the status of Arab companies, commercial establishments, and professionals had to be resolved. These included nearly all those who received their certification under the former Jordanian regime or in Arab countries (physicians, engineers, and the like) and who now needed Israeli licenses in order to continue practicing. This also involved many commercial establishments—ranging from pharmacies to butcher shops—which had functioned according to standards different from those normally authorized by the Jerusalem Municipality. Moreover, according to the municipal decrees of Israeli Jerusalem, shops must be closed on the Jewish Sabbath and holidays, the Hebrew language must be employed on shop signs, and the sale of non-kosher food (and bread during Passover) is largely restricted. In other words, the strict imposition of Israeli laws to the East Jerusalem business community not only implied bringing most economic activities to a halt, but would also have greatly impinged upon different cultural norms and habits.

Under these circumstances, the Israeli authorities once again tended to forego legal formalities in the face of practical considerations. East Jerusalem businesses were generally permitted to continue operating according to their previous norms, and Israeli laws and standards were gradually and only partially introduced. What this means in practical terms is that sectoral divisions in Jerusalem are related not only to the ethnic identity of economic entities but also to their authorized modes of conducting business. West and East Jerusalem business establishments are closed on different days (those in the Arab sector on Friday or Sunday rather than the Jewish Sabbath); similarly, while retail shops in the Jewish sector must display fixed prices, this rule has never been enforced in the Arab sector. In East Jerusalem, to cite yet another example, money changers are allowed to continue operating, an activity not authorized in West Jerusalem and the rest of Israel. More significantly, commercial transactions in the two sectors are in effect subject to different currency laws: Arab businesses are permitted and actually continue to deal in Jordanian dinars, a practice which is prohibited by law in the Jewish section, where all dealings must be carried out in Israeli shekels.

These institutional divisions also imply that the parallel business functions continue to operate mainly within their own sectoral markets. This was clearly the case when East Jerusalem firms, such as gas distributors and public bus companies, were allowed to maintain their pre-1967 concessions. Foreign airline companies also continued to maintain parallel offices in West and East Jerusalem, those in the Jewish sector linked to headquarters in Tel Aviv, while those in the Arab sector operated through Amman. At the same time, Arab enterprises that were permitted to operate according to norms unauthorized by Israeli regulations were in some cases denied access to the Jewish market. The two main instances in this regard are agricultural products and pharmaceutical items produced on the West Bank; although widely distributed in East Jerusalem, they may not be marketed in the Jewish sector of the city or anywhere in Israel. The official reason given is that production norms in the Arab sector do not conform to Israeli health regulations. But there are also underlying economic reasons, mainly involving the desire and ability of Jewish producers to protect their own market against Arab competition. Thus the organization of an ethnically divided market often involves not only legal aspects but also various economically based motives. As a consequence, Jewish and Arab retail markets continue to be distinguished from each other, even with respect to the origin of fruit and vegetables or the kind of aspirin to be found on either side of the ethnic dividing line.

These distinctions have several additional dimensions. The distribution of butane gas for daily household use is a case in point. Like so many other items, gas is divided according to the ethnic origin of Jewish and Arab companies and consumers. This distinction is made visible by the appearance of the containers themselves: gas containers of Jewish companies are painted silver-white, while those of Arab companies are painted blue. In this particular case, the differentiation has been imposed by the Israeli authorities and serves a double purpose. On the one hand, it was meant to prevent accidental interchanging of containers, since this would create technical problems related to the different pressure standards and modes of handling followed by the Jewish and Arab companies, distributors, and users. On the other hand, it was also meant to avert security risks, inasmuch as the gas containers might be used for terrorist purposes.

A similar combination of practical and security-related considerations explains the fact that following reunification all East Jerusalem cars were provided with Israeli license plates bearing serial numbers different from those of Jewish-owned vehicles.[3] This differentiation was introduced for administrative convenience, but it was also meant to facilitate identification of Arab cars during security checks. Similarly, the license plate numbers of Arab taxis always begin with a "triple six," as compared to the "double six" on Jewish cabs. As a result, whenever cars changed hands between Jews and Arabs, the license plates had to be replaced. Interestingly, with the rapid growth of these transactions over the years, the practice of issuing different numbers to private cars was abandoned. This is one of the few cases in which sectoral distinctions have been eliminated and normalization has, in effect, been dictated by market forces.

Apart from these institutionally imposed distinctions, divisive aspects of the Jerusalem commercial market are also expressed in various voluntary attitudes and patterns of mutual avoidance followed by Jewish and Arab business firms. This can be seen by the fact that media messages in West and East Jerusalem rarely inform their audiences about opportunities offered on the other side. For example, even with respect to films screened in Jerusalem cinemas, the information available depends on whether it comes from a Jewish or Arab newspaper, or whether one consults a municipal billboard in West or East Jerusalem. Other useful information regarding everyday life in the city—such as listings of the hours that pharmacies remain open at night—are also only published on a sectoral basis. This information barrier applies even more generally to commercial advertisements. Within the Jewish sector a number of Jerusalem weekend editions are in great demand and are distributed free of charge due to substantial advertising and a host of useful details on events taking place in the city. Rarely, however, have either Jewish or Arab business establishments inserted advertisements in newspapers "on the other side."

The use of both Hebrew and Arabic on shop signs in East and West Jerusalem has also remained extremely limited. In the Jewish sector Arabic has been introduced on the signs of a small number of clothing and furniture shops, law offices, and driving schools. In East Jerusalem, Hebrew signs stating "We speak Hebrew" or "Checks are not accepted" can occasionally be seen in shop windows. What this shows is that it is nei-

[3] It should be emphasized, however, that by providing East Jerusalem cars with yellow license plates as commonly used in Israel, this mainly differentiated them from West Bank vehicles which were issued different colored and hence distinguishable blue plates signifying the Occupied Territories.

ther the language barrier nor a lack of initiative that explains why this practice is not widespread. Jewish and Arab shopowners alike are certainly interested in attracting the greatest number of customers irrespective of their national identity. It is the social and political barriers which deter them from fully exploiting their potential consumer market.

The role of ethnic identity in commercial behavior can also be seen by taking a closer look at the pattern of marketing of Israeli and Arab goods in the East and West Jerusalem retail markets. Continuing sectoral divisions are reflected mainly by the fact that Arab products can rarely be found in Jewish stores, even when the marketing of those items is not officially restricted (which is mainly the case). One obvious and striking example is that of Arab-produced cigarettes. Although they are manufactured in two West Bank factories located near East Jerusalem, widely distributed in the Arab sector of the city alongside Israeli brands, and even sold in certain remote Arab towns in Israel, they cannot be found and purchased in West Jerusalem. Arab cigarettes do not differ from Israeli cigarettes, either in quality or in price. Nor is there a lack of potential demand for them in West Jerusalem. For one thing, the thousands of Arabs who are daily employed in the Jewish sector would welcome the convenience of finding their accustomed brands in local retail stores. In addition, Jews occasionally purchase these brands while visiting East Jerusalem, particularly when Israeli cigarettes are in short supply. Interviewed about this, Arab cigarette manufacturers stated that they were reluctant to openly compete with the Jewish company monopolizing the Israeli market. But it is mainly the local Jewish wholesalers who are responsible for this situation: they avoid distributing Arab cigarettes because the marginal profit to be made from these sales is not worth the problems raised by Israeli producers or Jewish retailers and customers who would reproach them for handling "Arab products."

Whatever distribution of Arab-manufactured goods takes place in West Jerusalem is generally limited in scale and often subject to specific modes of marketing. Standard manufactured items rarely bear any indication of their origin. For example, simple plastic items produced in Bethlehem (such as bowls and jars) carry no identifying label in Arabic and are only innocently marked with a few English initials (JPC—Jordanian Plastic Company). Standard paper goods for household use and sweets, both manufactured in Ramallah, are likewise distributed under neutral brand names in English, such as "Tako" or "Silvana." Indeed, this need for camouflage is probably one of the underlying reasons why Arab manufacturers working for the Jewish sector are obliged to act as subcontractors for Israeli firms, which then distribute their products under Israeli labels.[4]

[4] A similar practice of "camouflage" is reported to be employed by Israeli firms which

This asymmetric pattern of conduct of Jewish and Arab businessmen can be seen most clearly by comparing the origin and content of items displayed in souvenir shops in West and East Jerusalem. In spite of national antagonism and cultural differences, East Jerusalem souvenir shops openly sell the full range of items popular with Jewish tourists and visitors, ranging from menorahs to "Zionist" posters and guidebooks. The sight of decorative Stars of David displayed beside crosses and crescents and other Jewish, Christian, and Muslim symbols or ritual objects in East Jerusalem tourist shop windows is perhaps the most vivid commercial expression of the religious diversity of the city's inhabitants and visitors. In contrast, neither Arab nor Christian religious items or symbols can be found in souvenir stores in West Jerusalem, despite the fact that numerous non-Jewish tourists as well as Arabs from East Jerusalem and across the Jordan River regularly visit this part of the city and comprise an important part of the local tourist trade. These differences in practice and attitude can undoubtedly be interpreted primarily in economic and symbolic terms, attesting to the dominant and subordinate positions of the Jewish and Arab communities. Arab merchants are willing—and in fact obliged—to sell all Jewish products, including politically and culturally contested symbols, since they are heavily dependent upon Jewish customers. Jewish businesses need not sell Arab products, because they are in a better position to adhere to their own cultural norms and to protect their symbols in the ethnically and politically divided marketplace.

To a large extent, a mixture of political and cultural factors also stands in the way of wider interactions between Jewish and Arab businesses. Language barriers and mutual prejudice are the most obvious explanations for the fact that the number of business transactions across the ethnic divide remains far smaller than could otherwise be expected in terms of purely economic considerations. Another discouraging factor is the major differences between the two sectors with regard to modes of conducting business. In the Jewish sector, business associations customarily involve the use of written contracts, usually formalized and endorsed by lawyers. Financial arrangements are made mainly through the banking system. In the Arab sector transactions are commonly concluded informally with payment made in cash, and disputes are brought before mutually agreed-upon arbitrators. Under these circumstances, it is hardly surprising that Jewish firms claim that they are hindered from engaging Arab entrepreneurs on a larger scale due to the latter's refusal to sign binding, long-term contracts, or to be remunerated with checks drawn

---

market certain goods to nearby Arab countries by way of Arab middlemen across the Jordan River bridges. But in this case the removal of all Israeli identifying signs is an obvious necessity in light of the generalized, declared boycott on Israeli products.

on Israeli banks, as is legally required and commonly the case with Israeli businesses.

Arab storekeepers generally refuse to accept checks or credit cards from Jewish customers, and very few deposit their daily cash receipts in East Jerusalem branches of Israeli banks. Among the reasons mentioned in both cases is their apprehension that they might find themselves at a disadvantage when suing for payment of unhonored checks from Jews before Israeli courts, or that bank accounts might be disclosed to the Israeli authorities. Yet the fact that the Arab business community tends to avoid the Israeli banking system altogether in intrasectoral transactions clearly indicates that this behavior can at least partially be attributed to politically related motives. Further evidence of this attitude is the fact that since 1967 East Jerusalem money changers and the local Chamber of Commerce have greatly expanded their financial activities in order to replace certain functions normally assumed by the banking system. Here too, as in other areas, the Arab sector has sought to limit its dependence on Jewish institutions.[5]

Finally, these patterns of avoidance are also reflected in the fact that the number of open, lasting business partnerships between Jews and Arabs has remained extremely small and has actually diminished over the years. Among the few known cases are a handful of East Jerusalem restaurants and law offices which were jointly operated by Arab and Jewish associates for several years following reunification. These joint ventures also involved underlying sectoral considerations: since Arab landlords were reluctant to lease property directly to Jews, Jewish entrepreneurs wishing to open a business in the Arab section of East Jerusalem had to go into partnership with a local resident who would rent the premises. The role of the Jewish partner would often be to help provide the necessary authorization from the Israeli administration. One example of this complementarity were the watermelon stands and outdoor cafes which operated for a number of years at a location along the former dividing line between East and West Jerusalem. Although these ventures were operated by Arabs, Jews from the nearby neighborhood were also involved as "hidden partners." Indeed, business associations between Jews and Arabs were often conducted "under the surface," with one partner operating in his own sector while the other's participation was concealed from the public. Business associations and transactions between members of the two communities are both possible and numerous, but as a

[5] The limited use by Arabs of the six local branches of Israeli banks established in East Jerusalem in 1967 can be demonstrated by the fact that this number never increased after this early date. Their operations mainly involved dealings with foreign institutions located in East Jerusalem, or payments to Arabs working in or with the Jewish sector. See Romann 1984.

general rule both parties prefer to conduct them only on an ad hoc basis, thereby avoiding permanent, formal, and equal partnerships.

CONSUMPTION PATTERNS AND BEHAVIOR

It is in Jerusalem's commercial centers where the greatest number of Jews and Arabs can be seen regularly meeting each other, engaging in the kinds of daily exchanges normally conducted between the providers of commercial services and their customers. To the casual observer, the sight of Jews, Arabs, and foreign tourists freely mingling in East and West Jerusalem's business centers attests to one of the more obvious and expected features of a multiethnic city. Yet a closer examination reveals that at the consumer level, too, interactions generally involve specific patterns and norms of conduct that reflect underlying ethnic and sectoral divisions.

Following 1967, Jewish visits to the Arab commercial centers in East Jerusalem became frequent and numerous, as evidenced by the large number of Jewish residents and tourists who often crowded the major arteries of the Arab Old City. Usually these visits were part of touring expeditions or weekend outings made by families from Jerusalem or elsewhere in Israel, for whom the Old City, with its historic sites and its oriental bazaars, represents a major attraction. While there, they shop for typical tourist items or other traditional commodities such as oriental rugs, leather bags, or copper jars and vessels that are sold in the Arab stores and are in great demand among Jewish customers. Jews, in fact, constitute the main clientele of Arab tourist-oriented commerce and related services like food stands and restaurants. Jerusalem Jews also occasionally cross over to East Jerusalem for their general shopping needs or to obtain a particular item or service. The places most often patronized are food, clothing, and hardware stores, as well as garages and various other workshops for items ranging from carpentry to shoe repair. Most of these visits are made on the Jewish Sabbath and holidays, when commercial establishments in the Jewish sector are closed; for many Jews this open Arab commercial sector represents a natural and convenient alternative.

Another strong motivation is the fact that products and services are generally cheaper in the Arab than in the Jewish sector. As already noted, a price gap often exists between the same goods in East and West Jerusalem even with respect to standard Israeli products or imported items; this is particularly true of services provided by local workshops on either side of the city. Many Jewish residents who wish to repair their car, hire a truck and movers, or even purchase a pair of shoes, go to East Jerusalem to see if they can obtain a better bargain there. This underlying motive may also explain why Jewish clients turn to the Arab sector for a broader range of services than might be expected. In light of the animosity and ethnic prejudice which prevail between Jews and Arabs, it is interesting to find that many Jews are treated by Arab dentists. Even more surprising are the number of Jewish women who go to private Arab clinics in East Jerusalem for abortions. The reason for this is lower costs—prices in East Jerusalem are as much as two-thirds lower than those in the Jewish sector.

Arabs also go to Jewish commercial centers in West Jerusalem for a wide range of purposes. They might be less noticeable there than the Jews in East Jerusalem, but this relative inconspicuousness is due mainly to differences in the size of the respective markets and consumer populations. Nevertheless, the sight of Arabs in Jewish shopping areas, workshops, and public institutions has become as common a feature of daily life in West Jerusalem as is the large number of Arab workers in that part of the city. Work and consumption in the Jewish sector are often closely linked for Arab Jerusalemites: Arab men shop in West Jerusalem on their way home from work there, and long lines of Arabs can be seen cashing their pay checks at Jewish banks. Moreover, many Arab women and families from East Jerusalem and its environs travel to West Jerusalem to shop, particularly on Sundays.

As in the case of Jewish visits to East Jerusalem, overall patterns of Arab visits to the Jewish sector can be classified into several categories. Unlike the Jews, the Arabs often cross into the other sector out of sheer necessity—to collect national insurance payments, to visit Jewish hospitals or clinics, to appear in court, or to place an international call from the central telephone exchange. Arabs also go to West Jerusalem to find specific goods and services that are not available in the Arab sector, such as technical equipment and vehicles (most agencies for the import of automobiles have dealers only in the Jewish sector); the business and personal services they are interested in range from insurance offices to medical specialists. Like the Jews, Arabs too visit commercial centers on the other side to satisfy their daily needs, even if shopping could be done in their own sector. This tendency is mainly due to the greater variety of consumer products offered by the Jewish commercial sector. One obvious case is that of West Jerusalem department stores that attract Arab women shoppers in search of modern or stylish clothing or household equipment.

For similar reasons, Arab youths and families visit Jewish recreational facilities, particularly the West Jerusalem zoo, the Israel Museum, and several public swimming pools. Attractions such as these are virtually absent on the Arab side. West Jerusalem city parks are also popular venues for Arab family outings on weekends and holidays. Several city parks located in the western sector and close to the old dividing line have become major areas of encounter between Jewish and Arab families. A similar role is played by a number of cafes which have opened near the former border, such as those close to the Damascus Gate or Jaffa Gate, affording easy access to Jewish and Arab youth.

The scale and nature of Jewish and Arab consumers' visits to each others' sectors cannot be precisely determined, even though several surveys do provide rough indicators. In a 1981 study conducted by the Jerusalem Municipality, among a sample of the adult Jewish population nearly two-thirds answered affirmatively when asked if they frequented business establishments in East Jerusalem. Similarly, over 60 percent of the Arabs interviewed stated that they had visited West Jerusalem in the month preceding the survey. Among those Arabs who also specified the purposes of these visits, about 40 percent mentioned that they had visited at least once for shopping purposes, other reasons being, in declining order, visits to government or municipal offices, work-related matters, and recreation.[6]

A 1982 survey conducted among Jewish and Arab high school pupils also revealed that the incidence of visits to the other side was substantial.[7] When Jewish and Arab students were asked about the purpose of their visits, some well-defined but not necessarily similar patterns emerged. Jewish pupils overwhelmingly indicated that the major purpose was general sightseeing, visits to historic and religious sites, museums, restaurants, and related tourist activities. Shopping was another commonly cited objective, reported by over 60 percent of those interviewed. Interestingly, the survey also revealed that over 10 percent of the Jewish pupils had visited East Jerusaelm cinemas, coffee shops, or clubs at least once. Although the overall rate of Arab pupils' visits to West Jerusalem remained lower than among Jewish pupils, the range of purposes was more diverse and also far more target-oriented. General shopping purposes were mentioned by only about one-third of them, while over one-half reported visiting public parks in West Jerusalem and one-quarter had been to swimming pools there. The percentage of Arabs who had visited Jewish cinemas was more then double that of Jews who had been to Arab cinemas. Arab pupils also reported visiting Jewish soccer matches whereas none of the Jewish pupils reported visiting Arab soccer games. No less significantly, the relative number of Arab pupils visiting the other side for purely administrative or related purposes was again far greater than that of the Jewish pupils; the reasons given included visits to hospitals, municipal and government offices, and the like.

[6] See Smith 1981.
[7] See Romann 1984.

As in other intersectoral exchanges, Arab and Jewish consumers have been mainly motivated by purely economic considerations when seeking complementary opportunities in each other's sectoral markets. But it is particularly in regard to private consumption that differences in consumption norms, business practices, and various ethnically related attitudes often serve as either a complementary or a deterring factor. Whereas many Jews are attracted to Arab shopping centers primarily on the Jewish Sabbath when their own shops are closed, this is precisely one reason why religious, observant Jews avoid shopping in the East Jerusalem markets. By the same token, while traditional, elderly Arab women generally avoid visiting West Jerusalem, young Arab couples often prefer to meet in Jewish cafes and cinemas since in the more traditional Arab community social norms discourage women from visiting these places. In this instance the proximity of the Jewish sector offers a convenient solution. Different considerations also come into play when members of the two communities turn to the other sector even in those cases where close substitutes are available on their own side. Jewish consumers usually do so under the explicit or implicit condition that they will pay lower prices, yet many among them maintain that they would rather not expose themselves to potential danger "just to save a few shekels on a pair of shoes." Others say that they avoid shopping in the Arab sector because this always involves bargaining due to the absence of fixed prices, that they do not trust "unqualified Arab work," or that they simply do not want to "provide Arabs with work." Many Arabs, on their part, state that they prefer to buy a television set and similar items in West Jerusalem, or go to a Jewish doctor, because they believe that they can thereby obtain better, more qualified professional services. Jews normally have their cars repaired in the Arab sector in order to save on costs, even though garages there might not measure up to official standards; Arabs, on the other hand, often go to Jewish garages, because they expect better quality service there, even though in these garages, too, it is mostly Arabs who do the actual work!

Nonetheless, the overall economic and institutional framework also implies that patterns of intersectoral consumption have been basically asymmetrical. The major distinction in this respect is that Arabs are often obliged to make use of Jewish public and commercial facilities, due to the mode of public service allocation and the sheer difference in market size; Jews, by contrast, can always rely on their own public services and generally have a far greater degree of choice as to whether to utilize Arab commercial establishments in light of the abundant alternatives within the Jewish sector. It is because of this situation that many Arab clients prefer to engage Jewish professionals, not only because of their qualifications, but in particular when they become involved in legal procedures or have to deal with the Israeli administration. In this respect, a revealing example is the fact that Arabs commonly take driving lessons at Jewish driving schools. Although there are a few dozen of these schools operating in West Jerusalem, for many years following 1967 none existed in East Jerusalem. This cannot be attributed to any official restrictions or lack of initiative, considering the fact that in nearby Arab cities on the West Bank, Arab driving schools are numerous and widely utilized. The major reason is that since the vehicle licensing authority in Jerusalem is located in West Jerusalem and is operated mainly by Jewish officials, Arabs believe that their chances of passing the test and obtaining a license will be better if they take their lessons at Jewish schools.

For the most part, however, consumer behavior involves patterns of segregation and avoidance. Arabs and Jews alike generally satisfy their daily needs within their respective sectors. For many persons, months and even years may pass without their making use of services provided on the other side of the city. The spatial segregation of residential and commercial centers, as well as the sectoral division of most essential public services, are principal reasons for this. Language barriers, different consumption norms, and the lack of consumer-oriented information are additional factors. In the previously cited study conducted among Jewish adults, over one-third reported that they never shop in East Jerusalem. More significantly, among those who stated that they visit the Arab shopping centers a substantial proportion also said that they were frequenting Arab shops less than in the previous year.

This latter development is a clear indicator that consumer avoidance is related to personal apprehension brought about by the violent incidents which sporadically occur on both sides of the city and in which innocent bystanders have occasionally been victims. Indeed, whenever a terrorist act occurs, like the stabbing of a Jew walking through the Arab market or a bomb explosion in the center of West Jerusalem, the first to disappear are those consumers who can afford not to be there if it is not absolutely necessary. As we have already observed, they tend to reappear after a sufficient period of calm, economic motives once again overriding personal fears. This pattern is both cyclical and long-term in character. Since the mid-1980s the number of Jews crossing over to East Jerusalem for shopping or tourism has clearly declined. In Jerusalem's dichotomous and potentially violent environment, it is the movement of consumers across the dividing line which represents one of the best indicators of the climate of interaction and segregation in everyday life.

Several concluding remarks can now be made, particularly regarding the significance of ethnic identity in the patterns of segregation and interaction between Jewish and Arab public institutions, commercial establishments, and customers. The most striking feature is the total and unequivocal sectoral distinction made between practically all of Jerusalem's public functions and economic entities. In the united city an ethnic identity can always be applied not only to residents, neighborhoods, or religious and national institutions, but also to each hospital, hotel, or taxi cab, and even to items ranging from tourist articles to a pack of cigarettes. Moreover, even foreign establishments or Christian institutions are, as a rule, either "Jewish" or "Arab," since they too are clearly differentiated according to their sectoral affiliation.

Jewish and Arab economic entities of a parallel kind differ from one another in many characteristics which can be defined, in turn, as sectoral "identity attributes." These generally involve the ethnic identity of owners, customers, and employees as well as location in the urban area. In addition, such distinctions often relate to the origin of capital, products, and other factors of production. Arab or Jewish economic establishments can further be distinguished with respect to mode of operation or business norms—the kind of services provided, employment conditions, the language used, weekly closing days, and the like. Finally, these distinct institutional frameworks and even contrasting identity marks of similar Jewish and Arab establishments also imply the legal status that has been selectively imposed by the Israeli authorities. A Jewish establishment is, as a rule, Jewish-owned, serves mainly Jewish customers, and is located in West Jerusalem, whereas an Arab establishment will be Arab-owned, employs and serves its respective ethnic group members, and is located in the Arab sector of the city. In the former case it will always be closed on the Jewish Sabbath, while in the latter it will remain open. Hebrew versus Arabic shop signs as well as various other identifying features are additional significant symbols perceived by both Jews and Arabs.

Obviously, Jewish and Arab economic entities are not all necessarily pure types possessing each or the same attributes that clearly define their sectoral affiliation, nor are the various identity factors of equal significance. In particular, the origin of customers, employees, or other factors of production is not a crucial element. Arab businesses that primarily serve Jews, or Jewish workshops mainly employing Arabs, will not lose their respective identity as "Arab" or "Jewish." Hence, branches of Israeli banks and medical services operating in East Jerusalem, although exclusively staffed and frequented by Arabs, are nevertheless considered by both parties to be Jewish establishments. In contrast, ownership, and in several respects also location, are determining factors. But this is even more true regarding the specific operational mode and different legal status which continue to differentiate Jewish and Arab functions. Since these are always closely associated with ethnically related norms of economic conduct and adhered to or selectively imposed on national grounds, they represent, in turn, unambiguous identity elements. In present-day Jerusalem, it is unlikely that a commercial establishment, or even a foreign-owned institution, which uses only Hebrew, serves kosher food, and is closed on Jewish holidays, will be part of the Arab sector.

Those cases where a distinct sectoral affiliation cannot be clearly defined are extremely rare but no less instructive. One such instance is the city's French hospital, which stands apart in this respect from all other medical institutions. Being neither Jewish- nor Arab-owned and located close to the pre-1967 dividing line, it is staffed by ethnically mixed personnel of all professional ranks and equally serves both Jewish and Arab patients. However, it is mainly due to the fact that Jewish and Arab norms are equally respected, regarding the language employed and the like, that neither of the two ethnic groups working or being treated in this hospital can consider it as "their own." Other, yet different, cases refer to East Jerusalem's public functions which came under Israeli control after 1967, but continued to serve only the Arab population. Indeed, it is precisely because of the unclear sectoral identity of the East Jerusalem government hospital or municipal schools that issues related to their identity remain subject to permanent contention. In spite of nominal Jewish ownership and control, the Arab population continues to consider these establishments as part of their own sector, one of the determining factors being, once again, preserving their distinct cultural identity and status.

The mutual desire of Jews and Arabs to preserve the identity of their economic entities may also explain the selective patterns of functional relationships between the two sectors. More specifically, both communities prefer to conduct intersectoral exchange by involving those identity attributes least significant or compromising in this respect. Since, as we saw, being dependent on the other sector's customers, factors of production, or goods and services does not involve crucial identity elements, this is precisely the reason why exchanges normally take place only on these respective levels. On the other hand, because interactions involving ownership or location more directly imply giving up some sectoral economic or spatial assets, business partnerships, organizational mergers, and location on the other side are opposed and avoided. Particularly with regard to business relations in the commercial market, intersectoral transactions can be accomplished in various alternative ways or forms of exchange. As we have seen, the Jewish demand for Arab products has generally been satisfied in the form of Jewish customers shopping in the Arab commercial center, or Jewish firms subcontracting with Arab entrepreneurs. Alternative and more significant modes of exchange such as the direct marketing of Arab products in Jewish shops, Jewish-Arab cooperation on an equal basis in joint production or distribution, and the relocation of Arab businesses to Jewish commercial centers, have not developed. As we have also seen, it has mainly been the Jewish sector which opposes the more binding patterns of exchange.

Intersectoral exchange also implies giving up, by at least one party, some customary, culturally related norms and practices. Here again, the desire to preserve these less tangible identity elements interferes with the scope of exchange, implying, in turn, selective, asymmetrical patterns. This can be seen in the fact that it was mainly Arab businessmen who became accustomed to using Hebrew, while few Jews had to adopt Arabic. The official use of the two languages and the selective application of a different legal status to the Jewish and Arab sectors can be viewed in similar terms. Seen more generally, in a city inhabited by two ethnic groups with different cultural norms, three possible patterns could be applied: (1) the imposition of the majority norms as the only authorized or practiced pattern; (2) allowing each group, and particularly the minority group, the legal right to preserve its specific norms within its own sector; and (3) institutionalizing both norms comprehensively in both sectors. In united Jerusalem, ethnic and national divisions generally ruled out this last, more balanced, formula. The Israeli authorities were willing to respect Arab norms, but only within their own sector and regarding intrasectoral relations. Nevertheless, in most cases, the Jewish sector imposed its own norms, particularly when this involved intersectoral interactions.

CHAPTER 7

Contacts in a Hospital Setting

JERUSALEM'S HOSPITALS are especially interesting places for studying interethnic encounters. While, in keeping with the now-familiar pattern,
Jews rarely if ever enter Arab hospitals, large numbers of Arab patients
and employees are daily present in Jewish hospitals. Like the bread factory described in chapter 5, these Jewish hospitals provide a rich context
for analyzing the scope as well as the consequences of repeated contacts
between members of both groups. It is for this reason that special attention will be devoted to the Jewish hospitals, and to one in particular: the
Hadassah Hospital on Mount Scopus. By any reckoning this is a fascinating place for exploring how Arabs and Jews interact in this deeply divided
city.

Historically, Hadassah has been the focus of a lengthy and at times
traumatic series of exchanges between Arabs and Jews. Sponsored and
partially financed by the world-wide Jewish women's organization after
which it is named, the Hadassah Hospital on Mount Scopus was founded
in 1939. Located at a considerable distance from what were then Jerusalem's Jewish neighborhoods, the new hospital was built next to the
equally new Hebrew University campus and became an integral part of
the university's medical school. Hadassah quickly gained a reputation for
high-level medical standards. It is fair to say, in fact, that it became the
premier medical facility in Palestine if not in the entire Middle East.
While the medical staff was Jewish, from the beginning the patients included both Jews and Arabs who came there not only from Jerusalem but
from throughout the Arab world.

When, during the 1930s and 1940s, hostilities between Jews and Arabs
in Jerusalem grew increasingly bitter, the fact that the hospital was located in a predominantly Arab area proved to be a serious problem. The
worst moment came in April 1948, when a convoy of armored buses and
ambulances carrying members of the hospital staff was ambushed by Arabs while on its way to Mount Scopus; seventy-eight of the Jewish staff
members were killed and another twenty were wounded. From then on
Mount Scopus was effectively cut off from Jewish Jerusalem. A small Israeli army unit held control of the buildings themselves, but they were
in turn surrounded by Arab forces. According to the terms of the 1949
Jordan–Israel armistice agreement, this zone became a Jewish enclave

within Arab territory. The hospital and university were closed, and for the next nineteen years under UN auspices twice each month a small Israeli army convoy crossed the Jordanian lines to resupply the tiny garrison that remained there.

When Jerusalem was reunited, Mount Scopus with its empty buildings and marvelous panoramic views suddenly became available; moreover, soon after the 1967 war a series of new Jewish neighborhoods was built nearby. The idea of reopening the hospital was irresistible; with the aid of volunteers the Israeli authorities began to clear and repair the buildings, and soon thereafter, plans were announced to rebuild an enlarged Hadassah Hospital and Hebrew University campus on the Mount Scopus site. Eight years later, in May 1975, the Hadassah Hospital on Mount Scopus was rededicated.

Organized within the framework of the city-wide regional hospital system, Hadassah serves the ethnically mixed population that lives in the adjoining areas. All of those who reside within the hospital's immediate radius—a population of about thirty thousand persons, of whom approximately two-thirds are Jews and one-third Arabs—receive their primary medical care as well as hospitalization at Hadassah. They include elite Christian and Muslim Arab families from Sheikh Jarrah, Arab villagers from nearby places such as Isawiyeh, veteran middle-income Jewish families living in French Hill, and recent Jewish immigrants from places as diverse as Soviet Georgia and the United States. All of these persons can, in principle, come to the hospital's emergency room if they have had an accident, just as both Arab and Jewish women give birth in the hospital's maternity ward. In addition to the area residents, some patients are admitted on those days when it is Hadassah's turn to receive emergency cases from all of Jerusalem. Like its sister hospital in Ein Karem, Hadassah is a university teaching hospital, and consequently it accepts persons who suffer from especially complicated and rare diseases. Israeli army personnel injured in combat or training exercises and civilians (both Arabs and Jews) wounded in terrorist attacks are also admitted to Hadassah. The patients entering this hospital are consequently extraordinarily diverse: Arabs from one of the nearby villages lie in beds next to Israeli army soldiers, and the emergency room is crowded with Arab and Jewish family members. It is a repeatedly colorful scene of mixed appearances, language, and custom.

This is one major dimension of the hospital as an arena of Arab-Jewish social exchange. In addition, while Hadassah's staff is mainly composed of Jewish medical professionals, it also includes a small number of Arab doctors and nurses. The original plans for the new Hadassah on Mount Scopus had envisioned an even more integrated medical staff. Before the hospital reopened, negotiations were carried on with a number of East

Jerusalem Arab doctors who had indicated an interest in joining the hospital. However, in most instances they decided against working there, and consequently, although it includes members of both ethnic groups, the medical staff is predominantly Jewish. The hospital also employs large numbers of Arabs who work in unskilled and semiskilled maintenance tasks (cleaning, washing, kitchen work, and so forth); these Arab workers are employed in all the hospital wards, and they too are regularly in contact with both the patients and the medical staff.

BEING SICK TOGETHER

How the hospital functions as an Arab-Jewish social system can best be introduced by briefly describing several common situations. Drawn from field notes, the following descriptions illustrate the tone and texture of everyday events at Hadassah.

It is about four o'clock in the afternoon. The usual crowd is packed around the emergency room entrance: people near the door, others leaning against the wall, some kids sliding down the polished marble incline. Several young Arab women in their modern religious costume, heads covered by a grey scarf, apparently waiting for their youngsters; what appear to be Hebrew University students, one girl trying to explain her problem in English to the clerk in the glass-enclosed entrance booth; several soldiers, tired, carrying their M-16 rifles, making inquiries about a buddy who was brought in the morning after an accident; a middle aged religious Jew dressed in black together with his wife, plus several women in various stages of pregnancy. The door opens and closes to let hospital personnel enter: young residents, the doctor in charge with his knit skull cap, nurses and student nurses. The usual hubbub and sense of near chaos. They wink at me and let me in through the door. I chat briefly with the head nurse: a quiet afternoon, she assures me. Not much happening. Behind the various emergency room curtains I pick out persons lying on beds: some with infusions tied to their arms, loud moaning from farther back in the room, a young doctor with his clipboard taking notes next to one of the beds. Some noise outside; a new patient is wheeled in. Apparently a young Arab man, covered with dust, eyes shut in pain. He is brought in hurriedly by fellow Arab workers and what may be some family members. Apparently a work accident; his left leg may be broken, the nurse tells me. They start to clean the wound. Dr. Fuchs, the head of emergency comes over to look. He asks a few questions, gets answers in a mixture of Arabic and Hebrew. He walks away, calls Avi over to join him. Avi is one of the residents, doing his assignment now in emergency. His real name is Ibrahim—an Israeli Arab from Galilee, but here he is called Avi. Fuchs asks him to take the record. Avi is not happy. "Why me again, just to translate?" He walks over to the new patient, begins to fill out the record, asks questions first in Hebrew, then in Arabic. Briskly, business-like, he listens, probes the injured limb, asks questions of the Arab workers who have brought the patient. Fuchs comes back; Avi asks more questions, translates into Hebrew, the nurses are all the time cleaning the leg. They decide not to transfer him immediately to one of the wards. First they'll take X-rays and find out if anything is broken. The patient is given some pills, and they walk away.

Incidents such as this are constantly taking place in the emergency room. There is a continual stream of new patients, rapid mobilization and initial treatment, plus preparation for diagnosis and care. The patients include Arabs and Jews, and the medical staff is also ethnically mixed. All of these features are part of the hospital's daily routine.

A second set of events takes place in the orthopedic ward, and it too is based upon our field notes.

It is about four o'clock in the afternoon, a little before visiting hours begin. Outside in the TV room some of the patients are watching a film; some are in wheel chairs, a few hobbling with casts on their legs, even one youngster on a bed rolled in from his room. Young men and women, a few kids, some older persons, all of them dressed alike in hospital pajamas and housecoats of blue for men and pink for women. All of the chairs are taken; a few are standing to see the film—a Western with lots of cowboys and Indians—and all eyes are bright as they follow the scenes. In the back, together, sit two male patients who are recognizably Arabs; they watch quietly, saying nothing. The group hardly changes places or makes a noise.

I go inside the men's ward: six patients, three on each side, some asleep, nodding, others reading, light pouring in from the windows. I say hello to everyone, ask how they are. The soldier who was operated on the other day is asleep, still recovering; his girlfriend sits next to him. I offer her some chocolate. In the corner bed, on the other side, there is a heavy-set Arab patient; there are several men and women seated around him. He sits up in bed; they talk softly. Apparently he is in pain. My friend Tuvyeh is still there; we chat, he tells me how he feels; nothing much happening, the doctors say little. He probably won't get out this week. He complains about the nurses at their station; they take too long to get to him when he has a problem, like pain at night. Batya, one of the nurses, comes in with the tea cart; she is brisk, smiles a little—a Georgian Jewess with high stockings on her legs. She pours tea for everyone, hands out some cake with it, plus their pills for the afternoon, the "cocktail." She stops by the Arab patient across the room; he complains about his leg, apparently. She answers him in Hebrew, asks Tuvyeh to translate. "He says that the plaster is too tight, it hurts him," he translates into Hebrew. She says alright, take the pills, she'll ask Dr. Posner to come and check. The Arab patient nods his head; his visitors are quiet, peering straight ahead. One of the maintenance workers, Ali I think, comes in with his long mop and cleans the floor again. He smiles at Tuvyeh, they exchange greetings. The visiting hours have apparently begun. People begin pouring in, visitors; in the other beds the patients wake up.

In common with the previous description of everyday moments in the hospital's emergency room, these events are routine daily happenings. Moments such as these are the rule, even though from time to time unusual incidents take place that are considerably more dramatic. What conceptual understandings regarding Jewish-Arab relationships can be gained from analyzing these routine social exchanges?

The social world of the hospital is divided between what in Hebrew is called *metaplim* and *holim* (or, in English, medical personnel and patients). *Metaplim* include a broad range of persons who are employed in a variety of medical, administrative, and maintenance tasks. These positions are hierarchically arranged and ranked in typical bureaucratic fashion; thus the medical personnel range from "professor" to "doctor," there are both "head nurses" and "student nurses," and administrative and maintenance personnel include bookkeepers and guards, or chief electrician and custodians.

What is significant for our purposes is that the Jewish staff members hold the dominant positions within these hierarchies, while the Arabs are in lower-ranked posts. For example, the skilled maintenance positions are filled by Jewish workers while Arabs are concentrated in the unskilled jobs; nearly all of the members of the administrative staff are Jews (secretaries, computer operators, hospital executives); and among the nurses and doctors, the Jewish members tend to hold superordinate positions. In this regard the hospital is similar to other Israeli social contexts in which Jews and Arabs interact: Jews monopolize the higher-ranked roles in the internal system of stratification.

Internal differentiation among the patients is much different. Patients hospitalized at Hadassah are divided into various categories or types. In common with hospitals throughout the world they are distinguished in terms of features such as age, sex, period of time that they have been hospitalized, previous illness, and most important, their present illness or complaint. The latter is certainly the most important feature: women about to give birth are assigned to maternity wards, those suffering from heart disease are in internal medicine, the children's ward includes infants and youngsters, and so forth. Obviously, these distinctions have nothing to do with ethnic-group membership. Indeed, the processing form filled out by patients before they are admitted to the hospital does not require them to indicate whether they are Arabs or Jews, nor does the hospital keep statistics in this regard. This does not mean that being an Arab or a Jewish patient at Hadassah is unimportant or irrelevant—as we shall shortly see, ethnic-group membership is an important dimension of the patient's experience. The point to be emphasized, however, is that it is not the most salient feature of hospital identity.

In a variety of different ways Hadassah Hospital is organized and represents itself as a Jewish or Israeli institution. Even though both staff and patients are an ethnically mixed group, the hospital seeks to present itself unambiguously as belonging to Israeli society. Its Israeli or Jewish character is expressed in a number of ways. Language is one crucial feature. The fact that Hebrew is universally used has important symbolic as well as practical meaning. For example, nearly all of the signs that are prominently displayed throughout the hospital are written in Hebrew and English, but not in Arabic. Similarly the explanatory material distributed to patients when they enter the hospital is written in Hebrew. Conversations among medical staff members are commonly conducted in Hebrew (with English often used as a second language); a Jewish doctor or nurse who wishes to converse with an Arab patient or visitor must find someone (such as a Jewish patient who speaks Arabic, or an Arab maintenance worker) to translate. This use of Hebrew is important representationally as well as in regard to finding one's way through the hospital bureaucratic system. Arab patients and workers are made aware of the fact that they are within an Israeli medical institution, and what is more, that they need to accommodate to it.

The hospital's Jewish character is expressed in other ways as well. For example, when entering Hadassah patients are required to present evidence that they belong to a recognized Israeli medical insurance program, or that they have their own funds with which to pay the hospital costs. Nearly all of the Jewish patients are covered by hospitalization insurance, while many of the Arabs do not have medical coverage (particularly those who live in the West Bank) nor do they clearly understand what is required of them. This often leads to a grueling series of negotiations (often punctuated by angry shouting and recrimination) between the patient and family and the hospital officials. To be sure, these encounters may be difficult for all incoming new patients, both Arabs and Jews, but they are particularly complicated for those Arab patients who neither understand the language nor are able to make their way through the hospital bureaucratic maze. To cite still another example, the hospital employs a trained teacher who works with youngsters hospitalized for long periods of time—but the teacher speaks only Hebrew, and the lessons she teaches are the standard ones presented in Israeli schools. This is the case despite the fact that many of those in the ward are Arab children.

Commenting upon the fact that the Arabs seem to more openly express their gratitude to the hospital staff than do the Jewish patients, one informant ventured the explanation that this was "because they know that the care they receive is not really due them; after all, this is an Israeli hospital." This is not an isolated comment, and it expresses a sentiment held by many of the Jewish patients and staff members alike. It is an assumption, an intuitive understanding that while the hospital's population is mixed, Hadassah "belongs" to the Jewish group. The result of this attitude is, of course, that the Arab staff members and patients must adjust to the other group's norms and sensibilities.

With these introductory comments in mind we can now turn to an examination of ethnic-group relationships within the hospital. Social exchanges between Arabs and Jews take place along three broad parameters: between patients and medical staff members, between patients, and finally, between staff members. Analyzing each of these in turn can provide insight into this intense Jerusalem microcosm.

The Healing Profession: Staff-Patient Relations

Although there are contacts between hospital personnel (*metaplim*) and patients (*holim*) at various levels—medical staff, hospital administrators, and members of the maintenance crew—attention was primarily focused upon the interactions between medical personnel and patients. Some persons in the other categories were also included, but emphasis was placed upon examining how the *holim* and the medical staff interacted with each other.

The dimensions of these interethnic contacts should be kept clearly in mind. While almost all of the doctors at Hadassah are Jews, during the time of our study in 1982 there were four Arabs among the sixty doctors then attached to the hospital. Three of them were Israeli Arabs completing internship or residency requirements, and the fourth was an East Jerusalem Arab surgeon who was a senior member of the orthopedic department. Since the total number of Arab doctors was small they were not represented in each of the hospital's departments. On the other hand, probably one-third of the nursing staff were Arabs; all were Israeli Arabs, including both women and men, and they served on the staffs of nearly all of the departments.

As was previously emphasized, the patients also are an ethnically mixed group. Both Arab and Jewish women give birth in the delivery rooms, and Arabs and Jews lie side by side in the internal medicine wards as well as in the emergency room and outpatient clinics. In fact, certain clinical departments appear to have an especially high proportion of Arab patients. The reasons for this apparently have to do with the relatively underdeveloped state of medicine on the West Bank, as well as the staff's interest in admitting persons who have rare or unusual diseases; since Hadassah is oriented toward teaching and medical research the medical staff members are anxious to admit these interesting cases. To sum up briefly, at Hadassah Arab nurses bandage or give injections to Jewish patients, just as Jewish doctors operate on Arab patients.

Formally, all of the patients who are admitted to the hospital, both Arabs and Jews, receive equal treatment. This point—and it is an important one—can be stated categorically: the hospital staff does not differentiate between Arab and Jewish patients, and all of those who are admitted for medical care, whatever their particular background or ethnic membership, receive the same professional care. All of the patients wear the same standard hospital clothing, just as all of the medical staff members, both Arabs and Jews, wear identical white medical uniforms; at first sight all of the *holim* and *metaplim* have the same outward appearance. More importantly, no distinctions are made between Jews and Arabs in regard to the assignment of hospital beds or rooms; the hospital staff does not deliberately separate or mix Arab and Jewish patients, but rooms and beds are assigned to patients as they become available. Of course, the effect of this policy is that there frequently are Jewish and Arab patients in the same room, and consequently the rooms are often filled with both Arab and Jewish family members and visitors. Jewish patients are not tended by Jewish nurses, nor Arabs by Arab nurses, but rather the nurses serve all of the patients. Moreover, patient care is regulated strictly by medical considerations; whether a *holeh* is to undergo a complicated (and therefore costly) operation depends entirely upon the medical evaluation of the case, and not upon the patient's ethnic affiliation.

This poses some important questions. If, as has been emphasized throughout this study, the common Jerusalem pattern is for members of the two ethnic groups to be separated from one another, then why do the boundaries seem to dissolve in the hospital? What is there about the hospital setting that permits contacts between Arabs and Jews to be comparatively personal and close?

From the point of view of the medical staff patients are not so much defined as Arabs or Jews but instead as persons who are suffering from disease. Whether they are themselves Jews or Arabs, they have been trained to view patients in a neutral, professional manner; this is, after all, the meaning of the Hippocratic Oath that enjoins physicians to care for *all* of the sick. This does not mean that the doctors and nurses are unaware of whether a patient is an Arab or a Jew; it is rather that this identification is screened out or neutralized while attention is given instead to viewing the relationship on a professional dimension. In addition, in some instances the medical staff members' personal political views reinforce these attitudes. This is particularly the case among some of the Jewish staff members. For example, doctors who have nationalist or religious-nationalist political outlooks may wish to demonstrate egalitarian attitudes toward Arabs in order to show that Arabs and Jews can live together when the Arabs recognize that Jews are in control and that they will receive equal treatment; or, taking a contrary view, Jewish staff members who believe in peaceful coexistence also wish to show that members of both groups can coexist inside the hospital. Paradoxically, for their own different reasons both "hawks" and "doves" on the staff may wish to demonstrate egalitarian attitudes, and this too strengthens their professional orientation toward the patients.

The encounter looks quite different from the patient's point of view. Being hospitalized has many features of what Victor Turner and others have termed a "liminal experience": that is, becoming a patient in a hospital means entering into a new transitional situation in which novel, indeed, unusual, norms of behavior are required and become customary.[1] For example, becoming a patient means shedding normal clothing and dressing in another costume; the patient's daily routine is altered; and medical personnel (who also dress in other costumes) may ask intimate questions and perform physical examinations of a highly personal nature. The hospital is an "upside-down" social world, perched "betwixt and between" the normal outer world from which persons come and to which they will, presumably, also return in due course.

Under these unusual circumstances it is permissible for Jews to be touched and treated by Arabs, and for Arabs to put their lives in the hands of Jews. These are highly unusual conditions for members of both groups. Their own stereotypes, prejudices, and fears must give way to different attitudes and behaviors. Acts that would be totally unacceptable in another context are thus possible within the hospital. Of course, it is also a situation that typically lasts for only a brief period of time: a Jew who mistrusts Arabs knows that while in the hospital he must accept the fact that an Arab nurse will bathe him and give him injections, yet when he leaves the hospital he will return to a world in which he can avoid contacts with Arabs.

In general, both the hospital staff and the patients follow the rules of egalitarian, professional behavior; the anxieties and fears that members of both groups have about the others are apparently alleviated or "screened out" by the hospital context. However, from time to time these rules are bent or broken: intergroup frictions or confrontations take place that upset the normal patterns of relationship.

Outbreaks of national conflict periodically place strains on the medical staff's professional orientation. To cite two examples, during the

[1] Turner 1968.

Lebanese War the East Jerusalem Arab surgeon routinely operated on wounded Israeli soldiers, just as Jewish members of the staff have cared for Arab terrorists. Although their professional treatment was competent, in the latter case the Jewish nurses reported that they were at times angry and uncertain regarding how to behave: "Here I was taking care of an Arab who had planned to kill Jews; it was very, very difficult for me; I just couldn't stop thinking that he was a terrorist," one of the nurses recalled. Moreover, the normal hospital routine may also be disturbed by patients who refuse to be treated by members of the other group, or who voice ethnic slurs. Not surprisingly, these incidents usually involve Jewish patients. Arabs who come to Hadassah—a "Jewish hospital"—expect to be treated by Jewish personnel, whereas some Jews express surprise at being treated by Arabs in "their hospital." An informant described the following incident:

> When I came to the emergency room I could sense that something was wrong. You could just feel the tension. It took awhile, but finally one of the nurses told me. They had brought in a soldier who was injured in training, and he was lying on a stretcher. He was a Moroccan, and when Avi, the Arab resident, came over to check what had happened, he began yelling, "Get this dirty Arab away from me. I don't want an Arab around me here." Avi turned white, the other doctors and nurses were also shocked, no one knew quite what to do. Finally, one of the other doctors came over, shouted at the soldier and told him to shut up, and he finally quieted down. Believe me, it was awful.

When incidents such as this occur they shock and upset the normal hospital routine. Even though they are unusual, they place strains upon the accepted patterns of behavior.

While activity in the hospital is focused upon professional medical matters, ethnic-group membership is informally recognized and expressed. One way that this is done is through what may be termed "signaling behavior"; that is, patients and staff members may exchange subtle messages with one another regarding their attitudes or identities. Patients commonly attempt to interpret or better understand the behavior of the nurses and doctors upon whom they are dependent; they may form an opinion that a particular nurse is "friendly," that another is "clumsy," or that a certain doctor is "skillful and trustworthy." Similarly, staff members also form attitudes and opinions about their patients. One is thought to be a "nuisance," while a second is "always cooperative." Although the ideology of patient care at Hadassah emphasizes egalitarianism, both patients and staff members sometimes do attribute or explain behavior in ethnic terms. More specifically, if a Jewish patient is pointedly brusque with an Arab nurse he or she may be thought of as "not liking Arabs"; or, to cite the contrary case, should an Arab nurse seem to be "tough" with a Jewish patient this may be taken as a signal of the nurse's anti-Israeli sentiments. Arab staff members may also indicate their identification with Arab patients—a word, shrug, or wink of recognition means that the Arab patient is not alone in a Jewish hospital. Messages such as these are exchanged in various hospital encounters, and they provide nuances of meaning to otherwise universalistic forms of social interaction. Ethnic-group membership is therefore not entirely irrelevant to social exchanges between staff and patients; it flows around the edges of many of these contacts, radiating signals that alternately separate some persons and join others together.

In addition to signaling, patients may at times seek to cross ethnic boundaries. Earlier we saw that while the boundaries between Arabs and Jews in Jerusalem are tightly drawn, in certain circumstances individuals shift their identity from one ethnic group to the other. The hospital is a particularly fertile environment for changes in identity. At certain levels the hospital generates an intense, highly personal social environment in which, in contrast with other Jerusalem settings, Jews and Arabs are in close, regular social contact. In addition, the hospital is a "total institution" in which all of the actors, both staff and patients, are required to conform to norms over which they have little effective control. The pressures for conformity are consequently repeated and intense. Moreover, it is a stressful environment with repeated crises of life and death, and this too magnifies the element of personal identification and, in unusual circumstances, shifts in ethnic identity.

Not surprisingly, these changes tend to flow in one direction: it is typically the Arabs who adopt a Jewish or Israeli identity. Among the patients, these shifts are likely to take place in Arabs who are seriously ill and therefore hospitalized for long periods of time. Informants recall a number of Arab youngsters in particular who appeared to become "more Jewish" over time. These Arab youngsters were admitted to Hadassah with high expectations and equally grave anxieties; they had previously been treated (without success) at an Arab hospital, and their uncertainty and anxiety stemmed from being admitted to Hadassah, a Jewish hospital. The longer they remained there the more likely they were to learn and adopt new patterns of behavior. Some began to speak Hebrew, played with the Jewish children in the ward, and modeled their behavior after them; one child even adopted a Jewish name and insisted on being called by that name. Within the "total-institution" hospital environment some of the Arab youngsters sought to "become Jews."

Identity changes may also take place among the Arab members of the hospital staff. Generally speaking, most of the Arab staff members are thoroughly familiar with Israeli culture; nearly all are Israeli Arabs, born and reared in Israel, and many are also graduates of Hadassah's medical or nursing schools. Their behavior is in practically all respects identical to that of their Israeli Jewish colleagues: they speak Hebrew freely and with little trace of an accent, dress and comport themselves alike, and they also follow the hospital's norm of strict professionalism. Indeed, while at work the Arab staff members may call themselves by Hebrew names; Ibrahim, the Arab medical resident, was known as "Avi," a Jewish name, by his Jewish and Arab colleagues. Small wonder then that he was shocked when insulted by a Jewish patient: following years of medical training and successful identification he had again become an Arab in a Jewish hospital. This experience has been shared by other Arab members of the medical staff, and the nurses in particular: many of them adopted Hebrew names, yet they too report being periodically "reminded" that they were Arabs in a Jewish environment.

JEWS AND ARABS IN OTHER ROLES

In addition to contacts between *holim* and *metaplim*, there also are frequent social interchanges between persons within each of these categories. Jews and Arabs interact both as patients and as members of the medical staff. What features characterize these exchanges?

There are, generally speaking, few sustained social contacts among patients. Various reasons can be cited for this. Patients are hospitalized for different periods of time; frequent turnover affords little opportunity to make contact. The assignment to a particular bed is made by chance, and one's immediate neighbors change. Many patients are in pain or depressed by medicines and lengthy illnesses, and they do not wish to converse with the others. To be sure, patients often exchange stories regarding their illnesses and experiences, or sit together and converse while they watch television. But these are, in most instances, limited social encounters.

This is equally the case for all of the patients, both Arabs and Jews. Social contacts across ethnic lines are normally even more fragmented: the language barrier separates many of them, and even though some Jews are fluent in Arabic and some Arabs speak Hebrew, their contacts are usually limited. In some instances the Jewish patients may be hostile or resentful of the fact that they are in the same room as Arabs, or that they are being treated by Arab staff members: "I didn't know that there were so many Arabs here," is commonly heard. Similarly, Arab patients, who understand little Hebrew or are confused and uncertain regarding hospital procedures, withdraw and have no interest in attempting to converse with Jewish patients. During visiting hours family members and friends often stand in clusters; one can observe groups of Arab villagers gathered around the bed of a hospitalized family member, just as in the next bed an equally large group of Jewish family members visits with a member of their family. Persons in both groups peer at one another with interest or caution—but there is little in the way of contact between them.

The situation is different for those patients who are hospitalized for longer periods of time. They often become better acquainted with each other, exchange information as well as books or newspapers, and take a more active interest in the events taking place in their corner of the hospital. They may gossip about changes in staffing arrangements, or join in the celebration of a birth in the family of one of the patients or staff members. These more extensive bonds also extend between Arab and Jewish patients. To cite a common example, Jewish and Arab youngsters are commonly hospitalized together in the children's ward. They may have beds next to each other, sit and watch television programs together, and may take part in activities organized by the teacher assigned to the ward. Their parents also spend a great deal of time in the ward, and they too may come to recognize one another and exchange small favors. The mother of a Jewish patient may ask an Arab mother to watch her child while she leaves for a moment to make a telephone call. The children themselves tend to play with one another without barriers or restrictions. Of course, parental attitudes influence a child's behavior: Jewish parents who are reluctant to have their children play with an Arab youngster (or vice versa) manage to effectively communicate this to their children. As one informant reported:

> One evening I wanted to remain with my son who was not feeling well, and an Arab mother who was there, and who had been sleeping in an unused bed nearby, offered the bed to me. It was really sweet of her. We had become friendly since we both spent so much time here at the hospital. But I just could not bring myself to sleep on the same bed that she had been using. I know that it sounds silly, but I just could not do it.

Contacts are often limited by the perceptions and prejudices that each group has regarding the other. Even in these special "liminal" circumstances, the ethnic boundaries do not dissolve.

There are, finally, many contacts between the Arab and Jewish members of the medical staff. Indeed, in contrast with the patients the nurses and doctors enter into comparatively intense, long-term social exchanges with one another.

These contacts are, to begin with, eminently professional. In their daily routines the staff's focus of attention is concentrated upon medical matters. Work assignments do not take into account whether on a particular shift the nurses will be Jews or Arabs, nor is the medical diagnosis suggested by an Arab doctor viewed differently from that suggested by his Jewish peers.

One would be hard-pressed to discover significant behavioral differences between Arab and Jewish staff members. The nurses, for example, all dress alike, carry on the same conversations with one another and with the patients, and exhibit common concerns regarding pain or food—irrespective of whether they are Arabs or Jews. Of course, this does not mean that all of the medical personnel are alike, or that they behave in identical ways; but the differences between them are not necessarily linked to ethnicity.

While there seem to be effective collegial relations in many of Hadassah's departments, social ties between members of the staff do not normally continue outside of the hospital setting. To be sure, some staff members have become close friends and visit one another after work—but these are unusual cases, and with the exception of an occasional party or celebration staff members do not gather together outside of work. This pertains to both Arabs and Jews, all of whom are invited to take part in occasional social gatherings although they typically socialize separately with their own friends and companions.

In keeping with this professional orientation, within the hospital the staff members concentrate their attention upon medical topics and hospital events. During a break for coffee or at a staff meeting, they discuss new medical techniques and procedures, argue about their salaries and those of other doctors, or entertain themselves with hospital gossip. Political topics are rarely discussed; staff members often repeat the phrase that they "should not mix medicine with politics." As was noted earlier, the Jewish personnel include those with both right- and left-leaning political sympathies. These partisans consciously avoid political discussions. Not only do they maintain that political views have nothing to do with "good medicine," they also sense that political arguments might lead to divisions within the staff. Similarly, the Arab and Jewish staff members also avoid political discussions: they worry that their attitudes are so different that discussions will interfere with their routine medical tasks.

As a consequence the Jewish and Arab nurses and doctors are generally unaware of each other's actual political outlook. Even though they might work closely with one another while treating a wounded Israeli soldier or an Arab student injured in a political demonstration, they rarely exchange ideas or opinions. At the same time, however, they form opinions of the others' political orientation; that is, like the patients they too are sensitive to "signals" that presumably indicate their colleagues' real political outlook. In the course of events this uncertainty sometimes leads to tense, complicated situations. To cite one example, the son of a veteran Jewish nurse was killed in the Lebanese War. She later described how her Arab colleagues were uncertain of the proper way to respond to her grief; they wished to express their own personal sympathy, but, she said, they were uncertain regarding her reaction to their statements of sympathy. The Jewish nurse was herself aware that her Arab colleagues were avoiding her, and that none of them had spoken to her about her loss. Finally, they came to visit her and spoke quietly of their concern and sadness. In this particular instance the Arab staff members had wished to speak out—and the Jewish nurse had expected their expressions of condolence. Their mutual uncertainties and apprehensions had, in effect, made their relationship more complicated.

Judging from the depiction presented thus far, relationships between the Jewish and Arab staff members appear to be generally positive: the emphasis upon professional codes of conduct, as well as the shared Israeli cultural features, result in a wide base of mutual understandings. Indeed, social relationships develop with a good deal of spontaneity and harmony. Still, there is at least one significant area in which tensions and misunderstandings persist. This has to do with the issue of hierarchy and social status within the hospital. The question is whether at Hadassah, a Jewish hospital, Arab staff members can move to high-level positions of responsibility. Is mobility in the hospital system dependent upon professional accomplishments or ethnic-group membership?

The evidence is mixed and not entirely conclusive. The numbers are small and the period of time (1977–1983) is brief. Nonetheless, the evidence does suggest a number of conclusions. During the period of our research there were four Arab doctors at the hospital; two were young men doing their medical residency, one had been attached to a ward for several years, and the fourth was a senior surgeon. The residents and the young Arab doctor were not permanently attached to the hospital; still, if their performance was at a high level they might receive a permanent appointment at Hadassah. The more interesting case is that of the surgeon. There seems to be no question of his professional qualifications; he was highly regarded by the staff, and in addition to his work at Hadassah he was also attached to several Arab hospitals on the West Bank. The question is whether he, an East Jerusalem Arab, might reasonably aspire to become professor of medicine and chairman of his department at Hadassah Hospital.

Before attempting to answer this question let us consider the Arab nurses. There were seventeen Arab nurses working at the hospital at the time of the study; they were assigned to five of the hospital's departments, and in some instances had been at Hadassah for five or more years. None of them had been appointed as head nurse although one of the Arabs had become deputy head nurse. Hadassah's administrative procedure for promotion in rank is that when a vacancy exists persons announce their candidacy; the decision is made by an appointment committee that includes the hospital's head nurse plus several other medical and administrative personnel. Although in the past Arabs have been candidates for the position of head nurse, during the period of research none were selected.

This suggests, at the least, that a serious problem exists: while Arabs are employed at Hadassah in professional positions, they apparently can advance slowly, if at all in the medical hierarchy. The Arab surgeon may become the head of his department at an Arab hospital, but it is doubtful that he can attain that position at Hadassah. The same apparently is true for the Arab nurses. However devoted they may be, or however excellent their medical skills, thus far they have not been promoted to important positions. This is a delicate issue, and one that troubles some of the Jewish staff members as well as the Arabs themselves. The Jews feel that they are caught in a dilemma—they believe in professionalism and medical equality, but wonder if Jewish staff members and patients will accept an Arab as department head or head nurse. For the Arabs, the problem is much more immediate and abrasive: no matter how professional their skills and performance, will they always be relegated to lower-level positions in a Jewish hospital?

Some of the Arab staff members have resolved this problem by leaving Hadassah. Frustrated by their failure to be promoted, they seek positions in Arab hospitals in East Jerusalem or elsewhere in the Arab world. They may leave with bitter feelings against the hospital staff—even though, at the same time, their experience at Hadassah helps them gain good positions in other places. Thus, in part at least, the problems of status for Arab medical staff members have brought about an exodus of qualified Arabs from the hospital: their experience at Hadassah leads some to conclude that they can only advance within an Arab hospital.

In drawing this chapter to a close, it is instructive to view the bread factory and the hospital comparatively. While they differ in a variety of ways, there are many important parallels between Nimrod and Hadassah. Both are moderate-sized, hierarchically organized workplaces. More importantly, both are settings where large numbers of Arabs and Jews are in continuing interaction. In addition, the two are owned and organized by Jews. According to the realities of present-day Jerusalem each is defined as a "Jewish" establishment. What conclusions can be drawn?

The immediate conclusion is that Jews and Arabs do successfully cooperate with one another while at work. Surely a major finding of our study is that while baking bread or caring for patients, Arabs and Jews bridge the differences that often divide them. Even though members of the two groups may have different norms and values, and, more importantly, antagonistic political viewpoints, they are able to work effectively with each other. In part, as has been emphasized, this is made possible by avoiding political discussions ("we come here to work, not to talk politics"), and to an even greater extent by the fact that relationships are limited to the workplace itself. What this means is that members of both groups have real incentives and interests in working together. There are tangible economic rewards for all of those employed, and in addition, the hospital's emphasis upon medical professionalism also enables Arab and Jewish staff members to work together smoothly. Both places also experience similar strains and crises. Conflicts cannot always be kept out, and what is more, when Arabs are in authority roles within Jewish establishments this sets off powerful tensions. In the face of these and other problems, however, the success of these workplaces in maintaining cooperation is certainly impressive.

The question is how this should be understood or interpreted within the broader system of Jewish-Arab relationships: what implications should be drawn from the fact that an Arab surgeon operates on Jewish patients, or that, on occasion, an Arab foreman gives orders to Jewish workers in a Jewish-owned factory?

Two conclusions are indicated. First, cooperation between Arabs and Jews in workplaces suggests that the overall design of post-1967 Jewish-Arab relations may be well founded: that is, members of both groups are willing to meet in the workplace while, at the same time, they maintain separate services and continue to have opposed political aspirations. As long as they do not "talk politics," Arab and Jewish nationalists are prepared to work side by side. This leads to a second conclusion: working with one another does not necessarily lead to enhanced cooperation or interaction in any other arena. Jews and Arabs may agree to work with each other, but the post-1967 experience indicates that this has little effect upon their social or political attitudes and expectations. To be sure, some of the Jews and Arabs have also formed friendships that extend beyond the workplace, and in some rare instances ethnic identities have also shifted. But these represent a small number of cases; the general pattern appears to be one in which relationships formed at work rarely transfer to other contexts. These do not become multiplex relations, and they do not lead to broader forms of association based on strong mutual interests. What is more, work contacts seem to have little impact upon political attitudes or political events. Jews and Arabs may cooperate as staff and patients at Hadassah, but there is little evidence to suggest that these interactions lead to exchanges in any other sphere. For the present, these are islands of cooperation in a larger sea of tension and hostility.

CHAPTER 8

The Political Process: Politics in a Divided City

GOVERNING JERUSALEM as a Jewish-Arab city raises a series of complicated problems. The conflicts are deep and obvious: Jerusalem Arabs consider themselves to be in a condition of military conquest by Israeli forces, while Jews think of "united Jerusalem" as an Israeli city, the proper culmination of a lengthy historical process. Based upon these opposing views, Israel imposed its municipal government and police power upon Arab East Jerusalem, while the Arab population, in turn, rejected Israeli rule. The fact that Jerusalem is symbolically a holy religious city for both groups only aggravates these tensions. Political polarization seems, in short, to be total and complete.

These basic realities pose questions regarding the political process, or, to be more candid, whether a Jewish-Arab political process can even be said to exist. Phrasing it differently, one can ask whether Jerusalem's Arabs and Jews are linked within a common political system. If so, what are the components of this system, and how has it functioned in the period following the city's reunification? Finally, what are the consequences of these political arrangements, and how are they likely to fare in the future?

In contrast with many other cities, political issues in Jerusalem commonly involve several different layers of authority—municipal, national, and even, in the case of this Holy City, international. In practical terms what this means is that ordinary, simple-sounding matters such as granting a building permit may involve not just city officials, but also national cabinet-level ministers in Israel and Jordan and various international groups (church organizations, the United Nations, and others). The decision-making process thereby includes, in addition to municipal officials and their staffs, a great many others, all of whom are connected in complicated webs of negotiation, alliance, and, in many instances, dispute. Our study focuses primarily upon the municipal level. Although attention will also be given to how local actors are connected with other groups and interests, our main concern is with the interactions between the local Jerusalem actors, both Jews and Arabs, themselves. As will soon be evident, the issues that concern us have to do with problems of everyday city government, rather than Jerusalem as a fulcrum for Israeli or Palestinian national politics or Jerusalem as an international diplomatic issue.

DEFINING THE CONTEXT

Some features of the framework of Arab-Jewish political contacts have already been suggested. They need to be further clarified and elaborated, however; the political context is complex, ambiguous, and not the least, laden with ironies.

East Jerusalem Arabs have a dual political status: they are both citizens of Jordan and residents of Israeli Jerusalem. They live in Jerusalem, but at the same time they also maintain ties with their families and others who live in Jordan or in other Arab countries, as well as with the Jordanian state authorities. In common with Arabs who live in the nearby West Bank towns and villages, Jerusalem Arabs may apply to the Israeli authorities for permission to cross to Jordan, and then, following a family visit or business trip, they may return again to their homes in Jerusalem. What makes this simple-sounding behavior so unusual is the fact that, since 1949, Jordan and Israel have not had formal diplomatic relations. On the contrary, the two nations do not recognize each other, and the West Bank areas occupied since 1967 by Israeli forces are also claimed by Jordan. Israeli citizens, both Jews and Arabs, cannot travel to Jordan, although Jordanians can enter Israel or Israeli-occupied territory after receiving permission (thousands of Jordanians regularly cross the border and travel throughout Israel).[1] Paradoxically, even though there is a formal state of war between the two countries, Arabs who have Israeli identity cards travel in Jordan, just as Jordanian citizens may travel in Israel.

But the ambiguity is still deeper. In addition to private family contacts and visits, some state-level relations have also been maintained or established: in a number of complicated ways the Jordanian authorities have continued to be involved in issues and decisions regarding Arab interests in Jerusalem. The Jordanians have not recognized Israeli sovereignty; they have instead often acted as if they themselves exercised political rights in East Jerusalem. This Jordanian involvement centers primarily upon issues relating to the Muslim holy places, but it has extended as well to such topics as Arab education, local development, and taxation. Moreover, the Israelis have frequently been willing to hold informal discussions with Jordanian authorities or their representatives on a broad variety of local topics. Even though Israel annexed East Jerusalem and does not recognize Jordan's claims to control, discussions and negotiations have taken place between Israeli and Jordanian officials at different levels regarding many Jerusalem issues.

[1] The exceptions are Israeli Muslim Arabs who have recently been allowed to cross into Jordan on their way to Mecca in Saudi Arabia. Several thousand Israeli Arabs have taken part in the traditional haj to Mecca; they apparently are kept separate from other Muslim pilgrims in both Jordan and Mecca itself.

There is, finally, yet another level of complexity to this pattern. Israel's occupation of Jerusalem was immediately met by a total strike of Arab municipal workers; they were joined by the Jerusalem Arab teachers, lawyers, and judges, all of whom were employees of the Jordanian government. However, the municipal workers later returned to their jobs, and have since continued to be employed by the Israeli municipality. Some of the teachers also returned, but many of the lawyers and judges remained "on strike"; since that time their salaries have been paid by the Jordanian government, who in this and other ways has maintained its involvement in Jerusalem affairs. In effect, several hundred East Jerusalem Arabs were employed by the Jordanian government while "on strike" against the Israeli occupation. As can readily be appreciated, the continued Jordanian presence in Jerusalem has been, at one and the same time, both concrete and a fiction.

The Arab city council members also refused to take part in municipal affairs. This has meant that, since 1967, Jerusalem has been governed by a city council composed entirely of Jewish members, while Arabs have taken no part in formal city government or administrative processes. A minority of East Jerusalem Arabs have voted in the local elections held since 1967—yet none of them has agreed to run for election or to hold formal municipal office. During the lengthy period of time since the city's unification Jerusalem has undergone rapid changes, but, rejecting Israeli rule, thousands of Arab residents have had no direct voice in municipal decision making.

Not only have they refused to take part in the formal political process, many Arabs in East Jerusalem have also maintained their allegiance to Palestinian nationalist groups that actively, and sometimes violently, oppose Israel. Political interests, sensitivities, and debates are highly developed and intense among the Arab minority; a growing number of Arab newspapers and journals are published and distributed in East Jerusalem; the Old City coffee shops and stalls buzz with political talk and gossip; and Arab schools and universities are centers of intense discussion and political activity. However, since the political views being expressed are overwhelmingly Arab or Palestinian nationalist and anti-Israel, the Israeli authorities have refused to permit any formal organization of Arab political groups. The Israeli police and security services have been extremely active in controlling Arab nationalist organizations: a number of Jerusalem Arab leaders have been exiled to Arab countries, known activist supporters of the PLO or other Palestinian nationalist groups have been arrested or required to report daily to the police, and surveillance is constantly maintained throughout the Arab community. These issues are not idle or minor in scope. Since 1967 Arab nationalist groups have placed bombs in Jewish areas of the city, and periodically too, stones or explosives were thrown at Jewish buses or cars and Jews were attacked in mainly Arab areas such as the Old City. The point to be emphasized is that this continuous, bitter antagonism has severely restricted the Arab-Jewish political process. By means of their legal power the Israeli state authorities have sought to prohibit and control Arab nationalist opposition, and, in turn, the Arab minority has refused to collaborate or take part in governing the city.

THE IDEOLOGICAL POSITIONS

In addition to the elements that have thus far been described, Jews and Arabs also hold sharply contrasting expectations and ideologies regarding their political encounters. Political attitudes and political concepts certainly influence behavior. How do members of both groups conceptualize and explain the present state of affairs?

The Arab view is that they are living under a forced military occupation. They do not recognize the legal or moral basis for Jerusalem's reunification. On the contrary, they continue to insist that it is both illegal and morally wrong. At the same time, however, practical everyday matters have led them to avail themselves of Israeli state offices and government services. This is considered to be "proper" or "legitimate" since, in effect, there are no real alternatives. Beyond this, however, Arabs have also returned to work in certain local government offices where they serve under Israeli direction. The rationale for this behavior is that since Arabs have at the moment no choice than to live under Israeli control, it is best for them to be aided or served by fellow Arab city employees. This principle does not apply to all types of work. As was also pointed out, Arab judges and lawyers refused to serve within the Israeli legal system. In effect, each area has been considered on its merits and decisions made whether an Arab can properly work under Israeli state direction.

In addition to these practical considerations, previous historical precedents also provide a basis for Jerusalem Arabs taking part in some local affairs. The general principle is that Arab political institutions that had existed under previous alien regimes may also be permitted to function during the Israeli occupation. If, for example, Arabs took part in local government under the British, then this previous precedent may legitimize continuing some particular activities while under Israeli control. This is the ideological justification under which the Supreme Muslim Council has from time to time met with the Israeli authorities; the council is seen to be a parallel with the similar body that operated during the British Mandate, and its formal negotiations with Israeli authorities are therefore considered to be legitimate.

Practicality and previous precedents are essentially implicit principles that guide Arab behavior under conditions of external conquest and control. In addition, as we have seen, a more explicit ideology or doctrine has also developed: this is the ideology of *sumud*, or in English, "steadfastness." The *sumud* doctrine enjoins Arabs in East Jerusalem and throughout the West Bank to remain in their native land and to resist the efforts of the Israeli occupiers. As Frisch and others describe it, to "remain steadfast" means not leaving Palestinian soil (in contrast with those who fled from their homes during the 1948 war) and, equally, refusing to serve the Israelis while at the same time building Palestinian institutions that will sustain the population until its final liberation from Israeli control. In its early post-1967 form the *sumud* ideology called for the freezing of all public institutional life in the territories, minimum contact with the Israeli authorities, and censure of any local moves that went contrary to Arab consensus as expressed in the Khartoum Conference in 1969.[2]

In the 1970s and 1980s, *sumud* policies were enlarged to favor more active Arab local development. Significant sums of money were made available not only to pay the salaries of Jordanian civil servants who remained on strike, but also to build new homes and schools and to support newly established Palestinian newspapers and universities. In brief, the ideology of *sumud* not only called upon Arabs to remain steadfast against their Israeli occupiers, but it also supported a series of new institutions that were designed to serve the captive population.

Israeli attitudes and policies regarding Jerusalem were, of course, totally different. The key concept for them was political sovereignty. What was to be made clear and unambiguous was that all of Jerusalem, both East and West, was under Israeli political jurisdiction and control. Once their sovereignty was established, how to effectively govern the Arab minority was essentially a matter of developing appropriate day-to-day policies.

From the Israeli point of view what emerged following 1967 were policies and practices emphasizing a kind of quiet pragmatism. The essential point has been to promote conditions in which commercial and civic life would continue, and in which Jerusalem's Arabs would go about their daily lives with at least an outward sense of normalcy. Israeli officials did not require Jerusalem Arabs to formally or symbolically acknowledge Israel's presence or power; quite to the contrary, they sometimes were sympathetic with the plight of a minority that was being forced to conform to outside control. Since Israeli hegemony was firm, they could afford to compromise and be flexible on a variety of issues, ranging from the amount of taxes Jerusalem Arabs would pay to the curriculum to be

---

[2] *Jerusalem Report*, Jerusalem Center for Public Affairs, July 1984, p. 2.

followed in Arab schools. In regard to these and a host of other technical details Israeli policy sought to avoid becoming dogmatic and emphasized flexibility.

Teddy Kollek, Jerusalem's mayor, has been the principal architect of Israeli policies. Kollek, who was mayor when the city was unified in 1967, has been reelected to office in the five elections held since then, and consequently more than anyone else he has personally been engaged in designing policies regarding the Arab population. To be sure, many of the key decisions regarding Jerusalem were taken at the Israeli cabinet or national level, and the mayor has not always agreed with national government policies.[3] Nonetheless, as an activist mayor Kollek has been enormously involved in the daily management of Arab-Jewish affairs; insofar as there is an Israeli ideology regarding Jerusalem's Arabs, Kollek's views have certainly been especially influential.

Quiet pragmatism and practical solutions have been the guiding principles of Kollek's administration. The orientation has been to defuse or otherwise work around the difficult, vexing problems of Arab-Jewish relations. Writing in Foreign Affairs, Kollek stated his views in the following "four principles":

> There shall be free access to all the Holy Places irrespective of nationality and they shall be administered by their adherents.
>
> Everything possible shall be done to ensure unhindered development of the Arab way of life in the Arab sections of the city and ensure Muslims and Christians a practical religious, cultural and commercial governance over their own daily lives.
>
> Everything possible shall be done to ensure equal governmental, municipal and social services in all parts of the city.
>
> Continuing efforts should be made to increase cultural, social and economic contacts among the various elements of Jerusalem's population, while preserving the cultural and even the national identity of each group.[4]

The meaning of this manifesto is clear. Within the structure of Israeli political sovereignty, the mayor wishes to guarantee a kind of minority status to the Arab population, and pledges as well to do "everything possible" to reduce inequalities between the Jewish majority and the Arab minority. Any greater integration between members of these two groups is consciously rejected; the doctrine emphasizes separation and equality,

---

[3] Interestingly, changes in Israeli national politics do not seem to have affected basic policies regarding Jewish-Arab relations in Jerusalem. Most of the same features were present under both Labor and Likud governments.

[4] Kollek 1981, p. 1042.

not integration of, say, housing and services. Indeed, Kollek has emphasized the principle of "practical yet harmonious coexistence" between Arabs and Jews as the ideal goal for Jerusalem. According to this ideology, "peaceful coexistence" (Heb. *du-kiyum beshalom*) represents not only the most that might be achieved in Jerusalem, but also meets the aspirations of both groups.

THE PATRONAGE SYSTEM

Political contacts between Arabs and Jews in Jerusalem have operated in different ways and at various levels. Along one principal dimension these contacts can be said to form a kind of patronage system: a series of Arab and Jewish broker and patron roles have emerged, and these are linked in a regular, systematic fashion.

Whether they are Israeli citizens or "residents," Jews and Arabs who live in Jerusalem all have become part of a single overall municipal administrative framework. No matter where they live, from time to time they are likely to have some concern with municipal services. There are, after all, the myriad issues and daily problems that all residents of the city are concerned with: taxation, garbage collection, cleaning the streets, providing good schools for children, checking to make certain that the water bill is correct, or applying for a building permit. The Jewish residents normally deal directly with these problems. When they have a question about their tax assessment or a complaint that trash has not been collected they go to the appropriate office and pose their query or lodge a complaint. If they have a personal friend or an acquaintance in the municipal office they may also turn informally to them. As is the case with other Israeli bureaucracies, the municipal staffs may be ponderous and inefficient—but the Jewish residents are generally aware of how to approach and deal with these officials.

The situation is different for the Arab residents. To begin with, they do not always know where the particular municipal offices are located, or what the correct procedures are to obtain official permission, in order, for example, to add a room to their home or enroll their youngsters in a particular school. Since 1967 their experience with and knowledge about Israeli officials have grown; yet many Arabs voice uncertainty regarding the procedures. Most municipal offices are located in the western portions of the city, and Arab residents may be reluctant to go there. Language is another problem. The forms to be filled out are often printed in Hebrew, and the clerks in the municipal offices may not be able to answer questions in Arabic. Previous experience may lead the Arabs to conclude that these language differences are likely to provoke complications and misunderstandings. In addition, some of the Arab residents are ideologically opposed to dealing directly with the Israeli officials. This may be taken by them or by other Arabs as a sign of their collaboration with the Israeli city government, or even as tacit approval of Israeli sovereignty. For all of these reasons many Arabs have had difficulty in communicating or negotiating with Israeli officials, and they may be reluctant to expose themselves personally to these contacts.

In addition, some of the issues and problems that concern Arab residents are politically involved or politically sensitive. To cite several examples, Arabs may wish to know why they were refused permission to cross the bridges into Jordan, or the whereabouts of a family member who has been arrested by the police. These kinds of problems may not directly involve the Jerusalem city officials, but they are likely to know where and of whom to make inquiries. In brief, in order to receive correct information and to know what actions to take, Jerusalem Arabs tend to seek the intervention of more experienced and knowledgeable persons.

It is within this social and political setting that a series of intermediary roles have emerged that connect the Arab residents of Jerusalem with municipal authorities as well as with other Israeli officials at various levels. In effect, a number of both Jewish and Arab "specialists" often deal with the administrative problems faced by local Arabs. This system includes both formal broker and patron roles that have deliberately been conceived and set into practice, as well as more informal social networks where messages are exchanged and influence may be brought to bear. This patronage system thus serves as one of the principal political bridges or links between Jerusalem's Arabs and Jews.

One group of intermediaries are the Arab clerks and officials who have continued working in the Jerusalem city offices. In many instances Arab municipal employees sit in the same offices they formerly occupied under the Jordanian regime and continue to perform the same tasks. In some instances they were joined by Jewish municipal employees who worked in the same bureau or in different departments. Arab city workers also moved to new offices in the western zone of the city, and newer Arab recruits at times joined a department where many if not most of their colleagues were Jewish workers. The point to be emphasized is that since 1967 the Jerusalem municipal offices have included several hundred Arab employees who are chiefly engaged in various low- and middle-level administrative tasks.

These Arab city workers represent one bridge between the Arab population and the city administration. Arab residents who have questions about their water bill or tax assessment, or who wish to complain about a faulty sewer connection, often turn for help to their fellow Arab city officials. Since they commonly sit in the same offices and perform the same tasks they were involved in prior to 1967, these officials have been easy to locate and communicate with. Their offices are often filled with a regular stream of persons, mainly males, who come to pay their bills or to seek information and help. There is typically a light-toned, jocular air about these inquiries. The applicants may be slightly embarrassed as they plead for direction, while the officials adopt the role of "experts" who are instructing novices. In not a few instances the city workers also may be contacted outside of their formal work hours; friends or acquaintances may visit them at home and politely ask a question, or they may even be approached on the street for their advice. In nearly all cases the advice or information is of a technical kind—where and how applications can be made to the city authorities—rather than for direct help or favors. Indeed, the Arab municipal employees have few real resources under their control; all of the higher-level executive posts are filled by Israeli Jews, and the Arab employees have little influence within the city or allied state bureaucracies. They are brokers of a modest kind rather than true patrons or influentials, and they typically do not seek to accumulate wider political influence or power. Nonetheless, they represent one important link between the Arab population and the municipal authorities.

A second level of contact has a more formal component. Historically, within villages and towns in Palestine family elders had certain responsibilities for maintaining local order and negotiating with state authorities and other officials. The male heads of the large local clans were called upon to resolve disputes between villagers, and they often acted as spokesmen when negotiations were held with various higher-level, town-based state administrators. These local headmen were called *Mukhtars*, and during the lengthy Turkish rule they were responsible for maintaining order at the village or neighborhood level. This office was subsequently taken over and even strengthened by the British; they adopted the *Mukhtar* system (it fit well with the British concept of indirect rule) and elevated it further by lending them a formal government role and a small monthly salary. Under the British each Jerusalem Arab neighborhood had its local *Mukhtar*, and in more populous districts several headmen were appointed.

The *Mukhtar* system was also adopted by the Jordanian governors of Jerusalem. The Jordanians modified the authority structure by also organizing local councils in the settled urban areas; the headman might direct these councils, but they were meant to give a wider base of representation and expression to neighborhood concerns.

This system has, in turn, been retained by the Israeli authorities. While, as we have emphasized, Arabs have refused to take a direct part in governing the city, the local *Mukhtar* has continued to be active. From their point of view they are filling an office that has a lengthy history and many precedents; they are serving under Israeli occupation and rule, but their activities are considered legitimate since the office was established, at the least, under the previous Jordanian administration. The local headman may claim or imagine that he is merely maintaining an official task that is part of the ongoing Jordanian political system. However it may be viewed, following 1967 one or several persons were selected to fill this position in each Arab neighborhood. The process of selection is informal, and members of the largest or leading families meet to select their own representative. This is not an especially honored or esteemed position, and it is often assigned to a family member who has modest organizational talents. Those selected have typically been older males, and they usually served in the position for as long a time as they were physically able.

The *Mukhtar's* position is considered slightly differently by the Israeli city officials. From their perspective the headman is expected to maintain his traditional activities; that is, he is thought to have informal responsibilities for resolving disputes between residents, collecting vital statistics regarding births and marriages, and also in representing the neighborhood residents in their discussions or negotiations with the city authorities. Moreover, under the Israeli regime each *Mukhtar* receives a modest monthly salary from the Jerusalem Municipality, and he is also given an official city document that designates him as the headman of a particular locality. Thus, for the Israeli officials he is not just a spokesman or a carryover from the previous Jordanian administration, but rather is seen to be taking a part, however minor, in the system of local Israeli government.

On a day-to-day basis the *Mukhtars*—there are about sixty of them in all—are mainly engaged in performing a classic broker role: they serve as a bridge between their families as well as other neighborhood residents and the Jerusalem city administration. The system works more or less as follows. Residents regularly bring their queries and problems to the *Mukhtar*, such as a burst water main or collapsed wall, road repairs that have been dragging on, or complaints that a permit to open a roadside store has not been received. Having listened to their questions or requests, the headman may offer his own suggestions or analysis of the situation; he may also remark whether, based upon his previous experience, the particular request is likely to be granted. Following this he proceeds to bring the issue before the proper Israeli authorities. Depending upon the problem he may approach a number of different officials. For example, problems connected with a local resident's sewerage may be brought to the Arab officials who work in Jerusalem's water or sewer department. In this case the *Mukhtar* goes to the proper office and discusses the matter with the official in charge. If he is not successful, or if the topic is not entirely technical but also has policy implications, he may bring his request to a higher level. He is likely to request a conference with the mayor's advisor on East Jerusalem affairs—a city office created to deal with the "special problems" of the Jerusalem Arab population. The advisor is likely to hear a wide range of complaints and problems. Finally, if this level of consultation does not bring the desired results, the *Mukhtar* may turn directly to the mayor of Jerusalem or to one of his principal assistants. Meetings between a local headman and the mayor or members of his staff may take place in their offices, or they may be conducted during the periodic visits made by these city officials to the various local neighborhoods.

In addition to these tasks, the local *Mukhtar* is also supposed to be a participant in a number of ceremonial occasions. When Israeli city government or other officials visit his neighborhood, the headman (or several of them) receives the official visitors. They are welcomed into his home, offered coffee and sweets, and exchange conversation and pleasantries. On certain occasions the *Mukhtar* and members of his family may also be the hosts of a large, ceremonial meal where the mayor and his advisor are guests; the leading male family elders are expected to take part in these festivities, and the meal is followed by brief speeches in which both the *Mukhtar* and his Israeli guests dwell upon the problems and needs of the local Arab community. They are also expected to attend the yearly fetes organized by the mayor; these include large official ceremonies that are held during the major Muslim holidays, as well as an open house reception that is annually arranged by the mayor on Israel Independence Day. These various occasions may also be opportunities for a headman to ply his skills as a broker. When he is the host to the mayor or to his advisor, or even while he is a guest at some ceremonial occasion, he may find an appropriate moment for diplomatically requesting help for some neighborhood project or a more private family matter. Moreover, by taking part in the festivities organized by the mayor a *Mukhtar* is also publicly signaling his willingness to meet with Israeli officials. These official, open public gatherings are meant to demonstrate the possibilities of peaceful coexistence between Jews and Arabs in Jerusalem.

Although the previous description focused mainly upon the activities of the Arab political actors, mention was also made of two Israeli figures: the mayor of Jerusalem and his advisor on East Jerusalem affairs. In an important sense these two are the principal city officials who are in contact with the headman or other Jerusalem Arab representatives. To be sure, on many occasions some other city officials as well as Israeli government officials will have contacts with one or another of the Arab brokers, but political negotiations and exchanges are mainly concentrated around these two persons.

We begin by examining the role and activities of the mayor's advisor on East Jerusalem affairs. This is a comparatively new office. It was established in 1967 in order to provide a framework for considering and dealing with the "special problems" of the Arab East Jerusalem population. There is no parallel advisor on West Jerusalem affairs. The Jewish population is presumably served by the city's normal administrative apparatus and consequently it needs no separate office or special treatment. The assumption that underlies this position is consequently twofold: first, it supposes that the imposition of Israeli rule has produced problems for the Arab population that can best be dealt with by forming a special office within the city administration; and second, that it is most expeditious for this office to be directly linked to the mayor. This is not just an "office for Arab affairs," but rather it is under the immediate direction of the mayor. The advisor's office is located in a building close to the mayor's offices, and he is in continuous close touch with the mayor and his principal assistants.

The idea of having a special "advisor on Arab affairs" in the mayor's office was apparently based upon a similar arrangement within the Israeli national government. Since the early 1950s the Israeli prime minister has had an advisor on Arab affairs attached to his office. The prime minister's advisor deals with broad questions of policy regarding the Israeli Arab minority, and is also in a position to dispense patronage benefits to Arab communities as well as individuals. The prime minister's advisor has typically been an Israeli Jew who is an expert or scholar on Arab society (what in Israel is called an "Arabist") and who, together with a small staff, provides the prime minister with information, requests, and policy recommendations. The mayor's advisor in Jerusalem was modeled after this office. The idea was to provide the mayor with a specialist who could advise him on issues regarding the Jerusalem Arab population, and who would also undertake certain administrative as well as political tasks. In addition, the office was allotted a special budget that could be used for neighborhood development projects such as installing a local sewer system or paving roads. Since its inception in 1967 the advisor's role has been filled by five different persons. Each of the advisors has been an Israeli Jew, conversant with Arabic and Muslim custom, and who presumably possessed the expert knowledge and proper flair for working with both the mayor and members of the Jerusalem Arab population.

The advisor works from a modest suite of offices. He heads a small staff made up of a secretary and several assistants; the assistants—municipal employees who have worked in the office for many years—include both Arabs and Jews. The Jewish assistants are fluent in Arabic, and they and their Arab colleagues work together in solving problems connected with providing municipal services to the Arab zones of the city.

The advisor is involved in a broad range of activities. As the mayor's principal expert on the Arab Jerusalem population, he seeks to keep up-to-date in regard to persons and affairs in East Jerusalem; he pores over the Arab-language press and regularly exchanges information and gossip with other well-informed persons, both Jews and Arabs, in an effort to understand the complex, shifting social and political map of Arab East Jerusalem. He also keeps abreast of family quarrels and commercial intrigues, seeking to understand the sometimes subtle messages that indicate whether a particular person is a "moderate" or an "extremist," or what *really* lies behind an application to form a new sports club for Arab youngsters. Such information (and a great deal more) is necessary in order to properly advise the mayor. The mayor may not follow his advice, but he regularly calls upon the advisor to interpret the political meaning behind Arab requests or behavior.

The advisor also represents the mayor and the municipality in numerous wider forums that deal with issues relating to the Arab Jerusalem population. For example, as the mayor's representative he may meet with officials of the Israeli Ministry of Housing who are planning new residential zones in East Jerusalem, or with representatives of the police and army to discuss problems of terrorism or police protection. He is also involved in consultations regarding sudden crises. The mayor contacts him prior to deciding how the municipality should respond to a strike of East Jerusalem merchants, or how to react to Jewish nationalists who are planning to hold religious services within the Muslim holy places.

While these and other policy matters are of concern to the advisor, on a daily basis he and his staff deal with more mundane administrative matters. During the day their offices are often crowded with East Jerusalem residents who have come to make inquiries or to ask for help. Typically they include a wide variety of residents as well as a broad range of requests. The local *Mukhtars* are especially frequent visitors. Many come to his office early in the morning to raise some issue or describe a grievance that has arisen in their neighborhoods. The advisor listens politely to the complaint or problem, asks additional questions, summons one of his aides for a brief consultation, and then, depending upon the issue, he places a phone call to one of the Israeli government offices, or drafts a letter or a brief note to an official he thinks can be helpful, or politely defers and indicates that "nothing can be done about this problem." Together with his assistants he often spends part of the day visiting the Arab neighborhoods. They may drive to an area where a special project financed by their office is underway, check to see that road repairs that had been promised have in fact been made, or visit with one of the headmen and later inspect the roads or schools in his area.

The advisor is a member of the mayor's personal staff. Although he heads a separate office and controls a small budget, he is appointed by the mayor and serves directly under him. The point to be emphasized is that the advisor derives his authority entirely from the mayor. His is not an independent political office where power and prerogatives may be accumulated and used, but instead his position and influence depend upon the mayor's support and agreement.

This brings us to the question of the mayor's political role and activities. As has already been implied, his position is a critical one within the Arab-Jewish political pattern; more than that, he plays the pivotal role in the political system that has evolved since 1967.

Following a reform of Israeli municipal elections, since 1978 the Jerusalem system of government has been based upon direct election of both the mayor and the city council. The mayor is elected by the voters from among a list of candidates, and the city councilors are also elected at large rather than as representatives of particular districts. (In the previous system the mayor was elected by the city council members rather than directly by the voters.) The candidates at both levels are usually selected by the local branches of national political parties. In Jerusalem, for example, candidates for the offices of mayor and for the city council are selected by the Labor party, the Likud party, the National Religious party, the ultraorthodox Agudat Israel party, and several others. Since the mayor is directly elected and wields executive power, he may have considerable influence within the council. The latter must approve budgets and major policies, but a strong popularly elected mayor can have a decisive influence on local affairs.

In the period between 1965 and the present, Jerusalem has had a single mayor. The fact that Kollek has been mayor throughout this period has meant that his policies and concept of the office, as well as his own particular style and personality, have been fulcrum pieces in the Arab-Jewish political system. This is an important point in that there are a number of important personality and idiosyncratic features to the political arrangements that have emerged in united Jerusalem.

Kollek's political style is open and active. From early in the morning he is busy visiting in the different corners of the city, just as throughout the day and into the evening he bustles through a long series of meetings, ceremonies, political negotiations, and conversations with visiting celebrities or wealthy donors to special Jerusalem projects. In his office at city hall or during conversations at some official occasion he has successfully cultivated the image of a mayor who is humane, fair, and approachable. A parade of persons comes to the mayor's office—both Jews and Arabs— to ask for his intervention. The mayor has not only developed a wide series of personal contacts and acquaintances ("everybody knows

Teddy!"), but he has also been close to the daily concerns and problems of Jerusalem's exceptionally mixed population.

Although his advisor and other assistants work with the Arab population on a daily basis, the mayor has also devoted considerable time to direct contact with the Arab minority population. He is practically always present on official occasions—the dedication of a school, presenting formal credentials to a newly appointed *Mukhtar*, or installing a new extension of the city water system—and in these contexts he meets both formally and informally with the assembled Arab residents. Kollek does not speak or understand Arabic very well, and consequently his talks in Hebrew are translated or he speaks to the group in English. Nonetheless, his message seems to be conveyed in convincing personal terms. His speeches are direct, brief, and plainly spoken. When meeting with an Arab audience the mayor typically speaks about practical local problems and the ways he plans to solve them, and avoids more controversial political or ideological themes.

In addition to being an activist, as mayor of Jerusalem Kollek has also championed policies that would advance his doctrine of *du kiyum be-shalom* ("peaceful coexistence"). Even though his positions have not always been popular and are frequently criticized, he has adopted a strategy of moderation that would, presumably, guarantee Israeli sovereignty in Jerusalem while at the same time encouraging the Arab minority to live in peace and to prosper. As we have seen, under his administration the vast majority of public funds have been invested in the Jewish areas of the city, yet at the same time various development projects have also been undertaken in Arab areas. In fact, in a number of cases Kollek's administration has initiated or supported policies that were presumed to be in the Arab interest. For example, in describing Arab-Jewish land disputes in Beit Safafa (chapter 3), it was pointed out that the Jerusalem Municipality actively sided with the Arab residents in their court case against those Jews who had, in effect, illegally seized Arab homes. To cite a rather different case, following the 1967 war some Jerusalem Arab residents wished to erect a monument to the Arab soldiers who had been killed. Symbolic as it was, the Arab desire to place wreaths at a monument honoring fallen Arab soldiers aroused substantial Jewish opposition. Jerusalem was now an Israeli city, the opponents said, and there was no place in it for an Arab war memorial. Kollek gave his support to the Arab plan. He argued that there were monuments to the dead Jewish soldiers, and that the Arab residents had the right to honor their own fallen warriors. The mayor's view prevailed, and a simple monument to the Arab war dead was subsequently built.

As can readily be seen in these examples, since 1967 the mayor has given his support to policies that presumably would foster the practical interests of both Arabs and Jews. From his vantage point, the emphasis is upon pragmatic decision making that avoids ideological issues or disputes. The fundamental facts of Israeli physical control and hegemony over all of Jerusalem remain undisputed. These "fundamental facts" are, of course, not lost on the Arab population: while Arabs may have a grudging admiration for Kollek, they recognize that pragmatism is a tactic that leaves Israeli political control undisturbed. Quiet pragmatism may be preferable to unremitting Israeli police or Jewish ultranationalist pressures—but "peaceful coexistence," many Arabs would argue, is an ideology that cloaks what is, in the last analysis, the Israeli occupation of Arab Jerusalem.

It will be useful to pause and consider some of the implications of the political system that have thus far been described. What we have been calling the patronage system refers to a series of exchanges between Arabs and Jews in which Arab Jerusalem residents seek out specialist or well-placed, powerful persons who are asked to intervene on their behalf within the Israeli municipal and national bureaucracies. Not surprisingly, this system conforms well with the prevailing Jewish and Arab ideologies. Since *sumud* instructs the Arabs to "endure" the Israeli occupation, it is legitimate for a *Mukhtar* to bring a neighbor's problems before the advisor. Paradoxically, the Israeli advisor's help in resolving the issue may assist the Arab resident to "endure." Similarly, assisting local Arabs to cope with the Israeli bureaucracies or sponsoring neighborhood development projects is fully in keeping with the Israeli doctrine of peaceful coexistence.

What is more, the patronage system also encourages political moderation and dependency. Patronage systems are, by their very nature, conservative. the brokers and patrons who act as intermediaries have a solid stake in the existing political system, and neither they nor their clients are striving for radical changes. In the case of Jerusalem, the patronage system is certainly composed of moderates. In general, the more radical, nationalist Arab residents reject contacts with the Israeli authorities, and consequently both the headmen and others who come to the advisor's office, or who make an appointment to see the mayor, have a more moderate leaning. Moreover, to some degree the advisor's response to a request also depends upon who is asking; the Israeli authorities are more sympathetic to the problems and requests of Arabs who are known to be "moderate." This does not mean that the health problems or water supply difficulties of Arabs known to be Palestinian nationalists will be disregarded, or that each Arab request for intervention is first evaluated politically. But the response to certain persons and their problems is influenced by what is known about their political attitudes. In addition, the inherently dependent nature of the system should also be clear. Patronage in any of its forms is a political system that accentuates dependency, and Jerusalem is hardly an exception. The advisor as expeditor may assist Arabs in resolving their problems—but the creation of a special office that funnels Arab requests means that they are generally unable to resolve these issues on their own (as the Jewish population does) and are expected to depend upon intermediaries.

It is also important to point out that in this patronage system the networks of political contact are not wide-ranging; Arab clients in search of assistance or favors do not regularly come in contact with a broad array of Israeli Jewish officials. On the contrary, the links are compressed and limited to a small number of persons. The effect of this, of course, is once more to limit contacts and exchanges between members of the two groups.

There is, finally, yet another dimension to this patronage system. If patronage is understood as an exchange relationship, then what exactly is being exchanged between the brokers and their clients, or even more specifically, between an Arab headman and the Jewish advisor? Certainly the *Mukhtar* receives the personal assistance or intervention of the advisor, but how does he reciprocate?

To a considerable degree the *Mukhtar*'s very presence in the advisor's office, or the agreement to negotiate with the Israeli authorities, constitutes an "exchange." That is, by agreeing to take part in these relations the *Mukhtars* are exchanging a public, tacit recognition of Israeli sovereignty for the assistance rendered them by the advisor and others. From the Israeli point of view, their participation is its own reward. Beyond this, however, there are some more tangible features to the exchange relationship.

Political patronage systems are based upon clients' lending support to their patron. To put it differently, those who are assisted by a broker or a patron are expected to "return the favor" by expressing political support.[5] In fact, patronage machines throughout the world are based upon the expectation that clients, who regularly receive assistance, will return the favor by supporting the machine's candidates. Patronage in Jerusalem is no exception. The Arab residents, who are legally entitled to vote in local elections, are mobilized to support those who have helped them in the periodic elections for mayor and city council.

Beginning with the 1969 elections for mayor and city council, a minority of Arabs have voted for Israeli candidates for office. In his book, *Jerusalem, the Torn City*, Benvenisti, who was then the mayor's advisor on

[5] The literature on political patronage is, of course, enormous. Gellner and Waterbury's *Patrons and Clients* (1977) provides analyses of patronage systems in contemporary Mediterranean societies.

Arab affairs, describes the anxiety felt by Jewish political leaders before those elections took place. Palestinian nationalist groups as well as the Jordanian government had for weeks urged the Arab residents to boycott the elections; would Arab voters come to the polls in the face of nationalist threats?[6] As table 8.1 demonstrates, slightly more than 20 percent of the eligible Arab voters turned out in those elections, and while the proportion dropped in the 1973 elections that closely followed the Yom Kippur War, in two subsequent elections the numbers rose again. Most Israeli political commentators have taken this to be a mark of success: while the majority of Arab residents choose not to vote in Jerusalem elections, a minority did elect to go to the polls.

The months preceding elections are a period of concerted political activity in Jerusalem. The style of campaigning is rather different in the Jewish and Arab sections of the city. In West Jerusalem and generally among Jewish voters, prior to the elections the principal political parties hold many small "parlor meetings" where the candidates meet with potential supporters. Toward the end of the campaign large public rallies are also held. What are considered to be modern election techniques are followed. Residential districts are subdivided into smaller voting districts, and party activists equipped with computer printouts of potential supporters are responsible for bringing the party faithful to the voting booths. Posters announcing the candidates and their parties are plastered throughout the area, and on election day fleets of cars and taxis are mobilized to make certain that everyone on the list votes.

The organization is rather different among the Arab voters in East Jerusalem. Computer printouts may be available there too, and the parties may also attempt to organize meetings prior to the election. However, most of the electioneering effort consists of personal contacts. A small

TABLE 8.1
Arab Voting for the Jerusalem Mayor
in Municipal Elections, 1969–1983

Year	No. of Eligible Voters	No. Voting	%
1969	35,000	7,500	21.5
1973	43,000	3,150	7.3
1978	56,000	8,000	14.4
1983	63,090	11,603	18.4

Sources: Benvenisti 1981; Israeli Ministry of Interior, unpublished data.

[6] See Benvenisti 1976.

corps of Arab activists is mobilized to "bring out the vote" among persons whom they can influence. Typically, these Arab "vote contractors" are the *Mukhtars*, various city employees, small-scale Arab contractors, merchants who have developed ties with the Israeli administration, or ambitious younger men who are enlisted in the election effort. As political brokers they turn to members of their family and clan, friends, or others for whom they have done favors in the past, and ask that they go the poll and cast their vote. Particularly in rural areas on Jerusalem's periphery, local headmen may be able to deliver dozens of votes. Voting generally picks up in the evenings. Not only are the men then back from work, but it is also felt to be "safer" to leave one's home under the cover of darkness.

To a limited degree the major Israeli political parties compete for the support of Jerusalem's Arab voters. In fact, however, those Arabs who do vote have overwhelmingly cast their ballots for Kollek. Indeed, as many Arabs are quick to say, the question for them is not for whom to vote but whether to vote at all. The mayor has received their support for a number of reasons. His policies of quiet pragmatism and activism, as well as the promise of equality and the development of Arab neighborhoods, have earned him the good will and support of some Arab voters. Put in more modest terms, on the balance his administration may be perceived to be the "lesser of evils." Moreover, the political patronage system that is organized by his administration also brings some supporters to the polls; moderate Arabs who have received help or favors from his staff are likely to vote for "Teddy." In this regard Benvenisti makes the point that Kollek received a higher percentage of votes in the peripheral, poorer areas of Arab Jerusalem where persons are more dependent upon the local *Mukhtar* and various Israeli officials, while in the more fashionable, wealthier neighborhoods where Arabs are presumably less dependent (and also tend to be more nationalist) very few voters turned out in the elections. Finally, it is also important to emphasize that the Jerusalem Arab vote has become an important factor in Kollek's reelection. In several elections his slate for city council received a majority because of those Arab voters who overwhelmingly gave their support to him.

THE ELITE POLITICAL SYSTEM

The patronage system represents one avenue of Arab-Jewish political interaction. In addition, there is a second major format of exchange: the "elite system." In contrast with the patronage contacts that have been described, elite-level Arab-Jewish politics are principally concerned with broad matters of policy and decision making, and involve informal, often secret negotiations between Arab notables and Jewish political leaders.

In the face of the prolonged Arab refusal to take a direct part in governing Jerusalem, the elite system provides a mechanism for periodic consultation and negotiation.

Elites are, by definition, small in number, and the Jerusalem case is no exception. On the Jewish or Israeli side, negotiations at this level are almost exclusively carried out by the mayor; a few of his aides, and particularly his advisor, may also take a direct part in the consultation process, but the mayor certainly is the main Jewish player.[7] The Arab actors are more numerous and diverse, and it is important to describe them and their background in greater detail.

During the first half of this century Jerusalem was an important center of Palestinian national politics. Throughout this period the old Jerusalem elite families were among the main protagonists (and often, antagonists) in the struggle against the British and the Jews. The shattering blows of the 1948 war and the successful establishment of Israel, followed by Jordan's incorporation of the West Bank and Jerusalem, discredited their leadership and destroyed much of their political power. Under the Jordanian regime power shifted to include others from among the old-line Jerusalem families; in addition, Muslim Arab migrants from Hebron also began to play more important roles in Jerusalem's economic and political affairs. In fact, they began to dominate commercial life in the city, and also exerted an influence within various religious as well as political circles. When, in 1967, Israeli forces occupied East Jerusalem they found an Arab political leadership composed of Jordanian loyalists (such as the mayor, city council members, officials in the Muslim religious establishment, and the Chamber of Commerce) as well as the heads of the numerous Christian Jerusalem communities.[8]

With all of Jerusalem under Israeli control the Arab mayor and his councilors resigned from office and refused to take part in governing the city. Ruhi al-Khatib, who had been mayor under the Jordanians, was later banished to Jordan for opposing Israeli policies; a number of other leading figures also either fled or were forced to leave. However, the heads of the various Christian communities remained, as did some of the important figures in the Muslim religious institutions and business associations. Following 1967 this handful of persons began meeting informally with Israeli political leaders, and in particular with the mayor. Together with the Christian Church leaders, these Muslim notables have become members of the Jerusalem Arab political elite.

Following the 1967 war the Israeli political leadership was immediately

[7] A number of other Israeli government officials have also taken part in these negotiations.

[8] See Benziman 1973; Benvenisti 1976.

mindful that it was in control of all of Jerusalem's holy places—including the Jewish temple's Western Wall, the Muslim Dome of the Rock, and the great church built over the site of Christ's cruxifixion. The responsibility was enormous: the city was constantly filled with foreign pilgrims and tourists, and, in addition, throughout the world members of the various religious groups were keenly concerned with how the new Jewish regime would deal with their holy places, and whether the ancient sites and prerogatives would be properly maintained.

There are, as noted previously, literally a myriad of Christian groups located in Jerusalem. Each group maintains its own missions, in most cases within the Old City or close to the holy places themselves; a few include just a handful of persons, although in other cases the numbers of priests and members of religious orders are considerable. Several of the churches also are the center for a large resident Christian community. This is particularly the case among the Armenians, who are concentrated within one of the Old City's four quarters, and the Greek Orthodox, who make up the largest Christian community. The larger Christian denominations maintain their own separate communal institutions, such as schools and hospitals, in addition to churches and shrines.

The leaders or heads of each of these Christian groups compose one category within the non-Jewish political elite. Each is an elite member practically by definition. As the chief local delegate of a world Christian church they have what amounts to diplomatic status; for example, the heads of the Catholic orders and religious institutions are appointed by the Vatican, and they act as the Church of Rome's ambassador in Jerusalem. In some cases (as among the Armenians) the local church leaders are powerful figures within the ecclesiastical hierarchy, although typically they are persons of more modest status.

In addition to their religious duties the heads of the church groups also have many temporal interests. Since every denomination owns or is the custodian of property (churches, houses, hospices, hospitals, and so forth), they have a direct concern with various mundane matters such as taxes, the upkeep of buildings, or even the harassment of church officials. Then too the church leaders of the larger resident groups, such as the Armenians or the Greek Orthodox, also become involved in the daily problems of their followers. In regard to all of these issues the church leaders act as "patrons": combining both spiritual and temporal powers, they represent their community in discussion and negotiation with high-level Israeli authorities. The Israeli Ministry of Foreign Affairs and the Ministry of Religions are formally responsible for these contacts. However, for the mayor of Jerusalem, both the Christian elite members and their communities are "residents of Jerusalem," and he and his key assistants frequently meet with them to consider topics of common interest.

Meetings between the mayor and the various church leaders are closed, private affairs. The setting for these discussions is sometimes bare and formal, although on other occasions they are elaborately staged and practically baroque. These are meetings between two patrons—the mayor, an Israeli patron, and an archbishop, priest, or head of a particular religious order, all of whom are also patrons. During these encounters the church leaders may raise some of the problems they face and ask for the mayor's intervention and support. The mayor may agree to clarify the matter, and subsequently attempt to have the issue dealt with either within his own administration or elsewhere within the Israeli bureaucracy. In this regard Kollek acts as a kind of broker for the church officials. He makes use of his own status and influence in order to persuade high officials to be more cooperative regarding problems faced by the Jerusalem Christian community. Conversely, the mayor may also request the Christian leader's assistance in some issue or problem that he faces; the church head may at first react informally to the matter at hand, and then promise to raise the issue before a higher-level church authority.

Sectarian differences and conflicts within the Christian elite have generally inhibited any attempt to develop coordinated Christian policy or political activity. In addition, these Christian church leaders have also maintained a certain distance from the Muslim leadership. At this elite level the various heads of the church groups have sought to strike a neutral position in regard to the Arab-Israeli dispute. It is not hard to see why this should be. Christians are a small minority in Jerusalem, and since the churches' main interest is in maintaining access to and supervision of their holy places they need to maintain a working relationship with whomever rules Jerusalem. They may not be pleased with the Israelis, but then there is also a lengthy history of conflict and mistrust between Muslims and Christians. The problems of neutrality are particularly acute for the larger resident Christian communities such as the Greek Orthodox. Many are, after all, also Palestinians, and members of these communities have also supported Palestinian nationalist movements. With some exceptions, however, the Christian elite has avoided explicit involvement in the Palestinian cause; this would so complicate their position as to render their influence as patrons ineffective. From their point of view, the Israeli authorities do not require that the Christian officials compliment Israel's policies in Jerusalem or make pro-Israeli pronouncements. It is enough that they maintain a noncommitted stance, and that they attend various ceremonies or other occasions that symbolically attest to Israel's political rule in the city.

Although the Christian church leaders are one category within the East Jerusalem elite, they are by no means the most important. The Jerusalem Arab population is predominantly Muslim, and throughout the modern period Muslim leadership has been at the center of the city's turbulent events. Indeed, in order to understand how the Arab-Jewish political system is organized—and particularly how political exchanges take place in the absence of a formal Arab leadership—we need to examine the composition and activities of the Muslim Arab elite.

Earlier we noted that although they have consistently refused to hold government posts while under Israeli control, a small number of Arab office holders continued to retain various formal positions. In particular, these were persons who headed offices that either were connected with the Jordanian government authorities in Amman, or who represented the Jordanians, or both. Unlike the former Arab mayor of Jerusalem and his fellow councilors, there was no reason for these Arab office holders to resign; these were not Israeli government posts, and they therefore continued to fill them. Some of these Arab officials soon began holding informal meetings with the Israeli authorities; although they were not elected representatives, nor for that matter persons who had become accustomed to the Israeli occupation, they were men of considerable esteem and influence who were willing to exchange views with the Israeli mayor and other officials. These Arab office holders included a small number of persons: the head of the *Waqf*, or religious trust, who was responsible for supervising the Muslim holy places as well as the extensive property holdings that were under *Waqf* control; the head of the East Jerusalem Chamber of Commerce, a body that includes many of the Arab Jerusalem merchants and shopkeepers, and that began to oversee commercial links between Arabs in Jerusalem and in Jordan; the chairman of the board of the East Jerusalem Electric Corporation, the largest single employer within the Arab Jerusalem community; the heads of several professional associations; the former Jordanian governor of Jerusalem; and a small number of others. What they had in common was the fact that they were Palestinian nationalists and Jordanian loyalists who had the confidence of the authorities in Amman, and while they opposed the Israeli occupation they were also willing to hold informal discussions on a wide range of practical matters with the Israeli authorities.

These notables make up the second category within the Arab Jerusalem elite. In the period following unification they, the mayor, and several of his assistants have developed a remarkably complex, intricate system of political negotiation. Periodically, the mayor initiates a private meeting with one or another of them in order to listen to their views regarding recent political events and also to continue discussion of policy matters. Discussions, or better still, negotiations, typically advance in small steps. For example, at various times the mayor and some of the notables have considered questions having to do with assessing Israeli taxes on property owned by the *Waqf*, or the level of taxation to be levied on merchants in

East Jerusalem, or questions having to do with requests to build a new Arab hospital or school. Of course, these are only examples of the kinds of topics that are considered in these private discussions. Take the matter of taxes to be paid by the Arab merchants. For the Arab elite, not only is paying taxes to be avoided (a common enough attitude), but equally important, these are taxes paid to the Israeli authorities so that they can maintain and even solidify their continuing occupation. On the other hand, for the mayor and other Israeli officials taxes paid by Jerusalem Arabs are needed in order to provide them with adequate urban services, and (it is argued) the Jewish citizens should not have to pay for services the municipality provides for Arabs. Starting with these conflicting assumptions and attitudes, the two sides begin considering the issues. Each side may make proposals and suggestions regarding a fair tax level. The point to be emphasized, however, is that in these negotiations the Arab notables do not act on their own behalf or as free agents, but rather they represent the Jordanian and, indeed, the Palestinian organizations based in Amman. They frequently travel between Jerusalem and Amman, where they consult with the Jordanian officials. In Amman, Jordan's capital, the government maintains an entire ministry whose task it is to continue an active involvement in the affairs of the West Bank and Jerusalem. The notables meet with these authorities, report on discussions that they have had with Kollek and other Israeli officials, and then take part in discussions aimed at determining what the Arab position should be. Upon their return to Jerusalem they once again meet with the mayor and others and continue the negotiations until the issues are finally resolved, or, alternatively, simply set aside since they cannot reach agreement. In brief, by means of the notables a continuing dialogue is maintained between the Israeli and the Jordanian-Palestinian leadership, and a kind of Arab "shadow government" continues to have considerable influence in the city.

This small Arab elite was neither elected nor selected by the Arab populace; even so, since 1967 many of the same persons have been conducting negotiations with the Israeli authorities. What does their power and authority derive from? Where does their power lie?

As intermediaries between the Jordanian and the Israeli authorities, the notables face the extraordinarily complex pressures of being acceptable to both sides. Toward their Jordanian and Palestinian brethren they must exhibit patriotism, true allegiance to the cause, and support for the policies proclaimed by the reigning leadership. To the Israelis they must indicate that they reject extreme nationalist positions, and that they are in fact conveying reliable messages and can be trusted. Juggling all of these contradictory pressures is no small achievement. It is therefore not surprising that their political activities are nearly always private and without publicity (and, as has been pointed out, always denied by them). Nevertheless, once they have the acceptance and support of both sides they are able to martial considerable influence. This is particularly relevant within the Jerusalem Arab community, where there is constant gossip and frequent criticism of their activities.

A notable who has the reputation of being "close to the king" can muster political weight. Since practically every Arab Jerusalemite has close family relations in Jordan and since the Jordanian government's powers are extensive, being recognized as "close to the throne" lends authority in Jerusalem. Similarly, a reputation for being influential among the Israelis also affords a certain esteem. In a more direct, practical way, however, the Arab elite members are powerful persons since they have access to tangible resources. Several of them (the head of the *Waqf* or the director of the East Jerusalem Electric Corporation) control large bureaucracies, and others have an influence over business and financial matters. Moreover, the *sumud* funds that have been provided by the Jordanians or through the joint Jordan-PLO Committee, and which pay the salaries of hundreds of Arabs who continue to strike, as well as funding for Arab schools, hospitals, newspapers, and private mortgage loans, are supervised and distributed by some of the notables. To return to a phrase used earlier, in this and other ways the Arab elites are involved in managing the continuing Jordanian presence in united Jerusalem.

The previously mentioned Arab mortgage fund program is a good illustration of how this system works. New home construction has a high priority under the *sumud* doctrine. Not only does building new Arab homes allow the residents to persevere, but it also guarantees that the Israelis will not confiscate that particular piece of land for Jewish housing. Consequently, substantial sums have been set aside for building new homes or adding to existing dwellings. These mortgage loans are extended on excellent terms and are highly prized by the Arab residents. However, in order for an Arab applicant to receive a loan he must first show that he has already received a valid building permit from the Israeli authorities. As noted previously, for an Arab resident to be eligible to receive loans from Arab "nationalist sources" he must first obtain formal permission to build from the proper Israeli government bureau! Of course, the Israeli authorities are well aware of the source of the funds and the ways in which they are distributed. The facts are known to everyone—Arab applicants, notables, the mayor, and other Israeli officials—but in this instance, Israeli hegemony and the Jordanian presence have quietly agreed to cooperate with one another.

In contrast with the church elite who rarely meet together, the Arab elite do have occasions to exchange views and opinions. As widely recognized persons of authority they belong to a long list of Arab Jerusalem public committees and boards—groups that are concerned with such matters as hospitals, the care of the holy places, and social welfare and educational problems. These are often occasions for them to exchange views and opinions regarding the major political events of the day. The point is not that they regularly coordinate their policies, but rather that these are forums where elite members exchange views regarding political strategies and possibilities. Finally, it is significant to note that to a remarkable degree the list of notables has hardly changed. The same individuals who in 1967 or 1968 indicated their readiness to quietly discuss policy matters with the mayor continue in the same role practically two decades later. Although some have been replaced (the head of the *Waqf*, for example), the cast of characters with whom the mayor or other Israeli officials carry on negotiations has largely remained the same. To be sure, during this period of time other Jerusalem Arabs have been both economically and politically upwardly mobile—and yet the role of "notable" continues mainly to be filled by the same persons.

IMPLICATIONS AND DILEMMAS

In the previous sections the two major mechanisms of Arab-Jewish political interaction were described and analyzed. The patronage system and the elite system were, in effect, presented as if they were independent of one another. To some degree this view is accurate. There is no coordination between the broker functions of Arab municipal workers or headmen, on the one hand, and the Muslim elite or Christian church leaders, on the other. The *Mukhtars* are certainly not organized by the notables into separate patronage networks or factional groups; under the present circumstances there is no public, widely coordinated Arab political party or movement that unites the lower-level brokers with these higher-level elites. Putting it differently, a notable's position or influence will not be affected by replacing one or another of the neighborhood *Mukhtars*. Moreover, the patronage system deals exclusively with everyday problems and personal requests, while the elite system is generally concerned with broader topics of Arab public policy in Jerusalem.

In all of these ways the two systems are both analytically and effectively different from each other. At best it could be argued that they are the proverbial "two sides of the same coin" since they deal with different political interests of the Jerusalem Arab community.

Looked at differently, however, it soon becomes apparent that the two political mechanisms are closely connected. The *Mukhtars* and the notables are both elements in the overall Arab-Jewish political system, and they need to be seen in that light. Both are linked or connected with the same small number of Jewish political figures—preeminently the mayor of Jerusalem, his advisor on East Jerualem affairs, and their assistants. General matters of policy concerning Jerusalem's Arab population become the mayor's concern, and to an extraordinary degree he also maintains an involvement in many smaller daily problems as well. The patronage and elite systems are therefore closely connected since they involve interactions with the same Israeli political patrons. What this indicates, in other words, is the overall dependence of the Arab population and consequently of the Arab political actors as well. The 1967 war, plus the Israeli occupation and the Arab refusal to take a direct part in governing Jerusalem, have inevitably produced a political structure which is characterized by Arab dependence. Kollek and his close advisors may be benevolent and progressive—but the context within which they interact with notables or headmen is inherently unequal.

These remarks lead to an even more general question: why has this particular political system evolved and persisted? Is there some way to explain the forms that the Arab-Jewish political exchanges have taken?

These questions are difficult and complicated, and answering them fully would entail detailed information regarding a great many idiosyncratic personality features as well as historical and political conditions. However, the outlines of a more general explanation may be suggested. The Jewish-Arab political system serves the interests of both sides. More specifically, both the mayor's position and activities as well as those of the Arab brokers and elite can be seen to have come into being and persisted since, under the circumstances, they have been advantageous for both. This does not mean that the Arab actors have come to accept "the circumstances." And yet given the facts of Israeli occupation and political control each side had a considerable stake in this system of political exchange.

Let us begin with the Jewish side. How the notable system originally developed is a topic of some controversy. The problem that faced Kollek and his associates following the 1967 war was how to effectively govern a city that included a hostile minority population. One possibility was to convince some Arab leaders to take a formal role in governing Jerusalem; the political process would become normalized if Arabs were to take a direct part in it. The mayor and others relate that at various times in the past informal efforts were made to persuade politically moderate Arabs to join the municipal council, but that they were always rebuffed. According to these accounts the Israeli offers were genuine and had solid backing. On the other hand—and herein lies the controversy—in his book on Jerusalem as a Jewish-Arab city, Benvenisti makes the point that Kollek was not enthusiastic about having Arabs on the council; "they'll get in the way of my work" is Benvenisti's quote of Kollek's remarks.[9]

---

[9] Benvenisti 1976, 115.

Whatever actually did take place (both interpretations may be correct), the critical fact is that Arabs chose not to take part in formal Jerusalem councils.

Looked at in one way this may actually have strengthened the hand of Arab and Jewish moderates. This appears paradoxical, and yet it is based upon a powerful logic. According to this argument, Arabs who agreed to serve on a Jewish-dominated municipal council would always be in a position of opposing the Jewish majority, and they would therefore inevitably be driven into taking extreme positions. Any Jerusalem Arab who agreed to take part in a public Israeli forum would not only be vulnerable to personal attacks from extremists; he could only be "obstructive" and turn council sessions into propaganda debates. From this viewpoint it would be best not to have a public political forum, but instead to hold private negotiations with Arabs who could be persuaded to consider "real practical matters" with the Israeli authorities. Irrespective of how it actually developed, the "notable system" suited Kollek's desire to avoid sterile political arguments and to be pragmatic. It provided an avenue to open discussions with those moderate Arab political leaders who, in effect, subsequently became "the notables." The patronage system was certainly advantageous: a political arrangement in which Jerusalem Arabs were encouraged to make use of the local *Mukhtars* and the advisor on East Jerusalem affairs meant that the mayor would also acquire valuable political capital. Besides, it was a relatively effective arrangement that, under the circumstances, allowed Arabs to manage some of their own affairs and also to receive services from the municipality. In short, a system that emphasized Arab brokers and consultations with Arab elites had practical advantages as far as the mayor's, and more generally, Israeli interests were concerned.

The same can be said regarding the Arab side. They too found certain advantages in this system. Their problem was how to manage affairs and to persevere while under the Israeli occupation. Clearly it was impossible for Arabs to hold public Israeli political offices; that would signal collaboration and the acceptance of Israeli sovereignty, and was entirely unacceptable. The personal danger to an Arab who publicly cooperated with the Israelis should not be underestimated; there is a lengthy history of Palestinians who were assassinated as traitors for dealing with the Jewish authorities. However, there were real needs and outstanding issues confronting the Arab population, and the problem therefore was to find a political device that would serve local interests while never acknowledging or accepting Israeli hegemony. The "notable system" offered the way to accomplish these ends. The Arab elite members would carry on informal, always private negotiations with the mayor and other Israeli officials; it was a system of shadows, but it could be effective since it solved problems. Moreover, this was a way to involve and insure the continuing Jordanian presence in Jerusalem. The elite derived their power from the Jordanian authorities, and hence they could be depended upon to defend and maintain the Jordanian presence.

The fact that both sides had a stake in these political arrangements does not mean that they were developed consciously or purposefully; it seems more likely that they emerged as a result of trial and error and of various meetings and encounters between the Jewish and Arab political leaders soon after the 1967 war. Moreover, there is no reason to suppose that the two sides were deliberately engaged in an exchange relationship for example, that the Israelis were willing to accept the continuing flow of *sumud* funds so long as the notables took moderate positions and issues could be resolved in reasonable ways. Nonetheless, this system persisted because both sides shared an interest in maintaining it.

This does not mean, of course, that this Arab-Jewish political system is without internal tensions, flaws, and contradictions. On the contrary, it is laden with difficulties and pitfalls. As has been emphasized, this is a system that strengthens Arab dependence; the mayor's advisor and the *Mukhtar* system insures the dependence of Arab clients upon their Jewish patrons. This may be a way to strengthen what are deemed to be moderate Arabs, but it obviously opens the way to all of patronage's many evils. Or take the refusal of Jerusalem Arabs to take part in elected or appointed municipal bodies. It may be valid to predict that Arabs would refuse to serve, and that if they did serve they would only be obstructionist. This is the "realist's viewpoint," and even if it becomes a self-fulfilling hypothesis it may well be correct. On the other hand, Arabs serving on public bodies might form coalitions with various Jewish groups. For a variety of reasons the Arab minority and various Jewish minority interests (or even majority interests) might from time to time intersect in unpredictable ways.

A central problem in this political system is that it is entirely ad hoc and ad hominem: it is essentially a system of negotiation and exchange developed by a tiny set of elites, and it has no permanent constitution, charter, or set of rules. It is a temporary arrangement that was developed under certain circumstances—but these circumstances lasted for more than two decades, and the players hardly changed during this period. The system was designed by Kollek and the Arab elite, persons who were perhaps uniquely skilled and sensitive to one another's problems. Certainly it is to their personal credit that while constantly faced by enormous obstacles of hate and fear they succeeded in establishing an effective system of political exchange. However, one cannot lose sight of the fact that the private meetings and negotiations were limited to the same small group of persons. To what extent was the success of this system a result of the personalities of the participants? Will their successors be equally pragmatic? Finally, the fact that this system is without a mutually agreed upon legal or formal basis also contributes to its ultimate weakness. To be sure, ad hoc systems provide a maximum of flexibility; no one is bound by any prior agreement that is rooted in law, tradition, or a long-term system of checks and balances. At the same time, however, these political formats are easily torn apart and upset as it suits the parties. They are, even in the short run, only temporary devices by which antagonistic groups maintain a minimum of contact and exchange.

CHAPTER 9

Between Conflict and Accommodation: Trends, Comparisons, Conclusions

MORE THAN TWENTY YEARS have elapsed since Jerusalem was reunited under Israeli rule. This time span is actually longer than the pre-1967 period when the city was divided by walls and barbed wire. What began in 1967 as a sudden, startling conquest has become, for many, the only reality that they have known. Indeed, the majority of the present population, both Arabs and Jews, have in their lifetimes only experienced this most recent phase in Jerusalem's history. The figures are clear in this regard: by 1987 the median age of Jewish residents was under twenty-four years, that of Muslim Arabs barely seventeen years. Furthermore, many Jews and Arabs moved to Jerusalem following 1967. The demographic, urban, and economic trends during this same time period have also consolidated the act of reunification. Jerusalem's population grew at an unprecedented rate, nearly doubling in two decades, and by 1987 had approached the half-million mark. Well over one hundred thousand Jews, or about 30 percent of the Jewish population, were settled in East Jerusalem, and nearly half of the local Arab workforce was regularly employed in Jewish West Jerusalem. Indeed, from various perspectives, post-1967 Jerusalem has become a fact of life, a functioning, integrated urban system.

Yet within the framework of one city shared by two major communities, Jews and Arabs remain deeply divided. Basic, long-term social divisions and political conflicts persist, expressed not only in political attitudes but also in the structural features of this dichotomous urban environment. In present-day Jerusalem everything continues to be perceived in dual ethnic references of "us" and "they," "our side" and the "other side." Ethnic identity is constantly in mind whenever one passes strangers, and it largely dictates urban organizational structures as well as everyday behavior.

Under these circumstances the daily patterns of living together—the major topic of this book—are, as we have seen, exceedingly complex, with many seemingly contradictory, even paradoxical, features. In the light of the empirical evidence regarding the ongoing, practical relationships between Jews and Arabs, several concluding issues need to be addressed. First, to what extent is it possible to compare and evaluate the degree of integration versus segregation between Jews and Arabs in various areas of everyday life? More particularly, to what extent do the emerging patterns of daily behavior arise from voluntary cultural differentiation, or rather reflect imposed majority-minority power relations and political conflicts? Second, does this Jewish-Arab system represent a unique case, or can it be compared to other relevant models of community relations in Jerusalem itself, between Jews and Arabs generally in Israel, and in other ethnically mixed cities? Finally, recent events—in particular the Arab *intifada* or popular uprising—need to be presented and their implications considered and evaluated.

PATTERNS OF SEGREGATION AND INTEGRATION

There can be little doubt that one of the major features of Jewish-Arab relationships is the predominant force of persistent, widespread segregation. This can be perceived, as we have seen, by many measurable or otherwise observable indicators.

Residential segregation has remained practically complete. No mixed Jewish-Arab neighborhoods have developed during the more than two decades of coexistence—in spite of physical proximity and large-scale residential mobility. What is more, commercial centers, urban functional zones, and public institutions also remain essentially separate; this refers not only to religious or other culturally related institutions such as schools and theaters, but also to various public services ranging from urban transportation and medical systems to the provision of electricity and bottled gas. In all of these, as well as many other cases, aspects of separation are legally sanctioned, and ethnic facilities are distinguished by their ownership, modes of operation, and other distinct identity marks. In fact, one of the most striking features of the united city is that an Arab or Jewish identity can be and is attributed to all neighborhoods, public functions, commercial establishments, and even basic consumer goods. There is very little that appears to be neutral or that can be given a different label: practically everything is categorized as either "Jewish" or "Arab." The boundaries between group members are also tight and apparently impermeable: there are practically no marriages between Jerusalem Jews and Arabs, and as we have seen in previous chapters, it is rare for an Arab to adopt a Jewish identity or vice versa.

Aspects of segregation are also expressed in the daily conduct of Jews and Arabs, where the ethnic identity of places, people, and economic entities are always recognized. Crossing over to the "other side" is a highly conscious act that is often avoided, just as manifestations of avoidance and obstruction of intercommunal relationships are widely practiced in many everyday situations. Indeed, members of both communities have little information or knowledge regarding daily affairs or events on the "other side." Ethnic boundaries and barriers of estrangement are reflected in this division of perceptions, attitudes, and behaviors: Jews and Arabs continue to live in different social worlds, each sharing life experiences largely ignored by, or unknown, to the other.

A number of underlying factors help to explain this extreme pattern of deep segregation. One explanation of the divided structure rests upon Jerusalem's recent history. Certain features of the pattern of segregation can be traced to the two parallel urban systems that were created during the period when the city was physically divided. No wonder then that many of these dual systems continue to exist in the reunited city, particularly when they are attuned to the two communities' different social norms. However, the patterns of division are fundamentally the revealed expression of the continuing social distance between them. Given their basic religious, cultural, and national differences (not to say antagonism), neither Jews nor Arabs desire to assimilate to the other. It is for this reason that segregation, especially in housing and culturally related activities, is largely voluntary, advocated by both sides as most advantageous. Beyond this, the particularly high degree and persistent nature of segregation, as well as the widespread practices of mutual exclusion, undoubtedly also stem from the long history of conflict at the national level. Ethnic prejudice, fear, and repeated outbreaks of violence are significant factors keeping Jews and Arabs apart and leading to the present-day dichotomized urban environment.

At the same time, living together has also meant that Jews and Arabs are involved in a wide range of daily contacts mainly confined to the economic sphere. Overall, these are encouraged by geographic proximity as well as various mutual interests and opportunities. It is especially in this respect that contemporary Jerusalem has the apparent features of many other mixed cities where different ethnic groups work together in industrial, professional, or business associations, and where they interact as well in various other forms of exchange.

However, in Jerusalem ethnic identity more often than not also plays a crucial role in these encounters. Interethnic economic transactions are not only confined to limited areas but, in addition, are normally characterized by distinctive features that often differ from those practiced within each group. Jewish-Arab economic relations frequently involve special implicit or explicit conditions such as the necessity to use brokers, hidden transactions, and "camouflage," or, under certain conditions, specific "ethnic price" terms. In other words, even where Jews and Arabs do interact various kinds of segregative modes of conduct are required and practiced in order to circumvent ethnic barriers. Indeed, in this particular system aspects of integration are closely linked with features of segregation, and while they may not be obvious or apparent at first sight they nevertheless continue to constitute a fundamental element.

The willingness of members of both groups to engage in exchange relations differs with respect to the various areas of possible integration in everyday life. In a survey conducted among adult Jews in 1973 differential attitudes toward mixing with Arabs were clearly stated and ranked. Less than one-quarter of those interviewed expressed willingess to share schools or housing with Arabs; about one-half were positive regarding mixing in restaurants and hotels; while nearly two-thirds favored integration in hospitals, clinics, and playgrounds. The highest proportion of favorable attitudes—around three-quarters of the total—expressed their willingness to integrate public transportation and similar urban facilities, and favored mixing in employment and commercial activities.[1] Significantly, the actual observed behavioral patterns reveal that in practice Jews and Arabs interact much less than would be expected by these attitudes. Nevertheless, they do make selective choices depending upon the social context. Along this segregation-integration continuum, in addition to the complete separation in education and other cultural institutions, it is particularly the permanent mixing in space which appears to be least acceptable, and in fact falls at the segregative end of the spectrum. Spatial segregation not only relates to housing but also, and most significantly, to the location of economic activities. Hardly any business was located across the ethnic boundary during the first twenty years following reunification. On the other hand, integrative aspects are more common in the labor and commercial markets, as reflected by the varied and increased volume of employment, business, and consumer relations which developed over the years.

However, when evaluating the significance or degree of integration in those areas where Jewish-Arab interactions frequently occur, quantitative measures alone are not always sufficient. It is in this respect that the different and often particular modes, terms, and preconditions associated with interethnic exchange are no less relevant, and should also be scaled with regard to their integrative importance and significance. Thus, long-term, binding, open, and direct modes of intersectoral interaction similar to those practiced within each sector should be ranked higher in comparison with occasional, ad hoc, disguised relationships or those accompanied by ethnic-related elements such as brokerage functions or discriminative terms of exchange. In a similar vein, intersectoral interaction dictated by sheer economic necessity, institutional imposition, or lack of

[1] See Smith 1973. Later surveys commissioned by the Jerusalem Municipality and conducted by the same author showed that this ranking of basic attitudes was largely maintained. Significantly, attitudes among the Arab population have rarely been surveyed. Nevertheless, some hints in this respect can be found in Ashkenazi 1989.

choice are also less significant when compared to those involving a greater degree of mutual preference and choice despite the existing intrasectoral alternatives. It is in such a broader context that the large-scale employment of Arabs in the Jewish sector, in spite of its long-term, binding nature, represents a limited degree of integration since it is primarily dictated by the lack of self-employment opportunities for Arabs, or limited to types of work and conditions that were not acceptable to Jews. To put it differently, the employment of hundreds of Arabs in the municipal sanitation department is less significant, from an integrative point of view, than the employment of a number of Arab physicians in a Jewish hospital, or those cases in which Arabs have authority over Jewish workers. As was also observed, most business ties or consumer relations between Jews and Arabs are either of an occasional nature, or conducted on an ad hoc basis that is conditioned, in turn, by a host of ethnic-related imposed terms and economic or institutional constraints. Long-term open business associations on equal terms are rare and generally avoided, as are visits to commercial and administrative centers on the other side unless institutionally imposed or in search of opportunities that are unavailable within each sector. Here again, the frequent use by Arabs of Jewish buses which is imposed by sheer necessity could hardly be interpreted as a sign of significant integration, in comparison with those cases where Jews and Arabs take the first available taxi irrespective of its ethnic identity.

Drawing these observations together we conclude that one of the main defining features of Arab-Jewish relationships is that both parties seek to carry on their contacts in those forms and domains that represent only a low level of integration. It is for this reason that the location of businesses or residences "on the other side" is excluded, since it represents a higher degree of integration, as is implied by the permanent nature of occupying space. Likewise, out of the various alternative modes of intersectoral exchange in the economic sphere, the least binding and potentially compromising are generally selected and practiced. The prevalence of instrumental rather than multiplex ties is also in keeping with this pattern: the former are easily broken, while the latter indicate longer-term interests and commitments. This low level of integration not only reflects basic social and political divisions, but also enables both parties to avoid unnecessary friction and allows them to carry on exchanges while at the same time maintaining their mutually desired segregation. Both groups are able to live essentially within their own social world, even imagining that the other does not exist. A low level of integration may make it appear as if unification were a fiction, and that the city is, at a deeper level, thoroughly divided.

MAJORITY-MINORITY PATTERNS

The nature of Jewish-Arab daily interaction in Jerusalem must also be interpreted in terms of ethnic power relations. Looked at from this angle, the dominant Jewish position as against that of the subordinate Arab status represents an extreme case and is practically all-encompassing. This structure relates not only to population ratios and the Jewish demographic majority, but primarily to the coincidence of legal and economic status with ethnic membership, and most importantly, to differential access to political power and control. Hence, in addition to cultural-ethnic differentiations, it is mainly this system of dominance and dependency that explains the specific patterns of segregation, integration, and exchange between the Jewish and Arab sectors. More specifically, these are expressed in the collective policies adopted by members of the two communities, as well as in the asymmetrical nature of individual behavior and attitudes.

As we have seen, the objective differences in economic scale and structure between the Jewish and Arab sectors have basically determined the evolving patterns of functional relationships and the direction of exchange. Purely economic factors by themselves produced Arab dependency on the Jewish sector in areas ranging from employment to the provision of a wide spectrum of goods and specialized services. In addition, in a Jerusalem united under Jewish hegemony, Arab dependency further increased in those areas directly controlled by the Israeli national and city administrations. Under these circumstances one of the basic features which characterizes Jewish-Arab relationships is the underlying asymmetries with regard to the very necessity to conduct mutual interactions in various daily contexts. Whereas Arabs are more often obliged to rely on Jewish economic functions and institutions, Jews benefit from a larger degree of choice as a result of the broader economic alternatives at their disposal and the institutional patterns that they introduced following reunification.

By virtue of their dominant position Jews can also to a larger extent dictate the areas, forms, and terms of exchange with Arabs, or, alternatively, impose practices of exclusion. Jews are willing to employ Arabs or provide them with certain public or private services since this does not interfere with the sectoral identity of their own entities but rather reinforces Jewish economic control and Arab dependency. At the same time they are in a position to exclude the establishment of Arab residents and businesses in their own areas, or the distribution of certain Arab products, if these compete with Jewish products in their own market. By the same token Jews can more easily avoid visiting Arab commercial areas, or alternatively, they may select Arab services when these are offered on more favorable terms of exchange.

Arabs, by contrast, are frequently obliged to take any job offered in the Jewish sector, to work under Jews, to sell Jewish products, or to speak the Hebrew language—even if this conflicts with their own cultural norms and symbols. Similarly, it is mainly Arabs who have had to use Jewish brokerage functions or employ tactics of camouflage or other low-level ethnically related modes of exchange when in need of the Jewish sector. Indeed, one expression of this majority-minority pattern is that it is generally the Arabs who are more willing to cooperate with Jews in daily exchange and practical matters than the other way round.

Most importantly, minority-majority relations in Jerusalem mainly concern national political issues and are always closely related to the Arab-Jewish struggle for control. The dominant Jewish majority benefits from both political-legal power and economic supremacy. The imposed legal measures, institutional frameworks, and allocation of economic resources are all designed to consolidate the Jewish demographic, spatial, and economic dominance, and they are often based upon ethnic differentiation. Responding to the mutually desired voluntary segregation, the Israeli authorities are willing to respect different Arab cultural norms and separate institutions; but at the same time this is often associated with imposing a different legal status, and more to the point, with the discriminative allocation of public resources.

Arab attitudes and policies likewise reflect political motives and the desire to, insofar as possible, preserve their own separate entities and sectoral control. In political terms this involves the nonacceptance and nonrecognition of the unilateral annexation of their part of the city by Israel. In more practical terms this means that while as individuals they are obliged to engage in everyday relations with Jews for economic survival, collectively they deny any cooperation which implies acceptance of Israeli rule. To cite one example, East Jerusalem Arabs were interested in having Israeli resident status since this provided them easier access to the Jewish labor market and other social benefits; but at the same time they refused to accept Israeli citizenship, officially merge their own public institutions with Jewish counterparts, or present Arab candidates in municipal elections. It is particularly important to emphasize that the Arabs also reject any form of minority status since they consider themselves to be living under an illegal, enforced occupation. As a consequence they do not publicly organize to obtain a more equal allocation of resources, or use their political rights within the framework of the existing political system. Paradoxically, it is precisely this political attitude of total nonrecognition that has made it easier for the Jewish majority to pursue its own political goals.

EVALUATING THE JERUSALEM MODEL

The existing patterns of Jewish-Arab relationships in Jerusalem have often been the subject of different interpretations. Not surprisingly, these mainly differ between Jews or Arabs, or vary depending upon the contrasting political positions that are present particularly within the Jewish population and between Israeli political leaders. Some have emphasized the long tradition of Jerusalem as a pluralistic, culturally heterogeneous city where, it is claimed, the patterns of segregation are similar to those found in many other multiethnic cities around the world; whereas others would stress the ongoing political conflicts and related expressions of a deeply divided, polarized urban community.

Those supporting the pluralistic interpretation argue that the system of Jewish-Arab relations that has emerged in Jerusalem does not represent something new, but should rather be seen as the continuation of the traditional "mosaic structure" that has characterized this Holy City in the past. According to this argument Jerusalem has always been an amalgam of different religious, ethnic, and national groups, each of which lived within its own quarter and maintained separate community services, a significant degree of cultural autonomy, and its own occupational specialties as part of an ethnic-based division of labor. What is more, within this pluralistic system religious or cultural differences between the various groups were considered to be legitimate and proper, and there was neither the demand nor the expectation that the minorities would assimilate or that urban institutions should function as mediums of social integration.

The major change, to be sure, is that since 1967 power and control have shifted from the Arabs to the Jews. Under Israeli rule, this argument continues, the Arab minority rejects Jewish majority control just as it did all of the previous regimes, including that of the Jordanians. Yet it is precisely since 1967 that Jerusalem Arabs have benefited from a larger degree of self-expression and economic opportunities. Indeed, even though Jewish-Arab coexistence has faced many difficulties, these are essentially no different from the frictions that also exist regarding the other communal divisions in this heterogeneous city, such as those between ultraorthodox and secular Jews or Muslim and Christian Arabs. Despite the many problems, living together would be possible if the Israeli authorities would adopt liberal, tolerant attitudes and pragmatic policies. These should consist of insuring the Arabs' own way of life by allowing them a maximum of autonomous religious, cultural, and institutional authority within their own living areas, by providing them with municipal services that are equal to those received by Jews, and by encouraging voluntary, mutually beneficial social and economic contacts between Arabs and Jews.[2] Indeed, the Israeli doctrine of peaceful coexistence places value upon Arabs and Jews living side by side, although according to this formulation Arabs will have to accept their permanent minority status within a united Jerusalem under Israeli sovereignty.

While this interpretation may explain some features of Jerusalem's realities, it both ignores and fails to correctly represent certain key aspects of Arab-Jewish relationships. One major point concerns the different opportunities available to members of the two communities within the present framework of segregation and deep ethnic conflict. Given these circumstances, the formula of "separate but equal"—that is, Arabs and Jews maintaining separate residential and communal facilities while at the same time enjoying equal access to public goods and benefits—is largely fictitious, hardly possible, and rarely attained. As we saw in previous chapters, Israeli policies overwhelmingly favor the Jewish sector in both the allocation of public resources and in regard to determining urban priorities. Moreover, the Arabs' desire to preserve their own separate community structure is often used by the Jewish authorities as a pretext for not extending support to them. To be sure, benefits have reached the Arabs too as a direct result of the new opportunities made available by the Jewish economy as well as Israeli public funds allocated to the Arab sector. What is more, in several important domains both Arabs and Jews have received equal treatment and service. Indeed, when compared to their situation before 1967 it is fair to say that Arabs in Jerusalem have substantially improved their material situation while under Israeli rule. Yet, at the same time, in this united city Arabs compare their present level of well-being not with the past, but rather with the Jews with whom they daily interact. As we have seen, the inequalities in this regard have not only continued to be significant, but they have also tended to increase over time. What is more, given the fact of Jewish hegemony it has been the Jewish majority group which mainly benefited from new opportunities, particularly at the collective sectoral level, and this has largely been at the expense of the separate, yet dependent, Arab sector. Putting it succinctly, under the present structure of political and economic power the trend has inevitably been toward a system of "separate but unequal."

A second issue concerns the practical and dialectical problems arising from those Israeli policies designed to encourage voluntary ethnic separation, on the one hand, and Jewish majority control, on the other. Within the context of the continuing national struggle, Israeli policies are chiefly motivated by the desire for control, and this often at the expense of mutually desired segregation. This is particularly the case with regard

[2] The mayor of Jerusalem has been a major protagonist of this view. See, for example, Kollek 1977, 1988.

to spatial control; the expanding Jewish settlements in East Jerusalem and the nearby West Bank necessarily imply greater Arab-Jewish mixing, and this inevitably results in increased friction and conflict. These attitudes and practices are even more striking in the case of those Jewish nationalists who choose to settle within the Muslim Quarter of the Old City, or who wish to establish a Jewish presence on the Muslim-occupied Temple Mount. Their motives are do nance, not peaceful coexistence, and they are willing to live alongside Arabs and thereby forego desired separation in order to eventually dispossess them and thereby gain total control. In a related sense, we have also seen that voluntary segregation practiced by both Jews and Arabs is, in fact, closely associated with a policy of totally excluding others, intended, in turn, to consolidate one's own sectoral control.

It can readily be seen that the pluralistic or multiethnic mosaic model of Jerusalem fails to adequately emphasize the most critical aspect of Arab-Jewish relations: namely, the continuing Arab-Jewish struggle for control, and the antagonism and outright conflict resulting from the hegemony of the Jewish majority. It is for this reason that Jerusalem can best be thought of as a deeply dichotomized, or polarized, city system, not only in political terms but equally in regard to its urban structure and the everyday behavior of its residents.

The basic, underlying issue in Jerusalem confronting Jews and Arabs is political and national. The problems are not religious or cultural divisions—both sides agree to respect the different ways of life of the other community. Nor is the problem one of social and material inequalities or even outright discrimination: the Arab population does not regard the improvement in their incomes or living conditions as relevant to their political position as an occupied minority. The Israeli belief that improving the economic status of East Jerusalem Arabs would change their political aspirations has certainly proved to be unrealistic; political attitudes, as we have seen, are often reflected in economic conduct and interactions rather than the other way round. Significantly, Jerusalem Arabs have neither claimed nor struggled for their due share in economic terms or social rights so long as this implies recognizing the legitimacy of Israeli rule. In a fundamental sense the dispute centers upon the moral and legal basis of the city's political system and the mutual recognition of collective national identities, rights, and sovereignty.

In all of these respects Jewish and Arab positions are symmetrical and uncompromising, since each side denies the collective rights of the other and considers that all gains by one will mean the denial of the rights of the other. However, the basic asymmetries are also clear: while Jews wish to maintain the status quo of total control, Arabs want to completely change it and release themselves from their current occupation. Under these circumstances it is no wonder that Jewish-Arab daily relationships in Jerusalem continue to express patterns of extreme polarization. This is also the reason why conflicting claims cannot be accommodated merely by adopting policies or proposing even the best intended, carefully balanced technical solutions and compromises. As Benvenisti has shown, Jews and Arabs cannot even agree upon the same definition of "the Jerusalem problem." Jews perceive "the problem" as stemming from the fact that their just claim to Jerusalem is not recognized by the Arabs, and consequently Arab opposition undermines their attempt to bring about the desired goal of city-wide integration. For Arabs "the problem" is precisely their difficulty in achieving political autonomy and self-determination, as well as their inability to effectively resist unilateral Israeli actions undertaken to deprive them of control over their own affairs.[3] Jerusalem's emerging urban patterns and political orientations represent the encapsulation of the national political conflict between Jews and Arabs. Because the conflict is closely related to broader national issues, it becomes even more difficult to resolve.

THE JERUSALEM MODEL IN COMPARATIVE PERSPECTIVE

To this point our analysis has focused entirely upon Arabs and Jews in Jerusalem. However, some of this city's special features, as well as those that it shares with other urban systems, can best be seen by comparing Jerusalem's situation with similar cases.

In Jerusalem itself the social divisions and conflicts are by no means only between Arabs and Jews. Within each of these two major ethnic categories differences of origin, religious belief and practice are also significant. In the case of the Jewish population one basic division is between its secular and ultraorthodox segments; this latter group comprises nearly 30 percent of the Jews living in the city, and it maintains a completely separate regime that is governed by strict religious customs and rules.[4] Similarly, within the non-Jewish population the distinction between Muslims and Christians has also remained important. It is significant to note that the Christian population, which numbered over 30,000 persons toward the end of the Mandatory period, or close to 20 percent of the entire Jerusalem population, has since 1947 constantly declined both in number and as a proportion of the city's inhabitants. This trend under different regimes (Jordanian and Israeli) is undoubtedly related to the continuing Jewish-Arab conflict. Comprising by the mid-1980s no more than 14,000 persons, or merely 3 percent of the total population,

[3] See Benvenisti 1981b, 1985.
[4] See Shilhav and Friedman 1985.

Christian Arabs and non-Arabs (such as Armenians and others) nevertheless have continued to constitute well-defined, separate communities.[5]

Each of these main subgroups tends to cluster in separate neighborhoods and maintains its own school systems, communal institutions, and social networks. However, in contrast with the schism that exists between Jews and Arabs these other communal divisions are typically voluntary and by no means so deep and comprehensive. The comparative patterns of residential segregation can provide one useful indicator in this respect. In addition to the West-East, or Jewish-Arab, residential dividing line, the parallel north-south, or orthodox-secular division within the Jewish sector is in many respects no less visible and significant. Yet, unlike the boundaries between Jews and Arabs, the Jewish orthodox residential quarters have gradually expanded into the Jewish secular neighborhoods and in certain instances mixed zones or transitional areas have been created over time. In much the same way the Muslim and Christian residential areas and commercial centers have overlapped to form grey areas that include members of both groups. This tendency toward less rigid boundaries can also be seen in the political sphere. In contrast with Jerusalem Arabs, the ultraorthodox Jewish groups make effective use of the political system in order to enlarge their share of publicly allocated resources. The process has been different, but no less significant, among the Christian Arabs and Armenians: those that remained in Jerusalem have generally joined in support of the Arab national cause, thereby lessening the divisions between themselves and the Muslims.

Some of the other, more subtle distinctions within Jerusalem's heterogeneous population have also gradually been reduced over time. This is the case in regard to the great multiplicity of Jewish ethnic groups—that is, Jewish immigrants and their descendants whose origins are in numerous European and Middle Eastern countries—and, equally, with respect to the distinctions between Arabs who come from old-line Jerusalem families, others who are refugees from the 1948 war with Israel, and the large number of Arabs from the Hebron region who have migrated to Jerusalem. There can be little doubt that the frictions or conflicts between these subgroups have lessened partly as a result of the widescale Arab-Jewish polarization. Moreover, basic ethnic membership—that is, being a Jew or an Arab—dominates all other affiliations: each of the numerous subgroups resides within its own ethnic sector and tends to interact and compete for resources within its own ethnic boundaries. We therefore conclude that while Jerusalem is surely a heterogeneous, compartmentalized city, the basic division between Arabs and Jews is not merely deeper in degree but rather different in kind from the others.

[5] See Danilov 1981.

Enlarging our range of comparison, we turn next to compare Arab-Jewish relations in Jerusalem with the patterns of interaction between these groups in Israel as a whole. In chapter 1 it was pointed out that while the large majority of Israeli Jews and Arabs live in separate communities, there are also a number of places where members of both communities reside. Of special interest are those half-dozen or so Israeli cities or conurbations that have a significant Arab minority, such as Haifa, Acre, Tel Aviv–Jaffa, Lod, and Ramla. In each of these places a residual Arab population remained after the 1948 war in predominantly Jewish urban areas, and while the specific demographic proportion varies from place to place, some common features of Jewish-Arab relationships have emerged.[6]

To a large extent the social patterns and daily contacts between members of the two communities reflect the basic divisions between them. In each of the mixed cities the local Arab minority tends to be concentrated in specific, segregated residential enclaves that are typically located in the older, less favorable sections of the inner city (these are commonly areas where Arabs had lived prior to 1948). This form of Arab residential segregation is a consequence of both their own preference to cluster around their separate communal institutions, as well as the various institutional and economic constraints imposed upon them by the Jewish majority. Jewish interests have typically been given priority with regard to public housing policies, urban planning, redrawing municipal boundaries, and the expropriation of Arab land for new Jewish settlement. These practices have in particular been carried out in those urban areas where Arabs made up a significant and growing proportion of the population. Israeli policies have been aimed at limiting Arab expansion, preserving the Jewish demographic majority, and extending its territorial control.

This struggle over space and unequal opportunities available to Arabs and Jews are certainly reminiscent of Jerusalem. At the same time, however, there are significant differences both in regard to Israeli Arabs' political behavior and the actual boundaries that exist between the two groups. In contrast with Jerusalem, in several of the mixed Israeli cities Arabs have been elected to the local municipal councils, and they take an active part in local city affairs and administration. In addition, in contrast with Jerusalem, where Jews maintain tight boundaries around their own neighborhoods while at the same time seeking to forcefully pene-

[6] It should be noted that out of 120 urban localities in Israel, for the most part either Jewish or Arab, only eight, including Jerusalem, were defined in the 1983 census as "mixed cities." A "mixed city" was defined as one in which a significant number of non-Jews lived within the municipal boundaries in addition to the Jewish majority. Among the various studies treating the particular issue of Jewish-Arab relations in Israeli mixed cities, see, for example, Kipnis and Schnell 1978; Ben-Artzi 1980.

trate the Arab sections, in Israeli towns such as Haifa, Jaffa, and Nazareth local Arabs have in recent years been gradually moving into Jewish neighborhoods and have sometimes established their own businesses there.[7] These developments indicate that Israeli Jews more readily accept Israeli Arabs as their neighbors and business associates despite occasional tensions or expressions of prejudice and discrimination.

The differences are, in fact, even deeper. As a number of studies have shown, many Israeli Arabs have come to accept their minority status within the Jewish state.[8] Israeli Arabs vote in large numbers in municipal and national elections, have taken an active part in Israeli political parties (including exclusively Arab parties), and, in addition, have organized politically as a way to enlarge their share of government-allocated resources and thereby lessen or do away with the inequalities between themselves and the Jewish majority. In all of these respects they have behaved as "Israelis"—that is, despite their frequent sense of alienation they have chosen to act within the Israeli social and political system. This is, of course, in total contrast with the attitudes and behavior of the Jerusalem Arab population. We therefore conclude that the extent of Arab-Jewish polarization is far greater in Jerusalem than in Israeli cities and towns and, what is more, majority-minority relations also differ significantly in these two contexts.

These contrasts are well illustrated when we compare East Jerusalem Arabs with the small yet growing number of Israeli Arabs who remained in West Jerusalem following 1948 as well as those who have moved to the city and made it their temporary or permanent home. Unlike East Jerusalem Arabs many Israeli Arabs live in the Jewish sections of West Jerusalem, study at the Hebrew University, and are likely to be employed by a variety of Israeli government agencies. Even though their intermediary position often remains ambiguous and problematic, members of this group at times also serve as a kind of bridge and fulfill broker functions between the two sectors. As we saw in the analysis of Beit Safafa, they are often placed in marginal categories, considered by the Jewish population to be "Arabs" and by East Jerusalem Arabs as "Israelis." The significant point is that, beyond marginality, in many respects they continue to behave as "Israelis": they take part in Israeli local and national elections, and whether they make their home in East or West Jerusalem they have maintained a certain separation between themselves and the East Jerusalem Arab population.

By contrast, more than two decades of direct Israeli rule over East Jerusalem have failed to change the political attitudes and behavioral pat-

[7] See Soffer 1986.
[8] This is discussed and analyzed in Smooha 1984.

terns of East Jerusalem Arabs when compared to Arabs residing in the nearby West Bank territories. The legal boundary between these two Arab groups did have implications for their personal status, legal rights, and economic opportunities. Living under Israeli jurisdiction lent East Jerusalem Arabs certain rights such as more open access to West Jerusalem and Israel or the possibility of developing a free press,—rights essentially denied to West Bank Arabs. In addition, the fact that in Jerusalem Arabs have been directly exposed to the large Jewish majority population, in contrast with the all-Arab cities on the West Bank, has also provided some different life experiences and more frequent contacts with Jews. Nevertheless, in spite of Israel's original hope and intention that Jerusalem Arabs would adopt the positions of Israeli Arabs, the pattern of Jewish-Arab relations in Jerusalem has remained basically the same as the dichotomized model of Jewish-Arab relations that prevails throughout the other Israeli-occupied territories. The daily reality, institutional frameworks, and political attitudes of East Jerusalem Arabs remain practically identical to those held by Arabs in the West Bank; all share the same separate communal organizations, family ties, and economic relations; most important of all, they have continued to be Jordanian citizens. Regardless of the distinctions that Jews make between "united Jerusalem" and the West Bank territories, Jerusalem and West Bank Arabs express the same basic political attitude that rejects the Israeli occupation.

Finally, Jerusalem can also be usefully compared with other ethnically mixed cities where communal divisions are expressed in ongoing antagonism and conflict. Along the spectrum of cities that are not merely "heterogeneous" or "divided" but rather "deeply polarized," the best known cases include Beirut (Muslims and Christians), Nicosia (Greek and Turkish Cypriots), Belfast (Catholics and Protestants), Brussels (Flemish and Walloons), Montreal (English and French Canadians), and Singapore (Malay and Chinese). The particular definition of ethnic identities, historically derived social and political structures, and the specific reasons and manifestations of conflict, obviously differ from case to case. These various intercommunal urban conflicts may involve religious, linguistic, or related issues; the conflict itself may also be latent, overt, or violent. Similarly, the degree of social segregation, chances of mobility, or economic opportunity open to the opposing groups also differ, as do their respective attitudes and policies regarding the basic issue of whether to remain together or break apart.[9]

At the same time, however, all these cities share a number of essential features typical of polarized urban entities. As in Jerusalem, intergroup

[9] A comparative review of the Jerusalem case and several other ethnically mixed cities can be found in Kraemer 1980; Savitzki and Frank 1976.

conflicts are ethnically based, involving central values, world views, and symbols, and consequently are characterized by intense emotions, mutual distrust, and intolerance. Yet the most critical issue is the absence of consensus regarding political power sharing. This is the case irrespective of the actual majority-minority population ratios, or the economic status of the contesting groups. The principal grievances of subordinated groups are not merely related to their relative deprivation or discrimination, but rather concern the legitimacy of the urban political system. In addition, these polarized cities are also the reflection of macro-scale state-wide conflicts over nationality, sovereignty, and options of separation. Under these conditions not only is segmentation in everyday life expressed in many areas, but, in addition, practically all matters related to city administration, such as providing public services, housing, and employment policies or urban planning, are subject to fundamental disagreement and interpreted in zero-sum political terms.

In all these respects the closest analogical case to Jerusalem is Belfast and Northern Ireland.[10] In Jerusalem, as in Belfast, unresolved, often violent national-ethnic conflict is ever-present. In both cases diametrically opposed national aspirations involve a kind of a "double minority syndrome": the local minority considers itself part of an external majority, and the local majority, in turn, sees itself as a besieged minority. Consequently, the minority group refuses to accept its minority status and contests the legitimacy of majority rule. Both parties face political uncertainty, have a sense of insecurity, and fail to reach any effective compromise or agreement.

Given this overall context, in the particular urban settings of Jerusalem and Belfast the dominant group not only holds total political power, but is also the demographic majority and maintains economic hegemony. Yet, at the same time, the majority feels menaced by the presence of the large, well-organized, and growing minority, and both sides view all issues related to demography and territory in strategic, symbolic, and even sacred terms. But what makes these distant and different cities so similar is their all-encompassing dichotomized environment. This dichotomy relates to political, social, economic, and territorial interests, and has a direct impact upon both groups' perceptions and the psychological atmosphere that is created. Nevertheless, urban systems continue to function, daily interactions across ethnic lines are frequent, and an air of normalcy exists since, after all, "life must go on." But this does not mean that living together or daily exchanges are considered desirable: in the same way

[10] For a detailed analysis of the similar features of Jewish-Arab relations in Jerusalem and those of Protestants and Catholics in Belfast, see Benvenisti 1982. Analyses of the various urban patterns and related conflicts in Belfast can be found in Boal 1969; Boal, Murray, and Poole 1976.

that Belfast has been described as a city where Catholics and Protestants coexist on a "narrow ground," or that rather than being intermingled they are interlocked, so too these descriptions perfectly illustrate Jewish-Arab relations in Jerusalem.[11]

However, in spite of the many similarities, the contrasts or differences between the two cases are no less significant. Unlike Jerusalem's Jews and Arabs, Protestants and Catholics in Belfast share many basic cultural values (such as language) and there are no legal status distinctions between them; mixing or crossing over is therefore easier. What is more, social class interests sometimes override ethnic divisions; this has never been the case in Jerusalem at any level. In comparison with Jerusalem, the scope of daily segregation between Catholics and Protestants in Belfast is far less important; despite the high degree of residential segregation, many Protestants and Catholics continue to reside side by side in a number of mixed neighborhoods in various sections of the city, and they also share the same major commercial districts, public institutions, and services. In contrast with Jerusalem, there are no separate Protestant and Catholic urban transportation systems, universities or, for that matter, blood banks and cigarettes. Most importantly, unlike Jerusalem Arabs, many Catholics in Belfast have chosen to organize within the existing political system; enjoying equal political rights they have formed political parties and seek to increase their share in housing, schools, and other public facilities in spite of their continued minority status.

On the other hand, despite periodic outbreaks of protest and terrorism, the first twenty years of daily coexistence between Jews and Arabs in Jerusalem have been less violent in comparison with Belfast's open violence and widescale communal destruction. But this seemingly "normal" two decades of coexistence in Jerusalem should not be taken to mean that the conflict between Jews and Arabs has been less bitter or basic. On the contrary, it could be interpreted as resulting from the large degree of Arab dependency upon the Jewish economy and administration, and the effective tactics used by the Israeli security forces. Moreover, under the present political, economic, and social circumstances both Jews and Arabs have preferred a certain mutual restraint to open, outright conflict: the Arabs have not wished to provide an excuse for the Jewish majority to employ more extreme measures, and the Jews, who wield power and control, have had no reason to adopt more coercive means.

By most standards Jerusalem can be considered to be an even more polarized city than Belfast. To put it in more general terms, while Jewish-Arab daily relations in Jerusalem do not represent a totally unique case,

[11] See Boal and Douglas 1982.

they can nevertheless be classified as an extreme instance of polarization between ethnic or communal groups living together in mixed cities.

RECENT TRENDS AND PROSPECTS

During the first two decades following Jerusalem's reunification, the day-to-day forms of relationship between Arabs and Jews became well established. These patterns should not be thought of as constituting a "stable equilibrium" of expectation and action. To the contrary, they changed periodically as a result of both altered levels of conflict and, conversely, the dynamics of prolonged coexistence. Nonetheless, an overall framework of contact, marked by certain rules of the game and mutual understandings, was established.

It is in this respect that the examination of recent trends and events should be considered. This is particularly the case since to a certain extent these long-term trends and new developments moved in opposite directions, toward both greater integration and deeper division.

Among the recent developments indicative of enhanced integration are the growing number of Arab families who rented or purchased apartments in several of the new Jewish neighborhoods in East Jerusalem, particularly in the northernmost section of the city. Thus far this only includes Israeli Arab families, and it has also led to occasional opposition on the part of the Jewish residents. This process suggests that even in these most exposed, "frontier neighborhoods" of East Jerusalem the exclusivistic attitudes practiced by Jews have become somewhat relaxed, and the entrance into those areas by East Jerusalem Arabs may follow in the future. In a similar vein, the fact that a number of Arab businesses were able to establish themselves in West Jerusalem is no less significant. Even though these initiatives are small in number and took twenty years to develop, they illustrate the point that economic forces and mutual interest can enhance processes of broader integration.

On the other hand, trends indicating deeper divisions have also been evident, and in fact, much more pronounced. On an institutional level a revealing change was the modification of the concession rights granted to the Arab East Jerusalem Electric Corporation. According to a new agreement imposed upon the Arab company in 1987, it no longer supplies electricity to the Jewish neighborhoods located in East Jerusalem. These Jewish neighborhoods were directly connected to the Israeli electricity grid, so that Jewish consumers now receive "Jewish electricity" and Arab consumers "Arab electricity." This kind of Jewish insistence upon exercising greater control at the expense of the Arab population was also given concrete form, as we have seen, by those Jews who moved into the Old City's Muslim Quarter. In addition, trends reflecting greater segregation and conflict are indicated by the fact that since the mid-1980s the number of Jews who made their way to the Old City's bazaar or other Arab commercial centers has progressively declined; the intermittent violent incidents in which Jews were attacked while shopping or touring in Arab East Jerusalem led many of them to be more cautious about crossing the ethnic border.

On the Arab side, new political attitudes have also been voiced, proposing, in fact, two possible, although contradictory strategies. In 1987 a well-publicized, first-of-a-kind proposal was "floated" by an East Jerusalem political activist suggesting that Arabs run for municipal office on their own separate list. By making use of the political process they could become a formidable minority on the city council and thereby more effectively press for Arab rights. While this proposal remained theoretical (it was immediately attacked by both nationalist-leaning Jews and Arabs) it indicates the new conditions that would be brought about should Jerusalem Arabs actually exercise their political rights: the Arabs would be recognizing Israeli rule, while the Jews would have to choose between real democracy or discriminative control. Soon thereafter an alternative proposal was put forward—namely, that the Arabs adopt a strategy of all-encompassing civil disobedience. This was to include refusal to pay taxes, no longer using Jewish public facilities, and even stopping to work for Jews. This strategy would, it was suggested, enhance Arab disengagement from the Jewish sector, and in addition demonstrate in forceful political terms Arab resistance to the prolonged period of peaceful coexistence.

Overshadowing all these events, however, was the Arab popular uprising, or *intifada*, that broke out in East Jerusalem toward the end of 1987 following Arab rioting and protest throughout the West Bank and the Gaza Strip. These events have brought about a new phase in Arab-Jewish relationships and they undoubtedly constitute a watershed following the first two decades of Jerusalem's reunification.

The Arab popular protest at first took the form of spontaneous street riots. Arab youngsters set up barriers at various points throughout the Arab section of the city, stoned Jewish cars and buses, and attempted to set fire to branches of Israeli banks and other Israeli institutions located in East Jerusalem. At the height of the disturbances the Arab neighborhoods seemed like a besieged city, with tear gas fired at rioters, repeated police charges, and curfews imposed upon the Arab population. For the first time in more than twenty years Israeli military units had to be massively deployed in order to assist the local police in restoring order.

This sudden, violent Arab uprising came as a shock to the Jewish population. At one point Mayor Kollek dramatically proclaimed that "Jewish-Arab coexistence is dead," and while he later modified this assessment it appeared as if twenty years of efforts had collapsed overnight. The reactions of Jewish residents living along the contact line with Arab neighborhoods attest to this strong response; in some instances their homes were stoned by Arab youngsters, and the Jews began organizing for self-defense and called for direct retaliation. Symbolically, in Abu Tur Jewish residents erected street barriers in order to stop Arab rioters, thereby themselves reestablishing the old dividing line.

Once the Arab uprising moved beyond its initial spontaneous phase and became more organized and prolonged, its broader objectives and strategies were also more clearly and explicitly formulated. Beyond the continuation of street demonstrations and political unrest the major goal was disengagement from Israeli rule and Jewish domination in all practical, daily matters. The Arabs were urged by the leaders of the *intifada* to stop working for Jews, and, more particularly, to resign from all posts in the government and municipal administration, stop using these services, withdraw their money from Israeli banks, and boycott all Israeli products. In addition, the Arab population was called upon to take part in various acts of civil disobedience such as refusing to pay taxes and fines and joining the Arab strikes that closed the schools and shops. Printed circulars with explicit instructions in all these matters were issued by national and local "popular committees," and other, often violent, measures were employed in order to insure that their instructions were followed.

One of the central conflicts confronting the Arab organizers of the uprising and the Israeli authorities was who would be in actual control of Arab East Jerusalem. Long after it broke out, the practical outcomes of this struggle have not yet been clearly decided, and have also varied according to particular issues. For example, following the closure of Arab shops, as ordered by the *intifada* movement, the Israeli authorities at first tried to force the shopkeepers to reopen; this action failed, since, in addition to their political allegiance, the Arab merchants felt even more menaced and exposed to threats from their own fellow Arabs. Consequently, since these first confrontations Arab shops in East Jerusalem have been open for only a few hours a day with frequent strikes; the schedule is set by the Arabs according to their own rules and timetables. In other cases too the normal enforcement of city decrees, as well as the provision of certain public services to the Arab population, were interrupted, particularly when the Jewish authorities considered them to be nonessential or were reluctant to endanger their municipal workers. More generally, since the outbreak of these hostilities Jews have stopped visiting Arab shopping or tourist areas; fearing for their personal safety they have systematically avoided passing through the Arab sections of the city even when traveling to Jewish neighborhoods in East Jerusalem.

Arabs too have felt more exposed when visiting West Jerusalem. They typically undergo security checks and there is always the danger of Jewish violence. Within the Arab residential areas as well, the repeated intervention of the Israeli security forces and the accompanying curfews, house searches, and harassment place them under constant pressure. Indeed, since the beginning of the *intifada* a kind of "geography of fear" has characterized both Jewish and Arab movement across the ethnic boundaries; more than anything else this testifies to the psychological and practical effects of the deepening division of the city.

Nevertheless, certain day-to-day relations between Jews and Arabs have continued. While the previous air of "normalcy" may have left the city, the economic ties in particular cannot be entirely broken. After days or weeks of staying away from their Israeli workplaces, most Arab workers returned; at the Nimrod factory, for example, Arabs and Jews continued to bake bread together, and at Hadassah Hospital Arab and Jewish patients and nurses continued to interact with each other. By the same token, although the marketing of Israeli-produced bread, cigarettes, clothing, and similar items to the Arab sector drastically declined—the local population substituting Arab products—Arab customers and businesses could not forego the use of more specialized goods and services originating from the Jewish sector. Moreover, as the strikes and closing down of East Jerusalem's commercial activities continued, it appeared that the number of Arab visits to Jewish West Jerusalem may have increased (particularly among the more affluent) in order to both satisfy their daily needs and find temporary refuge from the burdens of the *intifada*. While all sections of the Arab population, including merchants, employers, and workers, were urged to share the efforts and personal sacrifices brought about by the uprising, these could not always be effectively imposed in light of the fundamental necessities of economic survival.

If, as we have suggested, the *intifada* punctured the Israeli ideology of "peaceful coexistence," this was nowhere more clear than in the realm of politics. Major components of the largely informal system of political exchanges that had linked Jews and Arabs for two decades came to an end. At the elite level there were few if any contacts between the Arab notables and Israeli decision makers: the notables, an older generation of Arab leaders, were shoved aside by the new *intifada* leadership, and, what is more, the Jordanian government took the position that it no longer represented the Palestinians living in the West Bank and Jerusalem. The Jordanians still retained a foothold in Jerusalem—employees of the Muslim *Waqf* continued to receive their salaries from Jordan—but Jordanian activity and influence had, in effect, ended. At the local level some of the neighborhood *Mukhtars* and others still met with Israeli municipal officials; as in the past, these encounters focused upon attempts to resolve local problems facing the Arab residents. Interestingly, neighborhood councils, or *minhalot*, that were established by the municipality in three Arab areas, continued to operate during the *intifada*. Nonetheless, all of the participants recognized that these local-level "broker functions" were irrelevant to the new issues being posed by the uprising. It was obvious too that the Arab doctrine of *sumud* had run its course. Arabs were no longer enjoined to remain "steadfast," but rather urged in bulletins issued by the *intifada* leadership to directly resist the Israeli authorities. Funds were not provided as in the past for mortgages assisting Arabs to build houses; they were directed instead to support the large number of families whose husbands or brothers were in Israeli jails. Finally, the patronage features that were a part of the old system also lost their effectiveness; Jerusalem Arabs chose not to vote in the local elections held in 1989, and as a consequence Kollek, although reelected, lost his majority on the city council. In short, as a result of the *intifada*, peaceful coexistence and *sumud* were replaced by direct action, violent confrontation, and greater uncertainty regarding the future.

Several observations can be made regarding this new phase in Jewish-Arab relations. To begin with, the Arab uprising was undoubtedly the most forceful expression of their refusal to live under Israeli occupation. Following two decades of living together, Jerusalem Arabs clearly demonstrated that they were willing and able to endure great economic and other sacrifices in order to gain control over their own affairs. The Arab *intifada* was also the outcome of many years of collective and individual frustrations resulting from the political deadlock, and, moreover, the daily humiliating experiences and repeated frictions with Jews and the Israeli authorities. Long-term social and economic forces, set within the framework of majority-minority relations as well as the particular policies adopted by the Israeli administration, also had a cumulative effect. A growing number of young, educated Arabs, knowledgeable in Hebrew and acquainted with Israeli norms, found it increasingly difficult to find appropriate outlets for their political and economic aspirations; these persons became the leading group in the uprising. To some extent this movement was based upon the structure and authority of the numerous Arab "national organizations"—universities, professional associations, and voluntary groups—that had been permitted to develop under Israeli rule. This institutional structure gave both direction and momentum to the *intifada*.

The Arab uprising in Jerusalem also did away with any Israeli illusions that East Jerusalem Arabs were different from those in the West Bank, and that they would grow accustomed to their unique status under Israeli sovereignty. At the same time, however, the *intifada* in Jerusalem was definitely less violent and comprehensive than in the West Bank and Gaza, in spite of the fact that the city was the center of the Palestinian national movement and organizations. Demonstrations mainly occurred or were initiated by Arabs living in refugee camps and villages in Jerusalem's periphery. Significantly, the number of Arab casualties in confrontations with the Israeli security forces was far less in Jerusalem in comparison with the other areas. Similarly, unlike the West Bank, in Jerusalem the Israeli administrative system did not collapse; only a few Arabs left their posts in the municipality and the police force, and Arab schools in East Jerusalem were not entirely closed. In part, this may be attributed to the fact that, within the Israeli jurisdiction of Jerusalem, law enforcement was in the hands of the police rather than the army, and to the moderating effects of the more liberal policies of Jerusalem's mayor and the municipality.[12] What is more, it may be that the Arab sense of being a minority facing a massive Jewish majority also acted as a moderating factor.

Finally, in spite of the far-reaching psychological and political implications of these recent events, in practical terms the underlying factors determining Jewish-Arab daily relationships have not fundamentally changed. This is particularly the case regarding the nature and implications of the continuing majority-minority power relations. Jerusalem's Arabs are seeking to change the rules regarding their daily relations with Jews. In effect, they have attempted to disengage themselves from Israeli control. But this has been difficult to accomplish in light of their basic economic and political dependency upon the Jewish sector and lack of sufficient alternatives. Quite to the contrary, it has instead been the Jews who were in a position to disengage themselves. Unlike the Arabs they could afford to completely avoid crossing over to the Arab commercial centers; faced with ongoing Arab strikes and political unrest, Jewish entrepreneurs also sought alternatives to employing Arab workers or maintaining ties with Arab firms. At the same time, both Arabs and Jews again appear to be looking for some way or avenue to accommodate their mutual economic interests and needs, even under changing political conditions. For example, since Jews became apprehensive about visiting Arab shops located within purely Arab areas, in recent years some Arab merchants relocated their businesses closer to the ethnic boundary so that they would be more accessible to Jews. Since the *intifada* Arab merchants have also attempted to channel their products through Jewish merchants rather than directly to Jewish customers. Similarly, facing a

[12] Although the specific features of the Arab uprising in Jerusalem and their differences when compared to the rest of the occupied territories have often been pointed out, the precise underlying reasons for these differences are obviously more difficult to confirm. This topic is considered in Zilberman 1988; Ashkenzai 1988.

decline in Arab demand for certain Jewish products, Jewish entrepreneurs have begun to use Arab brokers or even to camouflage the Israeli origin of their products. Paradoxically, these practices resemble those that were previously employed by the Arabs, so that the general rules of intergroup exchange have only marginally changed.

In conclusion, during the first two decades following Jerusalem's reunification, Arabs and Jews agreed to operate within a complicated framework of understandings and exchange. As we have seen throughout this book, the system that emerged was mainly concerned with everyday interests and practical matters. As recent events have shown, some features of this design have been altered and this process is still continuing. Yet the basic unresolved issue confronting Arabs and Jews has been, and undoubtedly remains, that of collective political rights, national identity, sovereignty, and control. Compromise and accommodation on these issues have been far more difficult to reach since they involve basic political principles and primordial symbols. Nevertheless, as we have also seen, what is possible in Jerusalem depends upon what both sides are willing and prepared to accept. Based upon their shared experience during the past twenty years, probably the only thing that Jews and Arabs presently agree upon is that whatever the future political situation, the city itself should not again be divided. Jews and Arabs are bound to live together in Jerusalem, even if they prefer to do so separately.

References

Abdul-Hadi, M. F. *Thoughts on Israel's Policies and Practices in Jerusalem.* Cambridge, Mass.: Center for International Affairs, Harvard University, 1985.

Amir, I. *An Evaluation of the Changes in the Economic Situation of East Jerusalem Arabs, 1967–1969* (in Hebrew). Jerusalem: Israeli Company for Economic Services, 1969.

Amiran, D. H. K., A. Shachar, and I. Kimhi. *Urban Geography of Jerusalem. A Companion Volume to the Atlas of Jerusalem.* Jerusalem: Massada, 1973.

Ashkenazi, A. *Israeli Policies and Palestinian Fragmentation: Political and Social Impacts in Israel and Jerusalem.* Policy Studies no. 24. Jerusalem: Leonard Davis Institute, Hebrew University of Jerusalem, 1988.

———. *Palestinian Views about Jerusalem.* Policy Studies no. 30. Jerusalem: Leonard Davis Institute, Hebrew University of Jerusalem, 1989.

Ben-Arich, Y. *The Population of the Large Towns in Palestine during the First Eighty Years of the Nineteenth Century According to Western Sources.* International seminar on the history of Palestine and its Jewish settlement during the Ottoman period, Jerusalem, Hebrew University, 1970.

———. *A City Reflected in Its Times* (in Hebrew). Vol. 1, *Jerusalem in the Nineteenth Century—The Old City*; vol. 2, *New Jerusalem—The Beginnings* Jerusalem: Yad Izhak Ben-Zvi, 1977, 1979.

Ben-Artzi, J. *Residential Patterns and Intra Urban Migration of Arabs in Haifa.* Occasional Papers (new series), no. 1. Haifa: Jewish-Arab Center, University of Haifa, 1980.

Benvenisti, M. *Jerusalem, the Torn City.* Minneapolis: Minnesota University Press, 1976.

———. *Jerusalem: A City with a Wall in Its Midst* (in Hebrew). Tel Aviv: Hakibbutz Hameuchad, 1981a.

———. "Some Guidelines for Positive Thinking on Jerusalem." *Middle East Review* (Spring-Summer 1981b): 35–40.

———. *Administering Conflicts: Local Government in Jerusalem and Belfast.* Thesis presented to the John F. Kennedy School of Government, Harvard University, 1982.

———. *Jerusalem: A Study of a Polarized Community*, Research Paper no. 3. Jerusalem: West Bank Data Base Project, 1983.

———. *The Jerusalem Question: Problems, Procedures and Options.* Rev. ed. Jerusalem: West Bank Data Base Project, 1985.

———. *Conflicts and Contradictions.* New York: Villard, 1986.

Benziman, U. *A City without a Wall* (in Hebrew). Jerusalem: Shocken, 1973.

Bigelman, S., ed. *Statistical Yearbook of Jerusalem.* Jerusalem: Municipality of Jerusalem and the Jerusalem Institute for Israel Studies, various years.

Bin Talal, H. *A Study of Jerusalem.* London: Longman, 1979.

Blumer, H. "Industrialization and Race Relations." In *Industrialization and Race Relations: A Symposium*, ed. G. Hunter. London: Allen and Unwin, 1965.

Boal, F. W. "Territoriality on the Shankill-Falls Drive in Belfast." *Irish Geography* 6/1 (1969): 212–29.

Boal, F. W., R. C. Murray, and M. A. Poole. "Belfast: The Encapsulation of a National Conflict." In *Urban Ethnic Conflict: A Comparative Perspective*, eds. S. E. Clarck and J. L. Obler. Comparative Urban Studies Monographs, no. 3. Chapel Hill: University of North Carolina, 1976.

Boal, F. W. and J. N. H. Douglas, eds. *Integration and Division: Geographical Perspectives on the Northern Ireland Problem*: London: Academic, 1982.

Clarke, F., D. Ley, and C. Peach. *Geography and Ethnic Pluralism*. London: George Allen and Unwin, 1984.

Cohen, A. *Urban Ethnicity*. London: Tavistock, 1974.

Cohen, S. B. *Jerusalem: Bridging the Four Walls*. New York: Herzl, 1977.

Danilov, S. "Dilemmas of Jerusalem's Christians." *Middle East Review* (Spring-Summer 1981): 41–47.

Epstein, A. L. *Politics in an Urban African Community*. Manchester: Manchester University Press, 1958.

Farchi, D. "Problems in Jewish-Arab Coexistence in Jerusalem." In *Ten Years of Israeli Rule in Judea and Samaria* (in Hebrew), ed. R. Israeli. Jerusalem: Magnes, 1980.

Gluckman, M. *Closed Systems and Open Minds*. Edinburgh: Oliver and Boyd, 1964.

———. *Politics, Law and Ritual in Tribal Society*. Chicago: Aldine, 1965.

Heilman, S. *A Walker in Jerusalem*. New York: Summit, 1986.

Hyman, B., I. Kimhi, and J. Savitzki. *Jerusalem in Transition: Urban Growth and Change—1970's–1980's*. Jerusalem: Institute of Urban and Regional Studies, Hebrew University of Jerusalem and Jerusalem Institute for Israel Studies, 1988.

Israel, Central Bureau of Statistics (CBS). *East Jerusalem: Census of Population and Housing 1967*. Jerusalem, 1968, 1970.

———. *Census of Population and Housing (1983)*. Various vols. Jerusalem.

Israeli, D. "Ethnicity and Industrial Relations." *Ethnic and Racial Studies* 2 (1979): 80-89.

Jackson, R., and S. J. Smith. *Social Interaction and Ethnic Segregation*. London: Academic, 1981.

Kapferer, B. "Norms and Manipulations of Relationships in a Work Context." In *Social Networks in Urban Situations*, ed. J. C. Mitchell. Manchester, Manchester University Press, 1969.

Kaplan, G. *Arab and Jew in Jerusalem*. Cambridge: Harvard University Press, 1980.

Kimhi, I., and B. Hyman. *A Socio-Economic Survey of Jerusalem, 1967–1975*. Jerusalem: Jerusalem Committee, 1978.

Kipnis, B. A., and I. Schnell. "Changes in the Distribution of Arabs in Mixed Jewish-Arab Cities in Israel." *Economic Geography* (1978): 168–80.

Kollek, T. "Jerusalem." *Foreign Affairs* (July 1977): 701–16.

————. "Sharing United Jerusalem." *Foreign Affairs* (Winter 1988/89): 156–68.

Kraemer, J. L., ed. *Jerusalem Problems and Prospects.* New York: Praeger, 1980.

Kroyanker, D. *Jerusalem Planning and Development 1979–1982.* Jerusalem: Jerusalem Institute for Israel Studies, 1982.

————. *Jerusalem Planning and Development 1982–1985: New Trends.* Jerusalem: Jerusalem Committee and Jerusalem Institute for Israel Studies, 1985.

Kutcher, A. *The New Jerusalem: Planning and Politics.* London: Thames and Hudson, 1973.

Lapierre, D., and L. Collins. *O Jerusalem.* Paris: Robert Laffont, 1971.

Ley, D. *A Social Geography of the City:* New York: Harper and Row, 1983.

Oesterreicher, J. M., and A. Sinai, eds. *Jerusalem.* New York: John Day, 1974.

Peach, C., V. Robinson, and S. Smith. *Ethnic Segregation in Cities.* Athens: University of Georgia Press, 1981.

Prawer, J., and O. Ahimeir, eds. *Twenty Years in Jerusalem, 1967–1987* (in Hebrew). Jerusalem: Ministry of Defence Publication and Jerusalem Institute for Israel Studies, 1988.

Romann, M. *A Social-Economic Survey of United Jerusalem* (in Hebrew). Jerusalem: Maurice Falk Institute for Economic Research in Israel, 1967.

————. *Inter-Relationship between the Jewish and Arab Sectors in Jerusalem* (in Hebrew). Publication No. 11. Jerusalem: Jerusalem Institute for Israel Studies, 1984.

Savitzki, J., and T. Frank. *A Comparative Study of Ethnically-Mixed Cities: Socio-Political Aspects, Public Policies and Programs.* Jerusalem: Institute of Urban and Regional Studies, Hebrew University, 1976.

Schmelz, U. O. "The Jewish Population of Jerusalem during the Last Hundred Years." *Jewish Journal of Sociology* 2/1 (June 1960).

————. *Modern Jerusalem's Demographic Evolution.* Jerusalem: Institute of Contemporary Jewry, Hebrew University and Jerusalem Institute for Israel Studies, 1987.

Shilhav, J., and M. Friedman. *Growth and Segregation: The Ultra-Orthodox Community of Jerusalem* (in Hebrew). Publication no. 15. Jerusalem: Jerusalem Institute for Israel Studies, 1985.

Shipler, D. K. *Arab and Jew.* New York: Penguin, 1987.

Smith, H. *Jewish Jerusalemites View the Arabs in the Eastern Part of the City* (in Hebrew). Unpublished, Sept. 1973.

————. *A Survey of Municipal Services* (in Hebrew). Unpublished summary of a public opinion survey commissioned by the Jerusalem Municipality, March 1981.

Smooha, S. *Israel, Pluralism and Conflict.* London: Routledge and Kegan Paul, 1978.

————. *The Orientation and Politicization of the Arab Minority in Israel.* Monograph Series on the Middle East, no. 2. Haifa: University of Haifa, Institute of Middle East Studies, 1984.

Soffer, A., ed. *Residential and Internal Migration Patterns among the Arabs in Israel.* Monograph Series no. 4. Haifa: Jewish-Arab Center, University of Haifa, 1986.

Turner, V. *The Ritual Process*. London: Routledge and Kegan Paul, 1960.

Weigert G. *Israel's Presence in East Jerusalem*. Jerusalem: Jerusalem Post, 1973.

Yuval, D. *The Delivery of Mother and Child Health Care in Jerusalem: Client Evaluation and Their Relationships to Ethnic Composition of Staff and Clients*. Unpublished Ph.D. diss., University of Michigan, 1988.

Zilberman, Y. *The Palestinian Uprising (Intifada) in Jerusalem: First Research Report* (in Hebrew). Jerusalem: Leonard Davis Institute, unpublished, 1988.

Index

Abu Tur (Village): Arab-Jewish relations in, 63–81; Arab residents of, changes for, after reunification, 66–67; changes during reunification, 65–66; contact and avoidance patterns in, 67–70; demographics in, 64–65; economic exchange activities in, 68; geographic description of, 63–64; Jewish neighborhood committee (va'ad shehunah), 79–80; micro zones in, 70–81; social exchanges among Arabs and Jews in, 70–81; urban services in, 68–69

Acre, 13–14; Arab minority population in, 232

Adolescents: Arab-Jewish relations among, 92–93; awareness of ethnic boundaries among, 51–54; educational integration in Beit Safafa and, 89–90. *See also* Students

Agricultural products, ethnic boundaries and, 160

al-Aqsa mosque, 4, 7. *See also* Dome of the Rock

al-Haram al-Sharif (Noble Sanctuary), 7

al-Isra Wal-Mi'raj, 4–5

al-Quds. *See* Jerusalem

Amman (capital of Jordan), 11; Arab Jerusalem's relationship with, 19. *See also* Jordan

Arab commercial centers, Jewish clientele for, 165–66

Arab East Jerusalem. *See* East Jerusalem

Arab elites, elite political system and, 212–15

Arab evacuation from West Jerusalem, during Palestine partition, 11, 11n.3

Arabic language: courses in, 152; fluency in, among Middle Eastern Jews, 88; Jewish knowledge of, in Abu Tur, 71–72. *See also* Language barriers

Arab-Jewish relations: in Abu Tur micro zones, 70–81; among patients, Hadassah Hospital, 184–89; apathy about, 77; apolitical nature of, 77–78; bibliographical notes on, 24–26; everyday work situations, Hadassah Hospital, 175–79; everyday work situations, Nimrod Bakery,

129–35; historical aspects of, 13–23; majority-minority patterns in, 225–26; national conflict, role of Jerusalem in, 9–13, 26–27; in present-day Jerusalem, 23–31; staff-patient relationships, Hadassah Hospital, 179–84; undocumented existence of business ties and, 158–59. *See also* Exchange relations; Labor relations; Social relations

Arab landlords: in Abu Tur, 71–72; patron or protector role of, 72–73

Arab medical professionals, at Hadassah Hospital, 174–75

Arab neighborhoods, Jewish migration into, 36, 38. *See also* Old City

Arab revolt (1936–1939), 11, 17–18

Arab workers: absorption of, by Jewish sector, 101–10; working conditions, Arab sector, 115–16; in every day work situations, 131–35; favoritism shown to, 135; menial positions held by, at Hadassah Hospital, 175–79; participation in va'ad by, 140–41; shaming and offense of, 134; vulnerability of, 139–41. *See also* Labor relations; Professionals

Arab zones in Jerusalem, map of, 32–46

Architectural styles, ethnic borders and, 46

Armenians, 230–31; elite political system and, 210

Artisans: Arab-Jewish relations and, 75–76; Arab self-employment and, 111

Asymmetry in Arab-Jewish business relations, 163; ethnic differences in consumption patterns and, 168

Avoidance patterns: in Abu-Tur, 67–70; Arab-Jewish business ties and, 164–65; in Beit Safafa and Pat, 86–93; commercial and business ties between Arabs and Jews and, 161; during everyday work relations, 136; ethnic differences in consumption patterns and, 167–72

Banking: Arab customers in Jewish firms, 166; Arab-Jewish business ties and, 163–

Publications by the Jerusalem Institute
for Israel Studies on Jerusalem

RESEARCH PAPERS

- M. A. Tagger, A Guide to Jerusalem Libraries, 1982
- U. O. Schmelz, Modern Jerusalem's Demographic Evolution, 1987 (joint publication with the Institute for Contemporary Jewry)

DISCUSSION PAPERS (OLD SERIES)

- O. Ahimeir (ed.), Jerusalem—Aspects of Law, 1983
- O. Ahimeir and M. Levin (eds.), Modern Architecture in Jerusalem, 1984

SPECIAL PUBLICATIONS

- M. Levin and T. Goldschmidt, The City as a Museum: Modern Art and Architecture in Jerusalem, 1980
- M. Choshen and S. Greenbaum (eds.), Jerusalem—Statistical Yearbook, 1988
- E. Onne, Jerusalem—Profile of a Changing City, 1985 (joint publication with Yediot Aharonot)
- N. Lichfield, Economics in Urban Conservation, 1988 (joint publication with Cambridge University Press)
- B. Hyman, I. Kimhi, J. Savitzky, and T. Soffer, Jerusalem in Transition: Urban Growth and Change 1970s–1980s, 1985
- T. Sawicki, The Jerusalem Handbook, 1987

ISRAEL STUDIES—THE REVIEW OF THE JERUSALEM INSTITUTE FOR ISRAEL STUDIES MAGAZINE Nos. 1–3